SCIENCE AND TECHNOLOGY INDICATORS FOR DEVELOPMENT

About the Book and Editor

The current indicators used to measure the impact of science and technology in developing countries have been formulated based on conditions and assumptions that are primarily relevant to developed countries. The contributors to this volume contend that these indicators, when applied to developing countries, often lead to inaccurate conclusions. An examination is made of the issues involved in assessing the effects of science and technology, and the problems of constructing and applying accurate science and technology indicators relevant to developing countries are analyzed. The contributors compare their firsthand experiences in the construction of social indicators, discussing the strengths and limitations of currently available indicators and necessary preconditions for their use. The book includes case studies of current programs in Brazil and China.

Hiroko Morita-Lou is associate scientific affairs officer at the United Nations Centre for Science and Technology Development.

Published in Cooperation with the United Nations
Centre for Science and Technology for Development

**Other Books in the United Nations
Science and Technology for Development Series**

*Research and Development: Linkages to
Production in Developing Countries*
edited by Mary Pat Williams Silveira

SCIENCE AND TECHNOLOGY INDICATORS FOR DEVELOPMENT

edited by

Hiroko Morita-Lou

Proceedings of the Panel of Specialists
of the United Nations Advisory Committee
on Science and Technology for Development
Held at Graz, Austria, 2–7 May 1984

Westview Press / Boulder and London

The United Nations Science and Technology for Development Series

The designations employed and the presentation of the material in this publication do not imply the expression of any opinion whatsoever on the part of the Secretariat of the United Nations concerning the legal status of any country, territory, city or area or of its authorities, or concerning the delimitation of its frontiers or boundaries.

The papers have not been formally edited. The views expressed in signed papers are those of the individual authors and do not necessarily reflect those of the organization with which they are associated, nor those of the Secretariat of the United Nations.

Mention of the names of firms and commercial products does not imply the endorsement of the United Nations.

Symbols of United Nations documents are composed of capital letters combined with figures. Mention of such a symbol indicates a reference to a United Nations document.

Published in 1985 in the United States of America by Westview Press, Inc.; Frederick A. Praeger, Publisher; 5500 Central Avenue, Boulder, Colorado 80301

Library of Congress Catalog Card Number: 85-51211
ISBN: 0-8133-0294-3

Composition for this book was provided by the United Nations Centre for Science and Technology for Development
Printed and bound in the United States of America

10   9   8   7   6   5   4   3   2   1

Contents

Tables and Figures

Foreword

During the last three decades, there have been many kinds of efforts to promote the use of science and technology in developing countries and to analyze their impact. The representative world-wide effort was undertaken in the latter half of the 1970s, resulting in the United Nations Conference on Science and Technology for Development, held at Vienna in 1979. The governments that participated in the conference arrived by consensus at a set of objectives and recommendations that constitute the Vienna Programme of Action on Science and Technology for Development.

The emphasis of the Vienna Programme of Action is on development and on the ways and means of harnessing science and technology to promote the cause of development. Its recommendations are directed toward how best to strengthen the self-reliant endogenous capacities of developing countries for this purpose, what can be done to reshape the international scientific and technological system, and the manner in which the capacities of the United Nations system can be strengthened, including the mobilization and deployment of adequate financial resources.

It is well recognized that one of the major impacts of the world-wide efforts launched in preparation for the Conference was raising the awareness of the developing countries about the various factors underlying their efforts to harness science and technology for development. This increased awareness has resulted in a wide variety of new initiatives in developing countries.

The United Nations Intergovernmental Committee on Science and Technology for Development, which is a body consisting of all states, and which came into existence in 1980 as a result of the conference, has been continuously engaged in defining the steps that could further encourage these initiatives. For this purpose it has categorized the related tasks within the framework of an Operational Plan under eight major programme areas: policies and plans; infrastructures; choice, acquisition and transfer of technologies; human resources; financing; information systems; research and development linkage to the production system; and cooperation among countries.

The Advisory Committee on Science and Technology for Development, which is a body of 28 experts serving in their individual capacities, assists the intergovernmental committee in refining the various concepts of the Vienna Programme of Action and its operational plan, providing specific suggestions to enhance the scope and impact of these initiatives.

During the five years since the Conference, while various initiatives have been underway, there have also been major and somewhat unexpected changes in the world economic and sociological scene, upsetting some of the original ideas of development strategies. Simultaneously, there have been several technological changes which could create major shifts in patterns of production, some of would undoubtedly affect the future prospects of developing countries. These changes require rapid adjustments and revisions in the policies and plans of developing countries, creating an increasing need for a better understanding of the influence of various factors on development perspectives, especially those factors relating to science and technology.

Policy makers and planners, under such situations, inevitably look for parameters or so-called "indicators" in reordering their priorities, redeploying their resources and revising their plans and policies. Construction of such indicators has to be based on a rational analysis of their own past experiences and present conditions, and must be supplemented by experiences of others in similar situations.

The Graz Panel considered the question of whether it is possible to develop science and technology indicators in the context of development, which would be especially useful as tools for policy makers and planners. Many developed countries over the years have been engaged in a variety of attempts to produce answers to this question. The panel reviewed a wide variety of science and technology indicators that are under development and experimentation.

The question of indicators, particularly science and technology indicators, presents a whole new set of dimensions in regard to developing countries. The numbers and statistics, in spite of their apparent appeal, do not mean exactly what they appear to signify. The use of indicators evolved in the context of situations in developed countries could be misleading if applied without proper modifications to developing countries. It must be kept in mind that developed countries have designed indicators reflecting their own scientific, technological and economic capabilities on the basis of established systems for collecting reliable data.

The image comes to mind of an iceberg. As one can predict that the tip of the iceberg accurately represents a much greater mass below the surface of the water, so too can one presume to judge from science and technology indicators the range of scientific and technological activity and its impact on the economy of developed countries.

This is not true, however, for most developing countries, where science and technology systems have often been created in isolation from the rest of the economy. As a result, there are major distortions in the relationship between scientific and technological activities and the development process, and what may have appeared at first glance to be an iceberg is, upon closer examination, only an ice floe, disconnected and independent.

The papers presented to the panel deal with different approaches to the question of science and technology indicators for development. They examine the potential for and the constraints on the existing approaches and difficulties for applying new methodologies. In many cases, the role of factors external to science and technology are calculated into the assessment process. Overall, these papers—and the concerns expressed during the panel meeting itself—provide additional dimensions to the use of indicators, with particular relevance to the needs of developing countries.

I wish to thank the government of Austria, the state of Styria and the Austrian Academy of Sciences for their support in organizing the panel. I express a personal gratitude to Dr. Leopold Schmetterer for arranging the meeting in the pleasant city of Graz. I deeply appreciate the leadership shown by the two co-chairmen, Dr. Leopold Schmetterer and Mr. James Mullin, in making the panel a successful one. I am also grateful to the participants for the presentation of the papers contained in this volume. Finally, I thank Mr. M. Anandakrishnan and Mrs. Hiroko Morita-Lou, and the staff of the Centre for Science and Technology for Development for the efficient organization of the Panel as well as for their efforts in editing this volume.

I sincerely hope that the interest of many governments, institutions, and individuals in this subject will continue and lead to further research and activities. I have no doubt that the Advisory Committee on Science and Technology for Development, through its panel, has provided an important initiative for the work on science and technology indicators for development.

Amilcar F. Ferrari
Executive Director
Centre for Science and
Technology for Development
United Nations

Preface

The problems associated with the generation and utilization of indicators of the impact of science and technology on development will prove to be of interest and of use to a wide audience of those many people in the developing world who have responsibilities for formulating, administering, and adapting the science and technology policies.

In today's world there are many needs, many goals, and many priorities felt by all countries, but everywhere, human and material resources are limited forcing difficult choices upon all societies. It was the aim of the panel of the Advisory Committee convened in Graz, Austria, to point out how adequate attention the improving of the availability of indicators of the impact of science and technology on development could assist in the making of such choices.

The few recommendations of the panel are deliberately quite general since it is a process that the panel hopes to see initiated rather than any one specific action, and this process is necessary in all countries.

If the report of this panel proves to be useful to developing countries as they seek to improve their capacity to take decisions on matters of science and technology policy, then the panel members will believe that they have succeeded in discharging the mandate given to them by the advisory committee.

Leopold Schmetterer
James Mullin
Co-chairmen of the
Ad hoc Panel of Specialists on the
Measurement of the Impact of
Science and Technology
on Development Objectives

PART ONE

REPORT ON THE MEASUREMENT OF THE IMPACT OF SCIENCE AND TECHNOLOGY ON DEVELOPMENT OBJECTIVES

Overview

Resource allocation represents one of the most difficult recurring problems facing all countries; in almost all cases the human and material resources available are quite inadequate to cope with all needs, and hence painful choices have to be made. This problem is certainly encountered in deciding upon allocations both to scientific and technological activities and to the scientific and technological system.

To improve the basis upon which these allocations are made, better methods are needed to assess the effects of scientific and technological activities on each country's economic and social development. Such assessments, in turn, make use of a variety of indicators but, at present, the range of well-established indicators useful for measuring the impact of science and technology is severely limited.

The purpose of the present report is therefore to bring to the attention of decision makers in developing countries:

- The contributions that can be made to policy management and assessment by sets of suitably constructed science and technology indicators, particularly for the assessment of national capacities to use science and technology and to evaluate the impact of science and technology on development;
- The limitations of applying science and technology indicators evolved in industrialized countries to the situations in developing countries in view of the markedly different problems of structure and linkages encountered in the scientific and technological systems of developing countries;
- A limited set of experimental approaches that could lead to some improvement in the availability and utilization of science and technology indicators for development.

The Panel has made the following suggestions:

- A number of "pioneering projects" should be supported that would attempt the experimental application of sets of new or old indicators in specific situations of practical interest to developing countries. Work has already been done in the field of agriculture in various developing countries to trace the impact of specific new technologies on food production. Such experiments should be carried out in other countries and should also be attempted in other sectors, such as health, the manufacturing industry or housing construction.
- Training courses should be held on the generation and utilization of science and technology indicators as management tools for policy makers in developing countries. These courses should be directed toward those who are involved in policy formulation or resource allocation related to the scientific or technological activities in developing countries. These courses would necessarily address such questions as the reliability and validity of science and technology indicators and the problems of data collection in developing countries.
- Workshops and meetings for professionals and researchers involved in the development and improvement of science and technology indicators should be held for the purpose of exchanging current experience and sharing ideas for further research.

It is essential that the pioneering projects should be carried out primarily by national teams in developing countries, though cooperation with international bodies or institutions in advanced countries could be valuable in some instances. Agencies engaged in the financing of science and technology in developing countries should assist in making the realization of the above-mentioned suggestions possible. In particular, they should make more explicit provision for research on science and technology indicators in the context of developing countries.

At the same time, non-governmental organizations, including professional societies active in issues involving science, technology, and development, would be of particular value in assisting national Governments to carry out such projects.

A few general conclusions emerged from the Panel's discussions:

- Science and technology indicators are tools, not ends in themselves, and so they should be discussed in the context of the improvement of policy management and assessment.
- The main assessment problem faced by countries is not one of making a list of indicators, but one of developing the skills necessary for the creation of indicators that respond to their specific needs.

- Further research on the determination and utilization of indicators and on the impact of science and technology on socio-economic development is necessary through suitable pioneer projects. Sources of support need to be identified in order to proceed with such research projects.
- Means must be found to demonstrate to senior decision makers the availability, utility and limitations of science and technology indicators;
- In order to construct indicators of the impact of science and technology on the development process there must be a clear statement of the development objectives being pursued, and adequate data are also necessary not only on scientific and technological activities but also on a wide range of development variables, including economic and social characteristics relating to the society involved.
- In scientific and technological research, as in many other fields of research, there are significant benefits to be obtained from cooperation among researchers, institutions, countries, and regions. It is essential that developing country researchers engaged in work on science and technology indicators exchange experiences, results, and research ideas not only among themselves but also with their colleagues in industrialized countries and in international organizations.

BACKGROUND

The creation of a sustained expansion of scientific and technological activities applied to the process of development was an explicit goal of the Vienna Programme of Action on Science and Technology for Development. To guide such an expansion, the task of policy setting, planning, and resource allocation requires convincing measures of the impact of scientific and technological activities on development priorities. The Advisory Committee on Science and Technology for Development, at its fourth session, pointed out that efforts were needed to develop appropriate indicators that would respond to the needs of decision makers responsible for development programs in countries at different levels of development.

The Vienna Programme of Action provides a perspective or orientation for science and technology for development, and is founded on a political consensus. Its key objective is the strengthening of the endogenous scientific and technological capacities of developing countries. Indicators to assess progress in attaining those capacities now need to be constructed, either at an aggregate level or at the levels of sectors, scientific disciplines, technologies, and problem areas, depending on the particular needs of individual countries or groups of countries.

The advisory committee emphasized that, in the context of the Vienna Programme of Action, scientific and technological research was one means of producing development, but not an end in itself. Therefore the impact of science and technology should be assessed in the light of specific social and economic objectives being pursued by individual countries and by the community of nations as a whole.

It is no longer enough to say that science and technology are promoters of development. There is a need to produce evidence of their impact in priority areas and to demonstrate their effects, be they positive or negative, short term or long term. This will help decision makers to obtain clear guidance on policy and investment options and permit judgments to be made about progress toward identified goals. The advisory committee felt that if indicators of the impact of science and technology were to be constructed, they should identify sets of social and economic objectives that had been defined with as much precision as possible.

The advisory committee suggested that the panel should look across the broad spectrum of possibilities to see what types of indicators could be useful and practical for decision makers in countries at various levels of development. The panel was also invited to examine the opportunities for and limitations of applying existing indicators and to outline pre-conditions for using them in developing countries. This implies four classes of indicators: indicators of science, indicators of technology, indicators of the attainment of socioeconomic development objectives, and indicators of the impact of science and technology on the attainment of socio-economic development objectives.

In undertaking that task, the panel examined its experiences in the development and use of not only science and technology indicators but also of similar indicators in various social and economic sectors, bearing in mind that it would be necessary to undertake critical appraisal of conventional science and technology indicators; of the relationship between science, technology and development; and of the methodological needs and constraints implicit in developing and using science and technology indicators for development.

SUMMARY

Scientific and Technological Capacity

If science and technology are intended to promote development, they cannot remain merely affairs of the laboratory, conference, or classroom.

They must culminate in innovations, in practical applications of the knowledge that is being generated or reworked. Decision-makers thus need to think of scientific and technological activities in terms of the complex of organizational practices and flows of knowledge encompassing pure and applied research, industrial and agricultural innovation, and the use of new technologies by households and by communities. As this discussion moves toward the narrower topic of indicators *per se,* it is important to mention briefly two topics of considerable importance: technological change capacity and their measurement.

Technological Change and Technological Capacity

Economists have long recognized the importance of technological change for long-term economic growth, for productivity increases, and for increases in living standards in general. Notwithstanding the existence of ample literature on the subject, technological change remains elusive, largely because of its complexity, because of over-emphasis on theoretical work, and because of the relative neglect of the empirical measurement of science and technology *per se.*

Endogenous technological capacity may be defined as the ability of a country to choose, acquire, generate, and apply technologies that contribute to meeting development objectives. The concept of technological capacity is clearly not absolute, but rather is relative to specific national objectives. Since countries have different development objectives, the nature of the technological capacity required to meet such objectives will vary from one country to another and from one period of time to the next. This definition implies that countries, as a matter of policy, have an influence on the production processes. For example, a country with a development strategy oriented toward basic needs would promote policies different from the policies of a country with a strategy of export-led industrialization.

Technological capacity can be further disaggregated. The capacity to search and select the appropriate technology among alternatives is, of course, fundamental. However, technologies that are known to exist may not be readily available. The capacity to acquire them includes the capacity to identify technology sources, to negotiate reasonable conditions, and to transfer technology from abroad or even from one internal sector of the economy to another.

If available technologies are not considered appropriate enough, alternatives may be created, but only after a time lag. The capacity to generate technology includes the capacity to upgrade traditional technologies and to adapt imported designs. It also includes the capacity to produce tools and machines and other capital goods required to generate technological alternatives. In order to maximize the effective use of different sets of technologies available, developing countries have to seek innovative combinations of traditional labour-intensive and advanced capital-intensive technologies. Finally, the crucial capacity to apply technologies that are technically and economically viable requires a capacity to promote their adoption, proper use, maintenance, and repair.

EVALUATING SCIENTIFIC AND TECHNOLOGICAL PROGRAMMES

Evaluation of scientific and technological programs implies the gauging of the impact of their performance, as judged by sets of criteria that may be either internal or external to science and technology. There are important reasons why such evaluations of science and technology are crucial.

First, science and technology, perhaps more than any other area of human undertaking, depend on the quality of the activity to produce results. As a consequence, and because the resources available are invariably limited—especially in developing countries—it is essential that creativity should be identified and supported.

Second, science and technology are strongly linked to the economic, cultural, and social fabric of countries. If they are to command a share of the meagre resources available in developing countries, it is important to assess the role of science and technology in overall development and thereby justify the necessary investments.

Assessing science and technology is not only an important but a very complex task. For example, in science, the appearance of scientific activity alone cannot be used to measure scientific productivity or progress. Also, the aims and influences of science and technology are complex, forming an intricate network that precludes development of a simple formula or a lone numerical indicator giving a realistic description.

For these and other reasons, detailed assessment is practically never practised in developing countries. It is ironic that exactly those countries in which resources are most scarce but in which the establishment of science and technology is at a most crucial and sensitive stage, the assessment of such activities is absent.

The techniques by which advances in science can be assessed should be different from those applied to technology. It would appear that at least four types of assessment of the scientific and technological capacities of countries should be developed. Specifically, measures would be needed for advances in the scientific capability of a country relative to its development goals; advances in the scientific capability of a nation relative to those of all other nations; advances in the technological capability of a nation relative to its development goals; and advances in the technological capacity of a country relative to those of all other nations.

Among countries, however, the contexts of science and technology, the patterns of development, the infrastructural conditions, and the capabilities and realities relating to science and technology are vastly different. Hence, the task of evaluation calls for different indicators or indicators specifically adjusted and modified to fit the differences in actual situations. No doubt science and technology have a large universal component, so that some indicators are likely to be universally applicable. The panel therefore considered both worldwide efforts to develop scientific and technological indicators in general, and special knowledge relevant to different contexts.

Prerequisites for Evaluation

The following are minimum prerequisites for evaluating the impact of science and technology on development:

- Knowledge of the development objectives being pursued;
- Understanding of the relative priorities among those objectives, to the extent that such priorities have been set;
- Availability of some basic data.

In almost all countries there will be an extensive set of development objectives being pursued at any one time and it is important to recognize that some of these objectives can come into conflict with each other, a circumstance that increases the difficulty of assessment.

For example, a large developing country decided to acquire indigenous capacity to manufacture tractors. A local enterprise designed a suitable tractor that now competes successfully with imported tractors. It then proceeded with a crash programme to design and manufacture combine harvesters. An analyst of the case could question the social merit of using indigenous capacity in a way which could result in further unemployment in the labour surplus economy of the country. It would appear that the goals of promoting a local capacity to generate technology and to substitute for imports was tending to contradict efforts towards the goal of employment generation. However, one can also argue that the design and manufacture of combine harvesters in the country was a rational economic response to acute agricultural labour shortages in the peak seasons and to real demand for such machinery.

From this example, it will be seen that an understanding of both the relative priorities of different goals (capacity building, import substitution and employment generation) and an understanding of the time-frame in which the assessment is to take place are essential if any conclusions are to be drawn that would be useful in development planning.

All assessments of impact rely on the availability of data; not only data that describe the scale and direction of the scientific or technological activity but also data on the economic or social factors of life which are presumably affected. As a minimum, census data describing the main demographic, economic, and social characteristics of the population undergoing development are necessary. In addition, administrative data routinely collected by different agencies within governments may be useful for evaluations of the type discussed here. For example, national customs services may have voluminous data on imports of technology or high-technology goods; agricultural extension services may have information on the use of new varieties of staple crops; public health authorities may have information on changing patterns of morbidity and mortality. All such data, in appropriate circumstances, can be of use in the evaluation of specific programmes.

It should be recognized that at times reanalysis of already available data will not suffice. It may be advisable to collect specific data to measure the impact of science and technology on development. This would require the capabilities of socio-economic research teams that should be progressively organized in interested developing countries or groups of countries.

A PERSPECTIVE ON INDICATORS OF THE IMPACT OF SCIENCE AND TECHNOLOGY ON DEVELOPMENT

There are many possible definitions of indicators in general and of indicators specific to science and technology. The common thread underlying the various definitions is that indicators are tools used to assist in the assessment of some activity, action, or consequence. Typically, assessments or evaluations make use of sets of indicators, each of which may display or highlight some facet of the object of the evaluation. In turn assessments and evaluations are important tools used in policy management.

The successful use of science and technology indicators is not solely a matter of conceptual clarity but of methodological realism as well. The relative success of science and technology indicators in the advanced countries is at least partly due to their data collection systems, together with the organic relationship between their scientific and technological systems and the socio-economic systems as a whole. Such an organic evolutionary relationship does not exist in developing countries, where large parts of their scientific and technological systems have been created in isolation. As a result there are major distortions in the relationship between scientific and technological activities and the development process. These distortions must be understood as a fact of development and any efforts in science and technology indicators need to take them into account. For example, the poor linkages between research and development on one hand and production on the other is a manifestation of a larger structural problem. Similarly, problems in data availability and reliability cannot be addressed through technical or institutional orientations, since these are reflections of deeper problems. Efforts to develop and use science and technology indicators for development must take account of these constraining factors and, therefore, methodologies should be developed that address the realities of the situation. For example, if available data are severely limited, techniques developed should facilitate the utilization of incomplete data. Similar techniques are available in such areas as survey and census research.

Types of Indicators

Indicators used in the assessment of science and technology can be of various classes and types, so that it might be worthwhile to utilize them in our evaluation scheme.

Generally, science and technology are grouped together. However, for conceptual clarification, empirical precision, and policy formulation, it is both useful and necessary to make a distinction between indicators of scientific knowledge on the one hand and those of technological change on the other.

Also, the relationship of science and technology to socio-economic development objectives needs to be evaluated. Thus, at least four different classes of indicators can be identified: science indicators; technology indicators; indicators of the attainment of socio-economic development objectives; and indicators of the impact of science and technology on the attainment of socio-economic development objectives. Within each such class, it is possible to determine several types of approaches.

The **input-output** approach is popular among economists. In applying this approach to science and technology, it quickly becomes evident that it is much easier to measure input than output. For example, one can measure the amount of funds invested in research, the number and kinds of buildings constructed for scientific activities, and the number of scientists trained and employed for research. In describing such input, however, difficulties may arise. For example, although it is easy enough to count the number of scientists employed, it is much more difficult to describe the quality distribution within such scientific manpower.

Nevertheless, measuring input is still very much simpler than measuring output. The product of science is knowledge, which is rather intangible and hence difficult to gauge. Although the product of technology is somewhat more concrete, the gauging of its quality is also difficult. On the other hand, disregarding quality altogether and placing all quantitatively equivalent activities on the same footing is unrealistic.

Moreover, the classical input-output analysis suffers from many limitations, including difficulties of measuring proximate output and of relating input to output. It is possible, for example, that the output of one system may be the input of another. Human resources in research and development is output of scientific and technological education but an input to technological development work.

To circumvent such difficulties, it is sometimes assumed that the output will be closely proportional to the input, and hence input indicators are implicitly used to measure the output. We know, however, at least in those cases in which the input-output relationship in science and technology has been studied at all, that the above assumption is very misleading.

Another useful distinction that can be made among indicators is along another dichotomy: utilization and impact. Utilization indicators are important for understanding the extent to which available resources and knowledge are effectively deployed toward stated objectives. Impact indicators are important for examining the actual influence produced in a particular context. At this stage, it would be more prudent to look at these indicators in a qualitative sense rather than in precise quantitative terms. Assumptions and models on which they are based, are no better than the reliability of the generation and collection of data used in arriving at the quantitative mark. Furthermore, some very crucial elements in the scientific and technological complex may not be amenable to quantification. In the panel's discussions, the usefulness of both quantitative and qualitative indicators was considered. Indicators can be strictly quantitative, thus assigning a definite number on a specific scale to describe some aspects of the scientific and technological activity. Strict quantitative indicators have a definite intellectual appeal, giving the impression of being more objective, more precise, and more reliable than qualitative indicators. Indeed, one should work toward the goal of developing quantitative indicators for as many aspects of science and technology as possible. A quantitative indicator, however, is not better than the reliability of the set of assumptions and models on which it is based.

Distinction is also made between micro- and macro-level indicators. Those indicators that pertain to the scientific and technological system as a whole, or to the performance of large parts of it, we define as macro-level indicators; those that describe some small, partial component of the whole system are defined as micro-level indicators.

In formulating an assessment system we must be ready to use both quantitative indicators and qualitative ones. The latter may involve consulting many scientists, technologists, and possibly other professionals and may also involve on-site visits. However, given the present state of development of indicators, we must conclude that assessing a scientific and technological system from a remote location using data-based indicators alone is not possible. The human element is indispensably a part of any realistic and functional assessment system.

Indicators for the scientific knowledge generated in a country itself are easier to find. New science is almost always published in one form or another, thus enabling us to use the number and quality of these publications as indicators. Indeed, such bibliometric indicators are among the best developed in the field. From the point of view of developing countries, however, the form of bibliometric indicators that is customarily used may be inappropriate for at least two reasons:

- The computerized compilations of data on publications are prepared in advanced countries and may use criteria for selection the range of which may not fully reflect publications of the developing countries.
- Bibliometric indicators frequently used in advanced countries cover only the formal journal literature, omitting publications in the form of reports and in popular media that could be significant in the case of research in the developing countries, particularly when in applied research.

It is to be hoped that developments in bibliometric indicators using data bases will provide more complete coverage of both formal and informal sources, as in the case of the International Information System for the Agricultural Science and Technology (AGRIS) of the Food and Agriculture Organization of the United Nations and the International Nuclear Information System (INIS) of the International Atomic Energy Agency. An improvement on such developments could be effected by extending them beyond the confines of a particular disciplinary approach.

To circumvent these two deficiencies, it has been suggested that developing countries, or groups of them, should establish their own bibliometric statistical systems. This, however, is not an easy task, not only because of the financial resources and the scientometric expertise needed for such a task, but also because of the necessity of dealing with some conceptual questions, such as what constitutes a scientific publication.

In spite of these difficulties, the measurement of the new scientific knowledge generated by scientists in a given developing country can be assessed, at least approximately. It is, however, more difficult to assess the function of those scientists who help to apply scientific knowledge generated abroad.

Examples of science and technology indicators and sources of indicators start on page 17. Some of the limitations in the development and use of science and technology indicators are listed on page 19.

Methodological Needs and Constraints

Several different kinds of variables might be appropriate to describe socio-economic development, depending upon what aspect of science or technology is being assessed. Indicators of the level of socioeconomic development, for example, must be constructed with several well-selected variables. Single-item indicators such as income, consumption of electricity, or percentage of the labour force employed in manufacturing are simply not appropriate. Thus, a multiple-item scale is usually required if the measure of the level of socio-economic development is to be valid. Furthermore, the careful choice of specific variables for inclusion in such multiple-item scales becomes important.

One concept of socio-economic development concerns variations in access to goods and services, which are measured by the socio-economic development (SED) scales. Another involves the distributional characteristics of variables describing access to goods and services (DSED). Gini, Kuznets, and Theil coefficients are examples of the latter type of indicators and attempt to measure the degree of socio-economic inequality.

In the context of science and technology for development, SED measures the changes in the total amounts of goods and services available to the population, while DSED is related to the changes in the equality of access to goods and services within the population. The output side of the input-output matrix should include both aspects to facilitate measurement of the impact of science and technology on both the general level of development and on the degree of inequality of development.

In measuring impact, the input-output matrix is one method; others include standardized path analysis, path regression analysis, and LISREL methods. All path analytic methods are designed to measure the total, direct, and indirect effects of antecedent variables on dependent variables as they are mediated by intervening variables. Standardized path analysis permits the measurement of the comparative influence of different antecedent variables within a single multivariate model applied to a single sample. Path regression analysis permits the measurement of the comparative influence of the same variable as it appears in repeated applications of the same multivariate model to multiple samples. LISREL methods allow tests of multivariate causal models. Such methods would be particularly useful in assessing the average total, indirect, and direct impact of scientific and/or technological development on socio-economic objectives. They would also be appropriate for comparisons of countries or for comparisons of research institutions in a particular country or in a number of countries.

Criteria for Indicators Useful in Assessing Impact

A set of indicators to be selected or constructed for the purpose of assessment should be designed to answer questions of decision makers and policy makers and to meet the particular purpose of assessment, whether it is for forecasting, monitoring, or evaluating the progress and effect of science and technology programmes.

Indicators do not necessarily have to be collected by expensive methods nor should they always attempt to be perfect measures. It is often important to pay attention to their timeliness, validity, or the availability of information.

The Role of External Factors in Assessment

A major array of statistical indicators has been developed to measure the inputs into national scientific and technological systems. A few statistical measures are also being developed to characterize the outputs from these systems. However, the statistical measurement of the impact of scientific and technological activity on the process of development is still a research topic and needs to be the subject of further investigation.

One element of an explanation analyzing the development of "impact indicators" has proven so intractable lies in the role of what may be described as "external" factors, that is, factors external to the scientific and technological system.

It is clear that, throughout the world, investment in science and technology during the present century has been immense and that the consequences of this investment for the development process, however defined, have been staggering. But it is equally clear that the range of factors that influence the ability of any advance in science and technology to cause some change in the level of national development is so complex and ill-understood that assessments of the impact on development of specific advances of science and technology have been extremely difficult and much disputed.

For example, recent research in a region of Brazil seeks to identify the impact of agricultural research for improvement of cocoa production on the quality of life of the cacao growers of that region. Such assessments will have to take into account the impact not only of technological changes but also of seasonal climatic variations and of fluctuations in the price of cocoa. Similarly, studies of the influence of technological changes on productivity would have to consider factors such as changes in the educational level of the labour force or the availability of capital.

The increased difficulty these external factors introduce into the process of assessment of the impact of science and technology provides some explanation of why the development of impact indicators is still in its infancy.

Some Lessons from Efforts to Develop Social Indicators

Some of the lessons learned in the development of social indicators may be of value in the development of science and technology indicators: indicators should be appropriate to the characteristics of the local social system, and indicator development must be related to research on the concrete characteristics of the formal and informal systems of science and technology in the types of society with which we are concerned.

Premature aggregation of different phenomena, for example by reducing all the impacts of science and technology to an economic cost-benefit analysis or to some idiosyncratic social welfare function should be avoided. Related to this is the need to avoid collapsing policy-relevant distributional issues into aggregate measures. The participation of different groups in the production of science and technology and in the receipt of its costs and benefits is a case in point.

Disaggregation of indicators by sector of activity is essential if one is interested in measuring the contribution of science and technology to the fulfilment of specific development objectives. For example, basic needs and employment objectives are more likely to be met if the bulk of expenditure on research and development is allocated for specific small-scale sectors rather than for a few large projects of a highly capital-intensive nature. Admittedly, the limited availability of data will create serious problems. Nevertheless, some bold attempts have been made recently to estimate research and development for appropriate technology in developing countries. Science and technology indicators may also be used to measure the effect of a given technology on the welfare of specific target groups.

The impact of different technologies may be empirically tested in individual countries in an input-output or social accounting framework. Such a framework enables, at least in principle, an integration of production, technology, and income-distribution data in an intersectoral manner.

As mentioned above, premature aggregation should be avoided. It is also necessary to avoid data overload. A systematization of indicators is required, and an integration of data into accounting systems appears to present one valuable way of proceeding. In the shorter term, attempts at national social reporting may be used as inputs into scientific and technological policy, and specialized reporting of science and technology may also be of considerable value. Additionally, it may be necessary to prepare specific science and technology indicators for the analysis of particular programmes and projects, ranging from the structure of basic research in some advanced field of activity to the implications of a technology-based development project for some locality.

There is also the need to avoid over-ambitious claims and to relate research to specific policy concerns and resource constraints. This demonstrates the importance of the work on science and technology indicators being carried out in relation to the concrete circumstances in which the indicators are to be applied.

RECOMMENDATIONS

As a result of the panel's discussions, the following steps are suggested as essential elements for the development and use of science and technology indicators in the assessment of the impact of science and technology on development:

- Specification of different parts of the scientific and technological system and their relationship;
- Specification of the purpose of the assessment, that is, whether it is for description, for seeking remedies, for planning, etc;
- Specification of the relationships between scientific and technological variables and other external variables;
- Construction of indicators that are relevant, functional, and feasible;
- Use of a combination of quantitative and qualitative methods to acquire information for the indicators; sometimes redundancy of methods may be useful for consistency checks;
- Specification of the manner of interpretation of indicators.

The goal in the development of indicators is not to create a fixed and finite collection of indicators for universal application, but instead to evolve methodologies and capacities for the improvisation of indicators best suited to the specific situation on hand.

EXAMPLES OF S&T INDICATORS
AND SOURCES OF INDICATORS

This listing is not comprehensive, but merely illustrative. It is designed to provoke further thinking on S&T indicators for development.

Each item has been marked according to whether it is an input indicator (A), output indicator (B), utilization indicator (C), or impact indicator (D). The assignment of these categories is suggestive and not definitive.

Funding

Extramural	(A)
Intramural	(A)
Government	(A)
Industry	(A)
Academic	(A)
Foreign	(A)

Literature

S&T paper counts	(B)
Citation counts	(CD)
Co-authorship counts	(BD)
Individual authorship counts	(B)
Institutional authorship counts	(B)

Manpower

Scientific	(A)
Technical	(A)
S&T Managerial	(A)

Education/training

By level	(AB)
No. of students	(AB)
No. of instructors	(AB)
No. of institutions	(AB)
Instrumentation budget/student	(A)
Literacy rate	(AB)

Patents

Patent counts	(B)
% Foreign patents	(BC)
% Worked patents	(CD)

Dependency indicators

Citation to foreign literature	(C)
Licensing of foreign technology	(C)
% of national patents held by foreigners	(BC)

Technology-specific

Health-related
Agriculture-related
Industry-related

S&T Information Indicators

No. of S&T Libraries	(AC)
No. of S&T Journals in univ. libraries	(AC)
No. of items accessible through computerised network	(AC)

Economic/demographic/ infrastructure

S&T Extension Service

Extension Budget	(A)

Gross domestic products	(AB)	No. of sites served	(A)
Population size	(A)	No. of extension workers	(A)
% urbanization	(D)		

Kilowatt hours of electricity	(AB)
No. of telephones per capita	(A)
No. of cars, trucks, buses per capita	(A)
Balance of trade in technology	(AB)
Management capacity	(AB)

Linkage indicators

% Scientists in industry	(ACD)
Patents citations to S&T literature	(C)
Licensing royalties	(ABC)
• domestic	
• foreign	
% Worked patents	(CD)
Energy saving per increase in output	(D)
Capital savings per increase in output	(D)

QUALITATIVE INDICATORS

Virtually all the above indicators are quantitative indicators. Qualitative indicators can also be useful in helping a developing country to take stock of its S&T. Qualitative assessments can be generated through Delphi methods, surveys, interviews, etc.

Examples:

- Public attitudes toward S&T
- Expert assessments of national S&T strengths and weaknesses
- Forecasts of future S&T needs
- Assessments of S&T impacts on the country
- Management capacity

LIMITATIONS OF INDICATORS

1. The problem of validity. Are the indicators really measuring what they purport to measure?

2. The problem of reliability. Will repeated measurements of a phenomenon yield the same results?

3. The problem of cost.

4. The problem of usefulness. Are the indicators really meeting user needs?

5. The problem of data collection. Can the needed data be collected?

6. The problem of cross-national comparisons. Are the indicators comparable from country to country?

7. The problem of a theoretical basis for development and analysis of indicators. Is there a clear rationale for the use of one type of indicator over another?

8. The problem of timeliness. Given the time it takes to develop indicators, will they still be useful when they are finally reported?

ORGANIZATION

The meeting of the *Ad Hoc* Panel of Specialists on the measurement of the Impact of Science and Technology on Development Objectives was held in Graz, Austria, from 2 to 7 May 1984 in cooperation with the Government of Austria, the State of Styria and the Austrian Academy of Sciences.

The following officers were elected:

Co-Chairmen: Leopold Schmetterer
　　　　　　　James Mullin

Vice-Chairman: Ang How-Ghee

The representative of the Governor of the State of Styria, Herr President W. Hofrat Dr. Werner Blanc, welcomed the participants of and conveyed to them the wishes of the Governor for success in their deliberations. In his view, Graz was an appropriate location for such a meeting for it has three universities, two of which are in the domain of science and technology.

On behalf of the Secretary-General, the Executive Director of the Centre for Science and Technology for Development of the United Nations Secretariat expressed his gratitude to the Government of Austria, the State of Styria and the Austrian Academy of Sciences for acting as hosts to the panel and to Prof. Leopold Schmetterer, a member of the Advisory Committee on Science and Technology for Development, for taking the initiative in arranging for the meeting to be held in Austria. He stressed the importance of the subject under consideration by the panel, focusing primarily on meeting the needs of developing countries. The policy makers and planners of these countries, facing rapid technological changes and major economic and sociological changes in the world, looked for guidance in reordering their priorities, redeploying of their resources, and adjusting plans and policies accordingly. The question before the panel was whether it was possible to seek such guidance, through indicators in so far as such problems were concerned with the use of science and technology for development.

List of Participants

Members of the Panel

Ang How-Ghee, National University of Singpore, Singapore

Tibor Braun, Hungarian Academy of Sciences, Budapest, Hungary

Hajime Eto, The University of Tsukuba, Tsukuba, Japan

Ivan Fabian, OECD, Paris, France

Davidson Frame, George Washington University, Washington D.C., United States of America

Maria Eduarda Goncalves, National Board of Scientific and Technological Research, Lisbon, Portugal

Archibald O. Haller, University of Wisconsin, Madison, Wisconsin, United States of America

Henri Hogbe-Nlend, Association Africaine pour l'avancement de la science et de la technique (AAST), Bordeaux, France

Isaac Kertnatzsky, Pontifical Catholic University, Rio de Janeiro, Brazil

Ian Miles, University of Sussex, Brighton, East Sussex, United Kingdom of Great Britain and Northern Ireland

Michael Moravcsik, University of Oregon, Eugene, Oregon, United States of America

James Mullin, International Development Research Centre, Ottawa, Ontario, Canada

Leopold Schmetterer, Austrian Academy of Science, Vienna, Austria

Giorgio Sirilli, Consiglio Nazionale delle Ricerche, Rome, Italy

Ivo Slaus, Ruder Boskovic Institute, Zagreb, Yugoslavia

Babatunde Thomas, African Regional Centre for Technology, Dakar, Senegal

Xu Zhaoxiang, Centre for Science and Technology for Development, Beijing, China

United Nations Secretariat

Department of International Economic and Social Affairs
   Nguyen Hong

Centre for Science and Technology for Development
   Amilcar F. Ferrari
   Ernst von Weizsacker
   M. Anandakrishnan
   Hiroko Morita-Lou

United Nations Industrial Development Organization
   A. Bromley

United Nations Environment Programme
   P. Bifani

Specialized Agencies and Other Organizations
of the United Nations System

International Labour Organisation
   A. G. Fluitman

Food and Agriculture Organization of the United Nations
   B. Muller-Haye

United Nations Educational, Scientific and Cultural Organization
   M. Abtahi

World Health Organization
   B. Mansourian

International Atomic Energy Agency
   David Kay
   Joseph Quartey

PART TWO

DISCUSSION PAPERS

1

Indicators of Science and Technology for Development

M. Anandakrishnan
Hiroko Morita-Lou

INTRODUCTION

Considering the hopes and cautions that have been raised on the impact of science and technology, and judging by the investments that are made in scientific and technological activities, it is but natural that efforts are undertaken to understand—in quantitative and qualitative terms—the associated cause and effect relationships. A meaningful assessment of impact requires careful examination of the scientific and technological endeavours in relation to the relevant economic and social system using different assumptions, diverse data sources, and analytical methods. One of the means attempted for this purpose is the science and technology (S&T) indicators, which have come into existence largely through the initiatives of developed countries and some international organizations.

Recently some attention has been devoted to examining the usefulness and limitations of these indicators from the points of view of developing countries. Such enquiries could be helpful in avoiding misleading interpretations of available S&T indicators and also perhaps in generating interests toward context-oriented S&T indicators for development (STD indicators).

USEFULNESS OF AVAILABLE S&T INDICATORS

The usefulness of a system of S&T indicators as instruments of planning, evaluation, and resource allocation has been advocated. As the scale of basic scientific research has grown and the costs of certain types of scientific research have escalated, and as growth rates in overall national science budgets have declined, so the need for an explicit and systematic science policy has increased. Equally important is the need for a technology policy to define the appropriate goals and standards for efficiency of technology used and its rate of change. S&T indicators, in this context, could:

- provide insights on the impacts of S&T efforts on national socio-economic development;
- help countries inventory their S&T capabilities;
- identify the extent to which a country's S&T system is integrated into or dependent upon the world system;
- help set priorities between different disciplines, institutions, or research groups competing for scarce funds, based on an assessment of their recent S&T performance;
- help research institutes better manage their research programmes.

CURRENT EFFORTS

The developed countries have, for a long time, been engaged in quantitative as well as qualitative analysis of their scientific and technological activities. Several S&T indicators have been evolved to assess their national policies, industrial productivities, institutional efficiency, scientific quality, comparative advantages, and relative international positions. The sheer size of their economies and diversity of their S&T activities have brought out the complexities of such assessments calling for increasingly sophisticated analytical procedures.

Quantitative studies relating to science and technology policy are thought of as having progressed through three stages.[1] The first stage was marked by the pioneering work of Bernal[2] and Roger Hahn.[3] The second stage evolving in the early 1960s, resulted from cross-fertilization between the Bernal tradition and what is now called bibliometrics, the search for quantitative laws in the statistics of libraries and literature, its writers and readers. This stage was greatly facilitated by the availability of large scale computers, which helped to create readily usable data bases. The third stage emerged in the 1970s when the persons concerned with understanding and managing S&T resources took interest in quantitative approaches.

Several large data bases were established in the industrialized countries and serious efforts in collection and analysis of S&T statistics were undertaken by a number of organizations such as the Organization for Economic Co-operation and Development (OECD); the European Community (EC); the Council for Mutual Economic Assistance (CMEA); the Scandinavian Council for Applied Research (NORDFORSK); and the United States National Science Foundation (NSF). Publications dealing with S&T indicators, including *Science Indicators* of NSF, OECD studies, numerous reports and manuals, and White Papers of Japan were brought out. The journal *Scientometrics* was founded in 1978.

At the international level, UNESCO has undertaken to establish data bases containing available S&T information with a more global coverage than the others.[4] At the regional level, the Organization of American States (OAS) has been compiling S&T statistics of countries in Latin America and Caribbean Region.

International Standards

Most of the early works on S&T indicators were devoted to the measurement of inputs of R&D expenditures, using incomplete statistics with a variety of non-standardized definitions that were progressively improved. In this process, one of the important steps has been UNESCO's recommendations concerning the International Standardization of Statistics on Science and Technology. These recommendations contain detailed outlines relating to the scope and definitions of terms, classification and presentation of statistical data, and long-term development of S&T statistics.

It is important to note that the UNESCO General Conference has recognized that the statistical systems of member states are not all at the same levels of development. In fact, in a large number of developing countries, most of these activities and factors are either nonexistent or at a relatively low level of growth. Thus it would be a waste of time and resources to attempt to deal with such a comprehensive set of data collection. Consequently, the UNESCO recommendations provide for the presentation of data at two levels of detail or complexity. The first level of detail consists of a limited quantity of basic information that is indispensable for establishing international comparisons and that should, if possible, be compiled by all member states. The second level consists of fuller statistical data, which not all member states are able to provide, but which, taken as a whole, could constitute a guide for those wishing to improve and enlarge their national statistical systems.

AVAILABLE S&T INDICATORS

Most of the readily available S&T statistics are generally at an aggregate level in a limited number of categories. These could be broadly grouped into:

• Human resource such as S&T and R&D personnel, student enrollment, women scientists, etc.;

- Financing such as R&D expenditure, total and by selected fields (it is rarely possible to find S&T expenditure);
- Publications such as journals, articles, patents, etc.

Much of these data are frequently outdated. In spite of their many inherent shortcomings, which will be discussed later, the available statistics are used extensively in quantitative methods for a variety of interpretations.

EXAMPLES OF QUANTITATIVE METHODS

Comparative Studies

One of the elementary uses of the available S&T statistics is for comparison of the status of science and technology among different countries. Such comparisons are sometimes questioned due to the lack of contextual validity of these indicators, especially when they are used to compare countries with widely varying levels of S&T activities. For instance, the number of R&D personnel in a developed country pre-supposes the availability of a variety of supportive systems such as a functioning infrastructure, viable demands, adequate funds, and effective utilization of skills. Similarly, publications and indicators implicitly assume a number of associated factors and an environment leading to such publications. If such preconditions do not exist, as is often the case in many developing countries, the comparability of these indicators becomes questionable. One suggestion in the use of these indicators is to view them as ordinal measures for selective rankings of countries in comparable situations.[5]

Correlation Studies

Often S&T indicators are utilized to examine the correlation among themselves or with other social and economic indicators. One of the economic indicators is GNP. On the basis of 1972 data on GNP and scientific publications for 107 countries, regression equations have been derived as follows:[6]

(a) For all the 107 countries together:
$$\ln Y = -26.34 + 1.383 \ln X \qquad \text{(eq.1)}$$
(b) For 33 developed countries only:
$$\ln Y = -18.063 + 1.066 \ln X \qquad \text{(eq.2)}$$
(c) For 74 developing countries only:
$$\ln Y = -20.848 + 1.115 \ln X \qquad \text{(eq.3)}$$
where,

Y = Number of scientific publications produced by a country
X = GNP of the country

From these equations, it was concluded that at a given GNP, the production of scientific publications is higher in developed countries than in developing countries; the GNP-publication relation is essentially parallel between the two groups; and the elasticities of publications with respect to GNP are nearly 1.0 (1.066 for developed countries and 1.115 for developing countries), implying that increases in GNP are accompanied by nearly proportional increases in scientific publications.

Similar correlation studies have been undertaken using other variables, such as patents and technology imports. For example, a correlation study has been attempted to link 12 indicators through regression analysis leading to correspondence values among these indicators.[7] It was based on 1965 data for 34 countries which, in the aggregate, represented 80% of world population and 90% of world GNP. The value of such an approach may lie in developing appropriate norms against which countries could evaluate profiles of their relative efforts in selected activity variables.

Performance Studies

Techniques of combining several indicators through the methods of *converging partial indicators* for the assessment of performance of basic research in specific disciplines in allocation of resources have been demonstrated by e.g., Martin and Irvine.[8] They argue that while there are no simple measures of the contributions to scientific knowledge made by scientists, there are a number of *partial indicators*—variables determined partly by the magnitude of particular contributions and partly by 'other factors'. Because of the impact or partial nature of the indicators, only in those cases where they yield convergent results can it be assumed that the influence of the 'other factors' has been kept relatively small and that the indicators therefore provide a reasonably reliable estimate of the contribution to scientific progress.

While examining the measures of output from basic research and performance of scientists, Martin and Irvine make a distinction between scientific activity, scientific production, and scientific progress. The three quantitative indicators of scientific performance they selected, quantitative indicators of publications, citations, and peer-evaluation could, at best, be regarded as measures of scientific production and not as direct and absolute measures of scientific progress. Nevertheless, these could be useful as partial indicators.

LIMITATIONS OF S&T INDICATORS

The most significant limitation of the S&T indicators is their lack of contextual validity to situations in a large number of developing countries. The magnitude and range of their S&T endeavours, either individually or collectively, are quite small compared to the activities in developed countries and hence, many of the yardsticks for S&T measurement become irrelevant. The fact that the major initiatives on S&T indicators come from the "relatively restricted group of wealthier countries . . . meant that attention was focused on a range of activities which were not necessarily the most important for the larger number of poor countries, most of whom had very little R&D."[9] Besides, individual developing countries are not all alike and do not follow the same patterns, priorities, and strategies for development. Indicators suitable to modern sectors and organized enterprises are not necessarily useful for informal and rural sectors.[10]

The data on S&T human resources are based on broad interpretations of the definitions of scientists, engineers, and technicians. This does not provide sufficient indication of the quality and nature of their occupation and the environment in which they function. R&D expenditure data are faced with definitional problems and do not reflect the total S&T financing. Many countries do not show a distinct budgetary item for S&T either in total allocations or in sectoral commitments of resources.

One of the drawbacks of publication indicators is that they define scientific activity too narrowly and ignore the research efforts of individuals who do not publish. Further, there is increasing reluctance by developed countries' journals to provide space to research papers originating in the laboratories of developing countries where emphasis on S&T activities is different, and even after they are published, to cite these papers. There are not enough scientific journals in developing countries to accommodate them either. There is some serious question as to the degree to which data banks such as the *Science Citation Index* (SCI) reasonably reflects the research efforts of developing countries. "The SCI coverage of the scientific literature is consciously designed to encompass the most significant research papers in the world. Coverage of LDC journals is certainly weak: this reflects the fact that LDC research is generally thought to be peripheral to the mainstream research effort. Consequently, SCI-based publication counts under represent the total publication activity of LDCs."[11]

Just as the S&T activity of developing countries may be undervalued by the publication counts, it is conceivable that the S&T activities of some developed countries could be overvalued due to the repetitive nature of some publications with minor extension or modification of contents and preferential citation of self-generated or "friendly" publications.

The data banks of national and international organizations are usually too highly aggregated to allow for fine-tuned investigations of specific sectors and are insufficient for purposes of internal assessments of national S&T systems.[12]

Valaskakis[13] argues that "most of the existing S&T indicators are essentially 'inward-looking' and cannot be used meaningfully by outsiders, as, for example, in designing and implementing technology-based economic and social development strategies. This poverty of S&T indicators is seriously hampering the development planning process and, in some cases, is misleading decisionmakers into making costly mistakes which either perpetuate under-development or worse, lead the particular nation into a path of increasing maldevelopment." He proposes that a priority on development research must be the construction of meaningful indicators of the impact of technology on development. He believes that reliance solely on the R&D indicator is particularly misleading for development planning: first, because it is an aggregate with very dissimilar components, fundamental research, applied research, innovation, and development spending; second, because the R&D figures from various countries are not comparable; thirdly, they are not indicators of performance in such aspects as technology-transfer strategies. R&D expenditures related to GNP are also misleading because GNP does not account for the informal economy and because methods of calculation of GNP vary from country to country.

SCOPE FOR NEW INTERNATIONAL INITIATIVES

It seems likely that in the coming years viable activities of data banks will grow considerably in developed countries, especially because of the potential use of such information to a variety of industrial and commercial enterprises. It is highly likely that many developing countries would take increasing interest in improving the collection and analysis of S&T statistics, as is already seen in such countries as Brazil and India. Therefore, it would be an opportune moment to look carefully into the directions that would be most beneficial to the largest number of developing countries.

Christopher Freeman[14] proposes three specific objectives for new international initiatives: "to monitor new world-wide developments in S&T indicators and to provide advice and assistance to policy-makers in the Third World interested in such developments; to sponsor a series of projects designed to develop and use such indicators in developing countries circumstances; to organize occasional workshops and training courses to promote mutual exchange of experiences. A relatively small programme of this kind would enable Third World countries both to benefit from the many new developments now in progress in the industrialized countries and to affect these developments in a direction more consistent with their interests and a balanced overall picture of world scientific and technological activities."

From the review so far of different approaches to S&T indicators, it is obvious that there is a clear need for reexamination of *a posteriori* use of the existing indicators in the light of situations in the developing countries. It does not necessarily mean that the available indicators should be discarded but that these would require contextual interpretations.

First, development perspectives should be the governing criteria and hence, the accent should be on Indicators of Science and Technology for Development (STD-indicators) rather than on indicators of science and technology *per se.* In the absence of universally acceptable development theories for science and technology, it would be useful to examine the various development perspectives—such as dependency, endogenous capacity, basic needs, distributive justice, sectoral development, world order, export-led growth, import substitution, etc.—in order to identify scientific and technological parameters most relevant to these perspectives. Some, if not all, of these perspectives are mutually inclusive. The intention is not to engage in the analysis of the merits of these paradigms but simply to establish their relationship, if any, to S&T domain.

The Vienna Programme of Action provides a perspective on science and technology for development, arrived at through an elaborate process of discussion and consensus among all governments. One of its basic objectives is to strengthen the endogenous scientific and technological capacities of developing countries. More specifically, the framework for its implementation emphasizes the capacities relating to S&T endeavours in policymaking and planning, infrastructure building, choice, acquisition and transfer of technology, development of human resources, financing, information systems, and cooperation among countries. The nature of STD indicators should be such as to provide the means for analysing the progress in attainment of these capacities in developing countries. Such indicators may also be constructed at aggregate levels or at the levels of sectors, scientific disciplines, technologies, organizations, or problem areas, depending on the particular needs of individual or groups of countries.

Second, the STD indicators should be based on an alternative sets of development objectives and fields of priority interest to developing countries.

Third, the STD indicators should lend themselves for interpretation under actual conditions within a country or in a cluster of countries under comparable situations.

In short, the STD indicators should be oriented toward a well-defined set of objectives and lend themselves to impact-assessment under real-world situations.

The challenges are enormous. However, the initiatives will have served at least one useful purpose if the basic problems associated with STD indicators could be brought into focus in order to mobilize the attention of the community of development experts. The role of the UN system and its pilot projects could help to catalyse interest at national levels and raise the state of awareness on the use and limitations of indicators.

NOTES

1. National Science Foundation: *Science Indicators,* published biennially (1972, 1973, 1976, 1978, 1978), National Science Board, Washington, D.C., United States. Reviews of **Science Indicators, 1978** by Yakov M. Rabkin and **Science Indicators, 1981** by J.D. Frame, all contained in *Scientometrics* 5 (1983).

2. J.D. Bernal, **The Social Function of Science** (George Routledge and Sons, London, United Kingdom 1939).

3. E. Garfield, E. **Citation Indexing—Its Theory and Application in Science and Technology and Humanities** (John Wiley and Sons, New York, United States 1979).

4. UNESCO: Since 1965, UNESCO has organized the world-wide collection and publication of data concerning science and technology including a computerized data base and dissemination of statistical information. Some of the important publications are **Statistical Year Books** since 1969; **Provisional Guide to the Collection of Science Statistics;** COM/MD/3(1968); **Manual for Surveying National S&T Potential** (1969); **Guide to the Collection of Statistics in Science and Technology** (1977); **Manual for Statistics on S&T Activities (Provisional)** (1980); Series of **Annotated Accession List of Studies and Reports in the Field of Science Statistics** since 1966; Series of **Statistics on Science and Technology** (Latest available data); and a number of analytical papers on S&T indicators.

5. *Scientometrics,* Vol. 2, No. 2 (Elsevier, Amsterdam, Netherlands 1980), pp. 133–145.

6. J.D. Frame, "National Economic Resources and the Production of Research in Lesser Developed Countries," **Social Studies of Science,** Vol.9, (SAGE, London, United Kingdom 1979). pp. 233–246.

7. UNESCO, "Study on the Planning and Measurement of Scientific and Technological Development," Meeting on Indicators of Scientific and Technological Development, 24–26 September 1974 (UNESCO/NS/ROU/316, part three, 1974).

8. B.R. Martin and J. Irvine, "Assessing Basic Research: Some Partial Indicators of Scientific Progress in Radio Astronomy," *Research Policy,* Vol. 12 No. 2 (North-Holland Publishing Co., Amsterdam, Netherlands, April 1983).

9. Christopher Freeman, "Recent developments in science and technology indicators: A review"; contains a comprehensive review and references on the subject. (Science Policy Research Unit, University of Sussex, Brighton, United Kingdom, November 1982 unpublished.)

10. United Nations Research Institute for Social Development "Improvement of Development Statistics, Report of a Group of Experts" (UNRISD, Geneva, Switzerland, 1976).

11. J.D. Frame, F. Narin, and M.P. Carpenter, "The Distribution of World Science," *Social Studies Science,* Vol.7 (SAGE, London, United Kingdom, 1977), pp. 501–516.

12. J.D. Frame, "Measuring Scientific Activity in Lesser Developed Countries."

13. K. Valaskakis, "Designing Technology-Based Development Strategies without Appropriate Indicators: The Problem and its Consequences" (First Pan-American Conference on Science Policy and Technology Forecasting, San Jose, Costa Rica, February 1983).

14. Christopher Freeman, "Recent Developments in Science and Technology Indicators: A Review."

REFERENCE

Brooks, H. "Science Indicators and Science Priorities; Science, Technology and Human Values," No.38 (M.I.T. Boston, United States, winter 1982). pp. 14–31.

CONICIT (Costa Rica). The First Pan-American Workshop on Quantitative Methods in Science Policy and Technology Forecasting was organized in San Jose, Costa Rica (7–9 Feb. 1983) jointly by CONICIT, IDRC and OAS. Several of the papers (unpublished) deal with S&T indicators with special reference to developing countries.

Hahn, R. A Bibliography of Quantitative Studies on Science and its History, Berkeley Papers in History of Science, California, United States. (1980)

India, Department of Science and Technology, **Research and Development Statistics,** 1980–81, New Delhi, India. (1982)

Irvine J., and Martin B.R. "Assessing Basic Research: The case of the Isaac Newton Telescope," *Social Studies of Science,* Vol. 13, (SAGE, London, United Kingdom, 1983), pp. 49–86.

Irvine J., and Martin B.R. and Oldham G., "Research Evaluation in British Science" (Science Policy Research Unit, University of Sussex, Brighton, United Kingdom. April 1983, unpublished).

Japan, Science and Technology Agency, **White Paper on Science and Technology,** Tokyo, Japan 1982.

Mazlish, B., "The Quality of 'the quality of Science'—An Evaluation," *Science, Technology and Human Values,* Winter 1982, No. 38, pp. 42–52.

McGranahan, D., Pizzaro, E. and Richard, C., "Methodological Problems in Selection and Analysis of Socio-Economic Development Indicators" (UNRISD, Geneva, Switzerland, 1982).

Morison, R.S. "Needs, Leads and Indicators," *Science, Technology and Human Values,* Winter 1982, No. 38, pp. 5–13.

Narin, F. and Woolf, P. "Technological Performance Assessments Based on Patents and Patent Citations" (First Pan-American Workshop on Quantitative Methods in Science Policy and Technology Forecasting, San Jose, Costa Rica, February 1983, unpublished).

OECD: One of the important contributions of OECD is the progressive development of the manual on **The Measurement of Scientific and Technical Activities: Proposed Standard Practice for Surveys of Research and Experimental Development,** generally known as "Frascati Manual" in four editions (1963, 1970, 1976 and 1981). The manual is specific to R&D and to the needs of OECD member countries. OECD also convened the first major International Conference on S&T Indicators in Sept. 1980: (a) Indicators of innovative activity—innovation proper and patents; (b) indicators of the impact of S&T on the economy—trade and technology; technological balance of payments, and technology and productivity; and (c) science indicators—publication counts, citation counts and peer reviews. These were mostly devoted to situation in OECD countries.

Price, D. "Role of Science Indicators in Science Policy Formulation" (First Pan-American Workshop on Quantitative Methods in Science Policy and Technology Forecasting, San Jose, Costa Rica. February 1983 unpublished). See also his papers "Measuring the size of Science," Proceedings of the Israel Academy of Sciences and Humanities, Vol. 2 (1969).

United Nations: In the 1970s the United Nations Economic and Social Council (ECOSOC) and its Committee on Science and Technology for Development (CSTD) and its Advisory Committee on Application of Science and Technology to Development (ACAST) initiated a number of studies, jointly with UNESCO, dealing with *Qualification of Scientific and Technological Activities Related to Development.* Following the Vienna Conference on Science and Technology for Development, the Intergovernmental Committee on Science and Technology for Development (IGCSTD), established by the General Assembly, has approved an Operational Plan (United Nations document A/CN.11/12, May 1981) for the implementation of the Vienna Programme of Action, which contains several proposals relating to S&T indicators. The IGCSTD has been interested in the question of levels of attainment of scientific and technological development among different countries (see United Nations documents A/CN.11/13, 25 and Add. 1). Its Advisory Committee on Science and Technology for Development (ACSTD) has proposed in-depth examination of the Indices of Measurement of Impact of Science and Technology on selected development objectives.

2
Science and Technology Indicators and Socio-economic Development

A. S. Bhalla and A. G. Fluitman

INTRODUCTION

Economists have long recognized the importance of technological change for long-term economic growth, for productivity increases, and for increases in living standards in general.[1] Notwithstanding the existence of ample literature on the subject, technological change still remains a "black box", largely because of its complexity, because of overemphasis on theoretical work, and because of relative neglect of the empirical measurement of science and technology *per se,* not to speak of the measurement of its contribution to growth and development. This view is supported by the fact that, in spite of work on socio-economic indicators for over two decades now, S&T indicators were either not included as **development** indicators or were treated very marginally.[2]

Indicators are variables that reflect or represent other variables. For example, school enrollment ratios are a measure of the amount of school enrollment, but may be used as an indicator of the educational level of a country; body temperature is an indicator of sickness; death rates may indicate the state of public health. In other words, "indicators are not simply statistics, and statistics are not *ipso facto* indicators—unless some theory or assumption makes them so by relating the indicator variable to a phenomenon that is not what it directly and fully measures."[3]

Originally published in *World Development,* February 1985.
Technology and Employment Branch, International Labour Office, Geneva. We would like to thank our colleagues, Dilmus James and Josiane Capt, for their assistance in the preparation of this paper. Views expressed in it are entirely our own and should not be attributed to the International Labour Organisation.

Although science and technology are invariably grouped together, it is useful for conceptual clarification, empirical precision, and policy formulation to make a distinction between indicators of scientific knowledge such as expenditure on R&D, number of scientific journals, and stock of high-level scientists on the one hand, and indicators of technological change such as labour productivity, use of mechanical power, and use of irrigation and fertilisers on the other.[4] Indigenous technological capacity cannot exist without a minimum threshold of scientific knowledge. However, while scientific activity requires conceptualization and analysis, technological activity and in particular the development of new technologies involves synthesis of existing knowledge and experimentation. Technological change depends much more on accumulated practical experience than on basic scientific research.

N. Baster[5] and others have pointed out that the systematization of indicators can be approached from two directions. Ideally, one should start from a broad concept such as development and break it down into its component variables; if these again are not directly measureable, they would be represented by indicators; the indicators are selected on the basis of plausible assumptions about their relationship, usually one of cause and effect, with the variable they represent. Once a conceptual framework has thus been established, data will be collected to give the indicator a value. Unfortunately, such data are usually not available. Alternatively, and this is the method more frequently used, one could start from existing inter-country data that seem relevant, and use correlation techniques to establish assumptions about the relationship between variables. This approach is simpler but likely to suffer from a number of limitations, in particular the fact that a correlation coefficient itself says nothing about causation. For example, a high and significant correlation between the number of television sets and per capita paper consumption in 150 countries does not indicate any cause-and-effect relationship, but is determined by a third variable such as per capita income; a high correlation between the number of television sets and days with rain in August is possible but can only be explained in terms of chance.

THE RELEVANCE OF SCIENCE AND TECHNOLOGY INDICATORS

S&T indicators that explain historical trends or relationships between variables at a point in time may be useful in determining the nature and level of resources to be allocated to scientific and technological endeavours and to sectors that support such activity. They may also provide the necessary data for assessing past performance in capacity building and utilization.

S&T indicators can thus make a contribution to the planning and evaluation of technological progress. However, such planning and evaluation have meaning only in a context of national development goals. This being the case, the formulation of indicators for given countries or parts thereof, deserves a higher priority than of indicators that facilitate cross-country comparisons. This is simply because review of planning and policy formulation is more meaningful and operational in terms of national action.

S&T indicators are no doubt more meaningful if they are related to outputs rather than inputs. Input indicators say little about the contribution of science and technology to economic aggregates like GNP and its growth over time. For example, the number of scientists and engineers involved in R&D may give some hints for the planning requirements of education, S&T, and R&D institutions. But it does not give any qualitative or efficiency indication of how scientific manpower inputs contribute to meeting objectives such as the fulfilment of basic needs and employment generation. Likewise, the number of doctors per 1000 population tells us nothing about the geographical distribution of these doctors, their specialization, or supporting medical services. Yet this is what would be required if we were to measure the contribution of medical S&T to the satisfaction of health needs of given target groups of a population.[6]

Disaggregation of indicators is essential if one is interested in measuring the contribution of science and technology to the fulfilment of specific development objectives. For example, basic needs and employment objectives are more likely to be met if the bulk of R&D expenditure is allocated to specific small-scale sectors, rather than to a few large projects of a highly capital-intensive nature. Admittedly, the limited availability of data will create serious problems. Nevertheless, some bold attempts have been made recently to estimate R&D for appropriate technology generation in developing countries. N. Jequier and G. Blanc have compiled data on the level and trends, size of funding, and geographical distribution of appropriate technology efforts.[7]

S&T indicators may also be used to measure the effect of a given technology on the welfare of specific target groups of people. One may consider a matrix approach in which alternative technologies represented by indicators such as the capital-labour ratio correspond to the attributes of different development strategies. Although it might thus be possible to show favourable influences, e.g., of upgrading traditional technology on the welfare of low-income groups, such indicators need not be unambiguous in demonstrating such influence. To quote Jeffrey James:

It is of course entirely possible that **none** of the diverse groups comprising the poor benefit from improved technology. This will occur, for example, if the improved technologies are adopted mainly or only by those with incomes above the poverty line and if wages and employment of those in poverty both fail to increase. Something like this appears to have occurred with the new technology of the Green Revolution in many countries. At the other extreme is the case in which all the poverty groups benefit but none of those living above the poverty line are able to do so. Of course, in reality most cases will fall somewhere in between these two extremes, with the final impact on inequality depending upon the particular combination of those who gain, those who lose and those whose position is left unchanged.[8]

As we shall examine in a later section, the impact of different technologies may be empirically tested in individual countries in an input-output or social accounting framework. Such a framework enables, at least in principle, an integration of production, technology, and income-distribution data in an intersectoral manner.

A BRIEF REVIEW OF EXISTING S&T INDICATORS

The development of statistics and indicators suitable for international comparison has long been a concern of UN agencies and other inter-governmental organizations such as the Organisation for Economic Co-operation and Development (OECD), the Council for Mutual Economic Assistance (CMEA) and the European Communities. Most of the work undertaken so far deals with the measurement of social progress and a large degree of disaggregation has been achieved for this purpose.[9] However, there have been relatively few attempts to link science and technology explicitly to socio-economic goals, presumably because of conceptual difficulties and inadequate statistics.

To the extent that conceptual difficulties are associated with indicators in general, the work of UNRISD needs to be mentioned since it constitutes a solid stepping stone for further work on S&T or any other types of indicators.[10] The UNRISD Research Data Bank of 73 Development Indicators includes only two technology indicators, namely:

- Professional, technical, and related workers (ISCO Divisions 0–1) as percent of the total economically active population; and
- Scientists and engineers engaged in research and development per 10,000 population.

In commenting on the first of these, UNRISD notes that although there are problems of comparability of classification in different countries, and although the number of countries with data (53) is limited, it appears to be one of the better indicators. But the second is less effective, and contrary to expectations, not highly correlated with the first.[11]

OECD work on the measurement of scientific and technical activities goes back to the early 1960s. In 1963, the first version of the "Proposed Standard Practice for Surveys of Research and Experimental Development," better known as the "Frascati Manual," was published. The manual is basically a guide for member countries for compiling and analysing statistics on inputs to R&D. That only R&D inputs are included is considered "regrettable since we are more interested in R&D because of the new knowledge and inventions which result from it than in the activity itself. . . . While indicators of the output of R&D are clearly needed to complement input statistics, they are far more difficult to define and collect."[12] The fourth edition of the "Frascati Manual" contains a short annex on the measurement of output of R&D, and refers, *inter alia,* to indicators of the number and cost of innovations, patent statistics, the technological balance of payments, and productivity indices.[13]

A recent report examines trends in the levels and structures of R&D efforts in OECD member countries during the 1970s and examines how these efforts may evolve during the 1980s. The report is "essentially intended to set the scene for further reports which will attempt to evaluate the output and impact of science and technology in general and R&D in particular on the economy and society at large."[14]

UNESCO undertook a study on the planning and measurement of scientific and technological development in 1974.[15] The work is based on a model of relationships between socio-economic development (SED), technological development, scientific and technological potential, and political, economic, and socio-cultural receptivity to scientific and technological development (STD). Through a process of elimination, 24 receptivity indicators and 32 STD indicators were retained for "semi-empirical treatment," which, following the UNRISD methodology, includes correlation and correspondence analysis. Finally, STD profiles are drawn for 31 countries "to measure in time and in a 12–dimensional space the advance or retardation of various aspects of scientific and technological development." The study "which at every turn . . . reveals its exploratory character," avoids drawing substantive conclusions, and ends with a note of warning about methodological limitations.

More recently, UNESCO has proposed to formulate a methodology for identifying "intrinsic" indicators of technological development by considering complex technologies in terms of unit operations and the way in which these are interlinked. A country's technological capability would thus be measured "at the micro level where the technologist takes over from the economist."[16]

In the course of preparing this paper and relying on the methodology developed by UNRISD, we undertook a correlation exercise not unlike the one reported in the 1974 UNESCO study mentioned above. We will not discuss the results, as they did not appear to be of much practical relevance. If anything, they convinced us that one needs to consider new directions and approaches. What indeed should a planner do with the fact that, for all 150 or so countries in the world, a certain correlation exists between infant mortality and the number of patents granted to residents, or between electricity consumption per capita and secondary school enrollments?

APPROACHES TO LINKING TECHNOLOGICAL CAPACITY TO DEVELOPMENT

Science and technology indicators should, in our view, give some indication of a country's technological capacity at a given point in time. However, before one can identify suitable indicators it is essential to be clear about what indigenous technological capacity means in various circumstances and at different stages of development.

Technological capacity need not always match national objectives. This is shown by the story of creating an indigenous capacity to manufacture tractors and combine harvesters in India. The Punjab Tractors Ltd., an enterprise specially commissioned by the state government, was successful in designing an indigenous tractor—Swaraj—which now competes successfully with imported tractors. Encouraged by this success in technological self-reliance, the Punjab Tractors Ltd. proceeded with a crash programme to design and manufacture combine harvesters. According to W. Morehouse:

> . . . creating the capacity for generating indigenous technology is like opening up Pandora's box. Once created, it can be used for good or for ill. What is the social merit, sceptics would ask, of using this indigenous capacity to design and build self-propelled job destroyers such as combine harvesters in the labour-surplus Indian economy? Yet that is exactly what has occurred and forms an integral part of the unfolding story of the Indian tractor industry. . . .[17]

However, one can also argue that the design and manufacture of combine harvesters in Punjab was a rational economic response to acute agricultural labour shortages in the peak seasons and thus to real demand for this machinery.

The ILO has made some attempts to incorporate technology as a variable in macro-economic planning models and to show interrelationships among income distribution, employment, and basic needs objectives, etc.[18] The idea of a social accounting matrix (SAM) as a basis for an economy wide planning framework was extended by E. Thorbecke and H.A. Khan to incorporate technology by introducing alternative techniques in different sectors so that a detailed examination of their impact becomes possible.

In an early attempt, Khan applied the SAM model to the Republic of Korea. However, the multiplier matrix that distinguished between traditional and modern techniques in seven sectors in the SAM of the Republic of Korea did not capture sharply the differential effects of technology choice on output and income distribution.[19] Subsequently, the energy and textile sectors were broken down into 11 categories each. For example, in the case of energy, of the 11 categories, three (charcoal, wood, briquette and dried coal) are produced only by labour-intensive techniques. One (coal) can be either capital- or labour-intensive. The rest are more or less capital-intensive. This classification was done on the basis of a number of technological indicators or ratios, namely, capital to output, capital to labour, value added by capital to total value added, value of foreign to domestic capital stock, and skilled to unskilled labour, etc.[20]

The lack of differential effect of different technologies on alternative production activities within sectors seems to be attributed to "an insufficient degree of product or quality homogeneity in the output-mix and the criteria used to define the technological alternatives which may not have been sufficiently precise or complete."[21]

In an ongoing research project for the ILO World Employment Programme, E. Thorbecke and H.A. Khan examine the efficacy of choice of technology as a macro-policy instrument as opposed to the more traditional macro-policy packages such as fiscal transfers. The question of the appropriateness of certain technology packages needs to be specified in greater detail. This is done by identifying the following sub-projects within a SAM framework:

- Developing a set of technological indicators for identifying different techniques that have analytical meaning and empirical relevance;
- Incorporating "formal" and "informal" production activities in SAM and exploring their interdependence. For example, in sectors such as trade and transport, macro-level interdependence between formal and informal sectors might be quantified. It is realized, however, that this would be fraught with formidable difficulties due

to the paucity of data. An attempt will therefore be made to collect information from sources like micro-level industry surveys.

- Incorporating one or two examples of alternative techniques in specific, disaggregated agricultural, industrial, or service sectors. To this end, reasonably homogeneous product mixes will be selected, and as a second step indicators such as those mentioned above will be calculated and used to identify sub-sets of similar products produced with alternative techniques.

- Attempting to understand more completely the quantitative link between research and development and the generation of technologies in certain specific activities.

The above research framework is being applied in Indonesia, where a SAM has recently been completed at two different levels of disaggregation, that is, 62 and 27 sectors respectively.

C. Dhalman and L. Westphal define technological mastery as "the effective use of technological knowledge through continuing technological effort to assimilate, adapt, and/or create technology." For the industrial sector, the application of technological knowledge is broken down into broad categories of activities:[22]

- Production engineering that relates to the operation of existing plants;
- Project execution that pertains to the establishment of new production capacity;
- Capital goods manufacture that consists of the embodiment of technological knowledge in physical facilities and equipment; and
- Research and development to generate new technological knowledge.

The relative importance of each of the four elements is likely to vary. Furthermore, from a policy and practical point of view, it is important to know the precise interrelationships between different elements. For example, how is the capacity for production engineering related to that for project execution? Similarly, how important is local capital goods manufacture for enhancing learning and adaptive capacity?

On the basis of their studies on the Republic of Korea, Dahlman and Westphal come to the conclusion that "high indigenous levels of all types of technological mastery are not necesary for the initial stages of industrial development."[22] In fact, they find that by relying on foreign sources of technology it is possible to choose a technology without having first mastered its use. Such transfers *per se* need not inhibit the development of indigenous technological mastery; they might be a first step in the exploitation of available knowledge. Likewise, technologies may be effectively applied without mastering their reproduction. "It appears that mastery of production engineering alone is nearly sufficient for the attainment of an advanced stage of industrial development."

These conclusions apply mainly to mastery in relation to given circumstances. A dynamic concept of capacity involves an ability to anticipate technological, market, and related changes that are likely to occur in the future. It is most unlikely that production engineering or project execution experience alone will be sufficient to develop a capacity to innovate and/or to manufacture capital goods.[23]

S. Langdon has examined indigenous technological capacity in two industries in Africa, namely, textile production and wood manufacturing. Not unlike Dahlman and Westphal, he defines the concept "at a simple level" as the ability of citizens of a given country to apply technological knowledge within their production systems, to improve upon that application over time, and to develop new technological knowledge usable in the future.[24] In order to determine the degree to which enterprises had absorbed essential technological knowledge for production in their industry and were able to use this knowledge to undertake new initiatives in their production, five indicators were investigated:

- The sources of technological knowledge, including the sources of machinery;
- The extent of present dependence on formal links with technology sources abroad;
- The propensity of enterprises to undertake product or process initiatives;
- The sources for technological knowledge to take such initiatives;
- The emphasis of enterprise on formal R&D facilities.

Langdon found indigenous capacity existing in a number of enterprises, developed usually from small beginnings via learning-by-doing and strengthened by direct managerial and technical experience overseas. For this reason Langdon suggests that governments should support small-scale domestic firms in acquiring the necessary learning experience rather than favour foreign technology projects.[25]

In examining technology policy studies for the Caribbean, Norman Girvan devotes considerable attention to the issue of strengthening local technological development. To obtain a framework for evaluation, he suggests that a national technological system be broken down into six major constituents, the educational system, the R&D establishment, specialist workshops and facilities, engineering and consultancy, information systems and mechanisms, and management, planning, and financing. These are grouped into three categories according to: the institution or system upon which they are based, the principal output, and the technological functions of the constituent group. In this analysis, the S&T indicators are implicit rather than explicit. We have tried to adapt Girvan's analysis slightly to bring out the relevance and importance of indicators under each of the constituent elements enumerated above. (See Table 2.1.) According to Girvan, for a country to have an effective technological capability, it is important that "each constituent of it must be supportive of every other, through a network of demand and supply relationships and through a pattern of pressure and response."[26]

Figure 2.1 shows the relationships among different constituents of national technological capability. For example, technical training centres produce technicians, which should be supplied to specialist workshops, which in turn will be required to make an effective use of this trained manpower; engineering and consultancy institutions should make use of the work of R&D organizations, but the latter must undertake projects relevant to the needs of the former. Furthermore, the system as a whole must produce technological outputs which are of relevance to and satisfy the demands of its users.[27]

Let us finally mention C. McGranahan, who has been responsible for a considerable share of the UNRISD work on development indicators. He points out that since indicators are meant to measure some conception, the nature and scope of the indicators, as well as the nature of the relations between them, will depend on this conception. He then reviews a number of major "conceptual models" that are used or assumed in the definition of development. According to one of these models, development is defined as enhancing the capacity of a society to function for the well-being of its members over the long run. This "capacity-performance model" of development "embraces not only technological and educational capacities but also structural and institutional capacities; it suggests the importance of structural and institutional indicators and of building up 'capacity indicators' in general. At the same time, it is made quite clear that quantitative indicators have their limitations and should not be confused with development as a whole. The problem is to devise a scheme of developmental analysis that combines quantitative and non-quantitative elements."[28]

TECHNOLOGICAL CAPACITY AND NATIONAL OBJECTIVES

In reviewing work on S&T indicators, one can conclude that the precise purpose of such indicators is not always clear. In any case, a variety of problems surround the definition and measurement of a country's technological capacity—a fairly complex concept that must be disaggregated in order to be better understood. In the previous section,

Table 2.1
Indicators of Technological Capability at the National Level

Input Indicators	Output Indicators	Technological Functions
(1) Educational System		
(a) Number and quality of primary and secondary educational institutions	Personnel with basic education capable of absorbing formal or on-the-job training in technologically-related skills.	Provision of basic infrastructure to support functions below.
(b) Number and quality of technical vocational and industrial training instructions.	Skilled technicians, workers, craftsmen and artisans.	Absorption, modification and adaptation of techniques and process; fabrication of specialist tools equipment and instruments.
(c) Number and quality of university and higher educational institutions.	Scientists (natural, agricultural, medical, etc.), engineers, researchers, consultants, etc.	Research and Development, design, engineering, consultancy, absorption, adaptation, modification, and innovation of technique, processes and systems.
(2) Research and Development Establishment		
(a) Number of research laboratories/ stations/facilities.	Basic scientific knowledge. Applied scientific knowledge of potential practical use.	Basic research. Applied research on techniques, processes and systems.
(b) Number of pilot plants/ experimental stations etc.	Economically useful knowledge.	Testing research. Applied research on techniques, processes and systems.
(3) Specialist Workshops and Facilities		
Number of mechanical, metalworking, repair and maintenance workshops and facilities.	Tools and equipment including prototypes, components and spares.	Repair, maintenance, modification and adaptation of hardware; fabrication of components, tools, equipment and plant incorporating results of technical change from other functions.

(4) Engineering and Consultancy		
(a) Number and quality of consultant firms.	Consultancy contracts embodying knowledge and advice of a specialist or a general nature.	Technology search, selection and evaluation; dissemination of technical knowledge.
(b) Number and quality of engineering (design and building) firms.	Project and plant designs.	Technology search, selection, evaluation and disaggregation; design, modification, adaptation of systems, incorporation or technical change.
(5) Information Systems and Mechanisms		
Research units in institutions, research institutions, survey departments, libraries, etc.	Brochures, leaflets, papers giving general and specific information.	Importation of knowledge, generation of local knowledge, dissemination of foreign and local knowledge to technology users to support (1) and (4) above.
(6) Management, Planning and Financing		
Science and technology plans.	Directives and guidelines for (1) to (5) above and programme of activities.	Orientation of science and technology towards goals and strategies of development; rationalisation, coordination and integration of technology functions and activities (1) to (5) above with development policy, planning and projects.

Source: Adapted from Norman Girvan, "The approach to technology policy studies", in Social and Economic Studies, Vol. 28, No. 1, March, 1979, pp. 19-20.

Figure 2.1. Relationships Among Different Constituents of a
Technological Capability

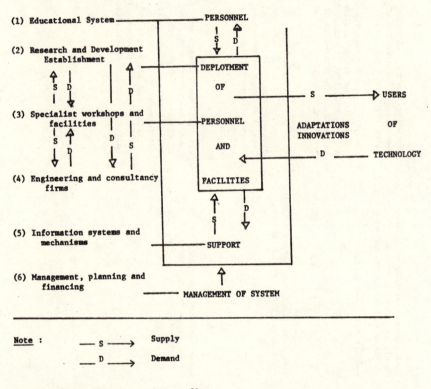

Source: Norman Girvan, op. cit., p. 21.

we referred to a number of approaches toward disaggregation. We will now suggest a somewhat different approach, which is both comprehensive and flexible. We argue that it is within such a framework that indicators of various kinds could play a useful role. A few points deserve reiteration and elaboration before presenting our approach.

The concept of technological capacity is not absolute but relative; the term needs to be used in relation to specific national objectives. In other words, technological capacity is a means and not an end: it is a necessary but not the only ingredient in a mix of factors giving rise to socio-economic change. As countries have different development objectives, the nature of technological capacity required to meet such objectives will vary from one country to the other, and from one period of time to the next.

A country that wishes to produce sufficient food, thereby employing as many of its citizens as possible, is likely to need and adopt technology policies which differ substantially from those of a country more interested in the conquest of space. A technological capacity that does not match priority objectives is not very useful.

The fact that a certain technological capacity exists does not necessarily mean that such capacity is exploited. It would appear that in many countries a certain latent capacity exists that is not matched with concomitant needs.

Because technological capacity is a broad and elusive concept, it should be defined in terms of its elements and, for reasons mentioned above, in terms of national objectives. Indigenous technological capacity may be defined as the ability of a country to choose, to acquire, to generate, and to apply technologies that are appropriate in the sense that their application contributes to meeting development objectives such as reduction of poverty, unemployment, and inequality. This definition implies that countries, as a matter of policy, decide, or have an influence on, what is being produced and how. Thus, a country with a basic needs-oriented development strategy would promote the production of more food per acre with improved tools, or the use of labour-based methods in building rural feeder roads; and a country with a strategy of export-led industrialization would facilitate the importation of advanced technologies so it is able to compete in international markets.

Technological capacity can be further disaggregated. The capacity to search and select the most appropriate from a menu of alternative technologies is of course fundamental: but known technologies are not necessarily readily available. The capacity to acquire them includes the capacity to identify technology sources, the capacity to negotiate reasonable conditions, and the capacity to transfer technology, when necessary from abroad or within countries, for example from one sector of the economy to another.[29]

If available technologies are not considered appropriate enough, alternatives may be created after, of course, a time lag. The capacity to generate technology includes the capacity to upgrade traditional indigenous technologies, and to adapt imported ones (e.g. through unpackaging), the capacity to innovate and to invent, as well as a capacity to test, to produce and to diffuse whatever has been generated. A capacity to produce tools and machines—capital goods required to generate and reproduce technological alternatives—is another element to be mentioned here. Finally, the crucial capacity to apply technologies that are technically and economically viable is composed of the capacity to see that technologies widely adopted, properly used, maintained, and repaired.

These partial capacities are interdependent. For example, it is not very helpful to invest in the capacity to generate technologies if there is no capacity eventually to apply whatever technologies are developed.

Bottlenecks may in fact occur throughout the system. This interdependence is illustrated in Figure 2.2.

Our disaggregation of indigenous technological capacity may clarify the concept, but it does not necessarily facilitate its measurement. To this end, the factors that determine the level and nature of each and all of the elements of indigenous technological capacity must be identified. In general, every partial capacity is a matter of abilities and opportunities as shaped by various resources, policies, institutions, environments, etc. Most specifically, indigenous technological capacity, whether considered *in toto* or in terms of its elements, depends on the following factors (these differ slightly from those of Girvan discussed in the previous section):

1. Human resources in sufficient number, where and when required; their quality in terms of formal knowledge and practical experience, as well as skill and attitude;
   Financial resources, domestic and/or external; the level of these resources and the conditions imposed by lender, donors;
   Useful information, e.g., on technological alternatives, on technology sources, on technology related health hazards, on research in progress, etc.
2. Technology policies and plans, objectives and targets, directives and incentives; their consistency, internally as well as with development objectives; distortions caused by other policies (e.g., fiscal and monetary).
3. Number, quality, and location of institutions for education and training; for research and development, for engineering, design, consultancy, and extension; for the collection and dissemination of useful information; for the promotion of invention and innovation outside the formal R&D framework; for screening technology imports; for other infrastructure and facilities.
4. Natural environment: natural resources, climate; socio-cultural environment: religion, customs, attitudes; political system.
5. Other factors: political situation, relations with other countries, impact of multinational enterprises, externalities.

As noted in the previous section, these determinants—and possibly others—are again interrelated; some of them, it might be argued, are inseparable. It should also be noted that some are more crucial than others, both *per se* and in the context of circumstances peculiar to each country. Disaggregation to this extent is nonetheless suggested because it facilitates a comprehensive analysis of technological capacity.

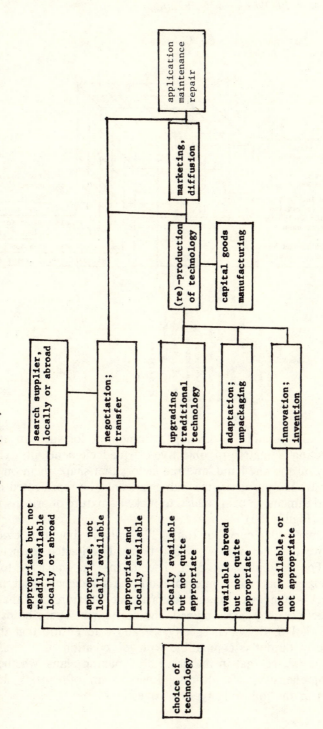

Figure 2.2. Elements of Indigenous Technological Capacity

Figure 2.3. A Framework for the Assessment
of Technological Capacity

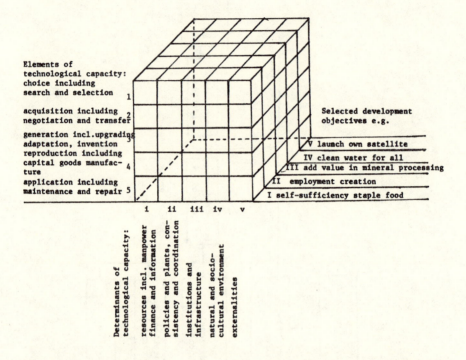

It is now possible to develop a framework for such an analysis by constructing a matrix of objective-oriented elements of technological capacity on the one hand, and the factors that shape them on the other. For illustrative purposes, the framework may be represented by a cube, the third dimension being added to make a mixture of priority objectives explicit (Figure 2.3).

This particular cube has (only) 125 cells; it should be evident from the above that the framework can be easily adjusted to include many more. For example, cell 3, i, I concerns the capacity to generate technologies that contribute to food self-sufficiency in terms of the resources—manpower, finance, information—required for that purpose. As objectives may be combined, the assessment could be extended to cover 3, i, I & II, which specify the above to ensure that the desired increase in output is compatible with job creation.

It is suggested that in the process of making plans, whether sectoral or comprehensive, a multi-disciplinary team of experts should find answers to the following types of questions:

- Does a given country have the technological capacity to achieve objectives X, Y, and Z?
- If the answer is positive, have the objectives been fulfilled in the past? If not, why were they not achieved?
- If the answer is negative, what remedial measures may be taken to remove the constraints in building such capacity?
- If such measures cannot be taken, how should objectives X, Y, and Z be reformulated? Or should their introduction be postponed?

This paper is mainly concerned with diagnosis, that is, with the use of indicators in answering the first of these questions. But our framework has the advantage that policy and planning prescriptions would follow rather directly from the diagnosis.

Since all cells of the cube are not equally important, the idea is to identify and estimate at least the crucial ones, where possible on the basis of facts and figures, and in their absence, on the basis of expert opinion. Taken together, such judgments may themselves be seen as a set of indicators of technological capacity. Speaking of facts and figures, it appears that discussions on indicators often amount to complaints about the lack of adequate statistics and problems of quantification as if figures were sacrosanct. Notwithstanding the usefulness of data, we argue that more stress should be placed on the significance of expert opinion or qualitative judgments.

An illustrative example

We will consider the priority objective of country X, which is to become self-sufficient in staple food (maize) in five years and in such a way that rural underemployment is eased rather than aggravated. The planner would like to know whether it can be done, and what the technological requirements are of this specific objective.

The example reflects a problem common to many developing countries. Moreover, it is particularly interesting in the context of strengthening indigenous technological capacities. Agricultural technology encompasses a biogenetic dimension; growth processes are affected by differences in soil qualities, temperatures, water availability, and a number of other environmental factors. Possibilities of importing appropriate varieties from abroad are therefore limited and local research capacity is all the more critical.[30] The biochemical dimension of agricultural technology (fertilizer, pesticides) is relatively less dependent on local R&D; the more important issue is that of imports vs. local production. But the mechanical dimension of agricultural technology is again primarily associated with an indigenous capacity to generate (improve, adapt, invent) technologies. In view of the employment objective, improved local tools and equipment would probably be more appropriate than relatively capital-intensive, imported machinery. Finally, the capacity to apply appropriate agricultural technologies must not be taken for granted; there are indeed a variety of case histories of farming practices that prove that more appropriate technologies are not automatically adopted.[31]

In order to assist the planner, a multi-disciplinary team of experts is constituted. It starts work with a general assessment of the status quo. How much maize is produced today, and where, by whom, and how? What role does technology play? How much should be produced for achieving self-sufficiency five years hence? To what extent are fluctuations in output explained by relative prices and by such non-economic factors as the weather? Is any maize exported or used for non-food purposes like starch-making? What are the post-harvest losses, if any? What can be said about the level and nature of rural under-employment? And so on and so forth.

It should be possible for a team of experts to draw certain tentative conclusions from such an assessment, or rather to indicate certain critical areas. For example, it may be found that pests, or irregular supplies of fertilizer, or lack of irrigation explain a large part of maize shortages. Or, it may be concluded that shortages can only be overcome by using high-yielding varieties.

Our matrix—the front slice of our cube—may now be used to formulate additional questions: a scanning device that should pinpoint the weak spots of the technology-development nexus. In our example, one might expect the experts to come up with such pertinent questions as:

- Is sufficient information available to select more appropriate pesticides (cell 1, i)?
- Are there any policies that favour the importation of capital-intensive machines (2, ii)?
- Do we have the necessary scientists to undertake bio-genetic research (3, i)?
- How much more should be spent on R&D to achieve the self-sufficiency objective (3, i)?
- Is the existing maize research institute properly equipped (3, iii)?
- Can improved tools be manufactured locally (4, iii)?
- Do farmers have access to credit to adopt improved technologies (5, i)?
- Is fertilizer delivered on time or not (5, iii)?
- Is enough water available to grow the additional output (5, iv)?
- Is average farm-size conducive to mechanical harvesting (5, v)?

In trying to answer such questions, the experts will have to rely on indicators, that is, on relevant facts and figures, but also on their expert judgement. The first question, for example, may be partly answered by searching the information bank of the maize research institute and possibly by comparing the results to what is available in the International Maize Research Institute. But there is judgement required in deciding what is most suitable for local conditions.

The experts would probably find it useful to answer the second question on policies that favour the importation of capital-intensive machines in the broader context of an enquiry into the availability of necessary capital goods for maize production. Information would be collected on various alternatives for meeting machine requirements, including data on imports and local procurement, on relative factor proportions, and on relative prices, the latter possibly indicated in "shadow" rates. Thus a variety of new and very specific indicators would be used to assess a fundamental aspect of indigenous technological capacity.

Answers to the third and fourth questions on the necessary R&D capacity would no doubt require the use of more traditional S&T indicators, be it in disaggregated form. Pertinent input and output indicators would have to be adjusted for qualitative differences. For example, to measure the input in inventive activity, one may need to spot individuals who, over a given period, engage in inventive activity, ascertain the hours spent on such activity, and weigh these hours by some scale of inventive ability. Multiplying the hours by the appropriate weights, we could then say that so many equivalent man-hours of inventive capacity have been "put in" during the year.[32] This type of approach can be extended to different categories of labour to measure their quality. For example, weights could be determined for such indicators of labour quality as primary and secondary education, on-the-job experience, health, nutrition (e.g., calories per capita), etc.[33]

Similarly, quantitative indicators like R&D expenditure have been followed up by more efficiency oriented ones like internal rates of return from research. Taking the specific case of food and agriculture, returns from investment in research may be measured by linking R&D expenditure with agricultural output using a production function model.[34] While this cost-benefit approach is an advance over the conventional input indicators, it suffers from conceptual as well as empirical difficulties, especially in developing countries because of the inadequacy of the quantity and quality of data on inputs and the yearly fluctuations in agricultural output. Interpretation of data is often difficult and simplistic. For example, the state-wide estimates of rates of return from investment in Indian agriculture would suggest that Punjab under-invests in agricultural research relative to West Bengal or Assam, which is not borne out by reality.[35]

A final example concerns the question of the timing of fertilizer deliveries. This may seem somewhat farfetched in relation to technological capacity, but it has in fact been noted in several countries that flaws in the distribution of fertilizer constitute a major bottleneck in augmenting agricultural output. It may be because the necessary trucks are not in running order, or petrol is hard to obtain; the organization of the effort may leave much to be desired, or perhaps the fertilizer factory cannot cope with the demand. In any event, it is of little use to blame seeds, scientists, or farm machinery if farmers find time and again that an essential component of their technology is unavailable when they need it.

This example is meant to show that the number of trucks required to deliver X tonnes of fertilizer, which are required to produce Y tonnes of maize, could well be one of the key indicators for experts to judge a country's ability to meet its priority objective. It is a good indicator for planners since it suggests a specific remedial measure, namely, providing for additional trucks as and when necessary.

CONCLUDING REMARKS

We have found in this paper that work on S&T indicators has so far remained limited, in particular to the collection and processing of input statistics. We have confirmed what others have also found, namely that such indicators are of little use in national development planning. It is not always clear what conclusions should be drawn from them.

A number of models have been presented in which science and technology are related to socio-economic development. We have ourselves suggested that an assessment of indigenous technological capacity must be related to specific socio-economic objectives and explained in terms of the factors that shape the various elements of such capacity. Indicators should be considered as facts, figures, and opinions that help in arriving at conclusions about the quantities that give substance to such a model.

In fact, we have suggested a framework that experts of diverse disciplines may use in development planning. In answering specific questions, the experts would identify indicators as and when necessary. Expert analysis should not therefore be treated as a mechanistic procedure in which standard indicators assume significance. On the contrary, imagination and flexibility are called for to arrive at meaningful conclusions.

It is hoped that such an approach to S&T indicators will be tested in practice and assessed for further refinement.

NOTES

1. See Salter (1960), Cooper and Clark (1982), and Freeman, Clark and Soete (1982), to name only a few.

2. For example, a "special issue on development indicators" of the *Journal of Development Studies,* April 1972, reproduced as Baster (1972), did not find it possible to include a paper on indicators of technological development; see Baster's introduction, note 14.

3. McGranahan, in Baster (1972), p.91.

4. See D. Bell, in Sheldon and Moore (1968).

5. e.g., Baster, in the introduction of Baster (1972), p.5, and Adelman and Taft Morris, in the same volume, pp. 117–118.

6. In general, for goals such as the reduction of poverty and the satisfaction of basic needs to show up in a measure of development, yardsticks other than output and growth are required. See e.g., Hicks and Streeten (1979).

7. See Jequier and Blanc (1983).

8. See James, in James and Watanbe (forthcoming).

9. See, e.g., United Nations (1978), particularly Annex I, WHO (1981), OECD (1978) and OECD (1982).

10. See, e.g., McGranahan et al. (1979).

11. See UNRISD (1976–77)

12. OECD (1981), p.17

13. Annex II "The measurement of output of R&D" op.cit., pp. 130–138. In lieu of a conclusion two works are cited "of interest to any reader wishing to pursue the study of the meausrement of output," namely Freeman (1970) and United States National Science Foundation (1972, 1974, 1976 and 1978).

14. OECD (1984), p.11

15. UNESCO (1974).

16. UNESCO (1983).

17. Morehouse, in Stewart and James (1982).

18. For a conceptual/methodological framework, see Gaude (1975).

19. See also Svejnar and Thorbecke, in Lucas and Freedman (1983).

20. See Khan (1982).

21. Thorbecke, in his proposal to the ILO (restricted). See also: Defourny and Thorbecke (1984) and Santiago and Thorbecke (1984).

22. Dahlman and Westphal, in *Annals* (1981), pp.13–15; see also Dahlman and Westphal, in Stewart and James (1982).

23. Dahlman and Westphal, in *Annals* (1981), pp.24–26.

24. See Langdon, in Fransman and King (1984).

25. Ibid.

26. Girvin, in *Social and Economic Studies* (1979)

27. Op.cit. pp. 16–18

28. McGranahan, in Baster (1972), pp.97–98

29. At this point a reference should be made to the significance of the word "indigenous" (native, belonging naturally). Although "endogenous" (growing from within) may be a better word, the term "indigenous technological capacity"

would seem to be used more frequently to underline the efforts made by developing countries at reducing their technological dependence. It is widely acknowledged however that such efforts are not meant to rule out technology transfers among countries. As in the case of "endogenous" and "indigenous," it appears from the literature that the words "capacity" and "capability" are used interchangeably.

30. Evenson, in *Annals* (1981), pp.54–67.
31. See e.g. Griffin (1974), Pearse (1980) and Ahmed (1981).
32. Kuznets, in NBER (1982), p.31
33. Galenson and Pyatt (1964).
34. See e.g. Ruttan (1982), Chapter 10.
35. See Mukhopadhyay (1983), pp. 58–59.

REFERENCES

Adelman, I. and C. Taft Morris, "The measurement of institutional characteristics of nations: Methodological consideration," in N. Baster (1972).

Ahmed, I., **Technological change and agrarian structure: A study of Bangladesh,** ILO, Geneva, 1981.

Baster, N. (ed.) **Measuring development: The role and adequacy of development indicators,** Frank Cass, London, 1972.

Bell, D. "The measurement of knowledge and technology," in E. Sheldon and W.B. Moore (eds.) **Indicators of social change: Concepts and measurement,** Russell Sage Foundation, New York, 1968.

Cooper, C.M. and J.M. Clark, **Employment, economics and technology: The impact of technical change on the labour market,** Brighton, 1982.

Dahlman, C. and L. Westphal, "The meaning of technological mastery in relation to transfer of technology," in *The Annals of the American Academy of Political and Social Science,* vol. 458, November 1981.

Dahlman, C. and L. Westphal, "Technological effort in industrial and development and interpretative survey of recent research," in F. Stewart and J. James (eds.), **The economics of new technology in developing countries,** Frances Pinter, London, 1982.

Defourny J., and E. Thorbecke, "Structural path analysis and multiplier decomposition within a social accounting matrix framework," in *Economic Journal* vol. 94, No. 373, March 1984.

Evenson, R.E., "Benefits and obstacles to appropriate agricultural technology" in *The Annals of the American Academy of Political and Social Science,* vol. 458, November 1981.

Freeman, C. **The measurement of output of research and experimental development,** UNESCO, STC/16, Paris, 1970.

Freeman, C., J. Clark, and L. Soete, **Unemployment and technical innovation— A study of long waves and economic development,** Frances Pinter, London 1982.

Galenson W. and G. Pyatt, **The quality of labour and economic development in certain countries—A preliminary study,** ILO, Geneva, 1964.

Gaude J., "A planning model incorporating technological choices and non-homogeneous supplies of labour," *WEP Working Paper,* WEP 2-22/WP.17, ILO, Geneva, June 1975 (mimeo).

Girvan, N., "The approach to technology policy studies," in *Social and Economic Studies* vol.28, No.1, March 1979.

Griffin K., **The political economy of agrarian change,** Macmillan, London 1974.

Hicks, N. and P. Streeten, "Indicators of development: the search for a basic needs yardstick," in *World Development,* vol.7, 1979.

James, J. "The Role of Appropriate Technology in a Redistributive Development Strategy" in J. James and S. Watanbe (eds.), **Technology, Institutions and Government Policies,** Macmillan, London (forthcoming).

Jequier N. and G. Blanc, **The world of appropriate technology: A quantitative Analysis,** OECD, Paris 1983.

Khan, H.A., "Energy, employment and balance of payments: Implications of technology choice in the energy and textile sectors in the Republic of Korea," *WEP Working Paper,* WEP, 2-22/WP.103, ILO Geneva, November 1982 (mimeo).

Kuznets, S., "Inventive activity: Problems of definition and measurement," in NBER: **The rate of directon of inventive activity Economic and social factors** Princeton University Press, Princeton, 1982.

Langdon S., "Indigenous technological capability in Africa: the case of textiles and wood products in Kenya," in M. Fransman and K. King (eds.), **Technological capability in the third world,** Macmillan, London, 1984.

Lucas, B.A. and S. Freedman (eds.) **Technology choice and change in developing countries: Internal and external constraints,** Tycooly, Dublin, 1983.

McGranahan D., "Development indicators and development models." in N. Baster (ed.) **Measuring development: The role of adequacy of development indicators,** Frank Cass, London, 1972.

McGranahan C., E. Pizarro and C. Richard: **Methodological problems in selection and analysis of socio-economic development indicators,** UNRISD, Geneva, 1979.

Morehouse W., "Opening Pandora's Box: Technology and social performance in the Indian tractor industry," in F. Stewart and J. James: **The economics of new technology in developing countries,** Frances Pinter, London, 1982.

Mukhopadhyay S.K., "Factors affecting agricultural research and technology: A case study of India." *WEP Working Paper,* WEP 2-22/WP.120, June 1983, ILO Geneva (mimeo).

OECD, **Urban environmental indicators,** Paris, 1978.

OECD, **The measurement of scientific and technical activities—Frascati manual"** 1980 fourth edition, Paris, 1981.

OECD, **The OECD list of social indicators,** Paris, 1982.

OECD, **OECD Science and technology indicators—resources devoted to R&D,** Paris, 1984.

Pearse, A., **Seeds of plenty, seeds of want: Social and economic implications of the Green Revolution** for UNRISD, Clarendon Press, Oxford, 1980.

Ruttan V., **Agricultural Research Policy,** University of Minnesota Press, Minneapolis, 1982.

Salter, W., **Productivity and technical change,** Cambridge University Press, 1960.

Santiago, C.E. and E. Thorbecke, "Regional and technological dualism: a dual-dual development framework applied to Puerto Rico," in *Journal of Development Studies,* Vol. 20, No.4, July 1984.

Sheldon E., and W.B. Moore (eds.) **Indicators of social change: Concepts and measurement,** Russell Sage Foundation, New York, 1968.

Stewart, F. and J. James, **The economics of new technology in developing countries,** Frances Pinter, London, 1982.

Svejnar J. and E. Thorbecke, "Determinants and effects of technological choice" in B.A. Lucas and S. Freedman (eds.) **Technology choice and change in developing countries: Internal and external constraints,** Tycooly, Dublin, 1983.

United Nations, **Social indicators: preliminary guidelines and illustrative series,** ST/ESA/STAT/SER.M/63, New York, 1978.

UNESCO, "Study on the planning and measurement of scientific and technological development," 3 parts, Meeting on Indicators of Scientific and Technological Development, Paris 24–26 September, 1974 (mimeo).

UNESCO, "Intrinsic indicators of technological development—Preliminary outline of the issues involved" by Jean-Claude Bochet, in collaboration with Y. de Hemptinne, Paris, 1983 (mimeo).

UNRISD, **Research data bank of development indicators,** four volumes, Geneva, 1976–77.

United States National Science Foundation, **Science indicators,** volumes 1972, 1974, 1976 and 1978.

WHO, **Development of indicators for monitoring progress towards health for all by the year 2000,** Geneva 1981.

3

Environment and Indicators of Technological Development: Methodological Considerations

Pablo Bifani

INTRODUCTION

Discussion of indicators always presents various conceptual and methodological questions. The difficulties are greater when the environmental dimension is introduced. The three concepts of technology, development, and the environment are elusive and controversial, while their interrelationships are rather difficult to identify and to quantify.

Apart from the traditional questions of why indicators are needed and for what purposes, additional questions need to be answered: why the environmental dimension should be considered in the concept of development, and why it should be reflected in the indicators of technological development.

The most powerful instrument for the transformation and use of nature and for fostering development is technology, but the increasing interdependence between science and technology has the negative impacts of disruption of ecosystems and depletion of natural resources. The systematic and increasing artificialization of the natural system has reached the point where socio-economic and political relationships are also affected by the use and control of science and technology at national and international levels. On the other hand, science and technology applications play a crucial role in distribution and as the cornerstone of development. Thus from food production to the arms race, there is not a single aspect of the modern world that does not have a scientific and technological dimension.

A SYSTEMATIC PERSPECTIVE FOR DETERMINATION OF INDICATORS

Technology, as a means of achieving concrete results, differs from science, which is oriented to expanding knowledge and to understanding the natural and social systems.[1] Today, however, science and technology are viewed as being in a symbiotic relationship, a consequence of the conscious, systematic, and increasing application of science to technological development. The practical and scientific character of modern technology is reflected in Mario Bunge's definition of technology, which includes the scientific base and method, the practical purpose of control, and the transformation and creation of objects and processes.[2] Such a conceptual approach helps in the identification of those dimensions that should be considered when determining indicators of technological development.

A second important aspect lies in the very concept of technology, which refers not only to a specific object, gadget, or process, but also to a complete set of methods, tools, instruments, machines, knowledge, and organization oriented to increasing the efficiency of productive activities designed to overcome concrete problems. In this context, the efficiency of each element or process depends on its interrelationship with the others.[3] Consequently, technology refers to an ensemble of interrelated operations and applications of scientific knowledge. Techniques, objects, machines, tools, methods, and know-how are not scattered and unrelated; rather, they are functional and interdependent structural components of a system. Thus the knowledge depends on the existence of a given scientific and technological infrastructure and an organizational and institutional base[4,5,6] and discussions about technology are in fact discussions on the characteristics, structure, functions, role, planning, management, and control of a specific system. Since technological development refers not to isolated processes or machines, but to the development of a complete system, the determination of indicators should take this systemic aspect into account.

The technological system has been created by the social system, and exists because society makes it function and develop.[7] This means that the technological system is not neutral, but has a purposive character. It has been created in order to overcome concrete problems, according to the interests, value system, and the prevailing ideology of specific social groups. As Bunge stated, the goal of technological research is the truth as it is useful to somebody, while the goal of scientific research is the truth for its own sake.[8] Technological knowledge is a means of controlling a fragment of reality and focuses on what it is possible to create, transform, use, control, or destroy.

This knowledge is an intermediate means for the achievement of specific objectives. The corollary of its pragmatic purposive character is that indicators of technological development should reflect its efficiency in relation to the expected achievement. In other words, they should test performances by measuring results.

This corollary brings into the discussion the difficult problem of measurement and type of indicators. The problem of measurement arises at two different levels. At the aggregate level, in which the attempt is made to assess the degree of technology achieved by a country, information is generated for international comparison, which provides a suitable picture of the situation and trends in each country. The second level comprises measurement of technological efficiency for operative purposes, either at the sectoral level using a branch-by-branch approach, or even at the plant level on a regional, subregional, or local basis. In this second case, indicators should provide suitable information for planners and managers.

It is clear that both levels are complementary and, in fact, disaggregated indicators should be translated into aggregated indicators, whenever possible. In both cases, it is necessary to distinguish between input and output indicators. Input indicators reflect the allocation of resources and therefore the intentions and priorities of governments, while output indicators show performance in the application of resources and achievement of goals, and hence need to be compared with prescriptive, normative indicators.

Where technology indicators are concerned, one tends to consider output indicators as more suitable because they are supposed to reflect levels attained, and hence of efficiency or performance. However, according to the concept of technology outlined above, efficiency is not an aim in itself, since technology is a medium for the achievement of specific societal objectives.

Technological levels and performance can be determined only by linking inputs with outputs, and outputs with goals. In seeking to determine indicators of technological development, therefore, it seems that there is no alternative but to consider three types of indicators: input, output, and normative indicators.

The problem of optimization and/or maximization of efficiency has several important implications: Who defines efficiency? How and on the basis of what criteria? What can be considered efficient in a given context and in relation to a specific society would not be considered efficient in a different context by a society with a different value system. The above questions are especially relevant when the environmental dimension is considered.

Historically, the environment has been neglected in the definition of efficiency. Hence the application of technology for the exploitation and transformation of the natural system has ignored the impacts on the bio-geochemical cycles of nature, on the use of natural resources and, in general, on the structure and functioning of the natural system.

Prevailing criteria have been those of short term utility maximization measured in monetary terms.

A society that assigns low priority to the preservation and improvement of the natural system, and whose planning horizon is the short term, will tend to disregard the effects of technology on the natural environment.

In order to take the environmental dimension properly into account, the system concept needs to be restated, but from a different perspective. It has been said that because of its pragmatic character, efficiency in the achievement of results has been emphasized. This efficiency has been determined in relation to immediate and direct results: to produce something in a short time and at a minimum cost. This traditional approach deserves two comments: the first is that there is a confusion between technique and technology, and the second is that it ignores that real fact that technology is applied in specific socio-economic and natural systems and consequently both are to a lesser or greater extent affected.

Technological application affects the productivity of different sectors, and hence the rate of growth of the economy, the level and distribution of income and wealth, the regional distribution of economic activity and, ultimately, the balance of economic and political power. At the same time, it modifies the structure and functioning of the natural system by extracting some of its elements or by adding new alien products or elements, thereby affecting the normal cycles of nature. Ultimately, this disturbance will affect the homeostasis and resilience of the natural system and consequently its stability.

The fact that technology is applied in a system implies that its application has no isolated single effect, but rather triggers a complete set of interrelated events with second and third order effects. Some of them are not expected, and may not even be foreseen, while others will materialize only in the long term and probably in parts of the system far away from the point which the specific technique has been applied. The consequences of secondary, side, and delayed effects can lead to changes that can either reinforce the direct results obtained or, on the contrary, cause negative modification which, from a social point of view and a longer-term perspective, cancel out the direct outcome achieved in a concrete sector or region, or for the benefit of a restricted social group.

The clearest example of the systematic character of technology and its effects is illustrated by the "green revolution." Sectoral beneficial results reflected in increased food production have been evident. However, the current debate indicates also a large number of negative effects, such as: regressive redistribution of income, wealth and agricultural land;

nitrite contamination; and loss of biological diversity, increasing vulnerability of natural ecosystems.[9]

Technological development cannot be evaluated solely on the basis of immediate direct output, but must rather be assessed on the basis of the set of effects and impacts on the socio-economic and natural systems, in the long as well as in the short term. Therefore, the level of technology development should be determined by the degree of optimization of as many expected outputs as can be identified in the longest time span possible. Indicators of technological development should be elaborated in this perspective.

For example, the indicators of scientific and technological development could include fertilizer consumption per hectare cultivated and total mass of chemical products (insecticides, fungicides, etc.) consumed per hectare cultivated.[10] It may be argued that these two indicators reflect only the economic power to acquire those products, and not necessarily technological efficiency and technology development. The level of technological development is determined by the above mentioned magnitude plus the capacity to use those products in the most efficient and rational form and the ability to control the effects of their application. What this means can be explained using the same example.

It is well known that even in the most efficient agricultural system, that of the United States of America, crops absorb only about 50 percent of the nitrogen and 35 percent of the potassium from fertilizers. These percentages are much lower in certain crops in developing countries: Nitrogen absorption in wheat and rice crops in India fluctuates between 34 and 39 percent and 29 and 35 percent respectively.[11] Typically, 30 to 60 per cent of nitrogen applied is directly absorbed into the tissue of the crops, and between 20 to 40 percent is lost from the ecosystem either by water or in gaseous form to the atmosphere. Not only is it a wasteful and inefficient use of nitrogen, but the fraction lost also causes disturbances of the natural system and constitutes a source of pollution. It has been reported that the crops harvested in the United States of America in 1977 removed only 7.6 million tons, or only 36 percent of the 21.1 million tons of nitrogen intentionally returned to the soil.

From the above example it may be concluded that technology development in this area is still at a rather low level, since the potential for improvement of the efficiency of crop use of nitrogen is great.[12] Perhaps the production of chemical fertilizer has incorporated advanced knowledge and used sophisticated techniques, but the know-how for their utilization and control needs a great deal of improvement, in addition to further development and better understanding of the absorption process by different crops in different soils and climatic conditions.

This lack of understanding and know-how results in wasteful use of resources and energy and in serious environmental problems: the release of large quantitites of nitrogen disturbs the nitrification-denitrification cycle, causes eutrophication, nitrate contamination, and methaemoglobinaemia, and ultimately also contributes to depletion of the ozone layer. These environmental problems are followed by economic damage: eutrophication negatively affects the fishing activity, reduces the efficiency of hydroelectrical investment, and has health impacts on man. Similar analyses can be made in relation to the other chemical fertilizers lost in the process of fertilization.

The concept of technology as a system is demonstrated in this case by the fact that the use of fertilizer is just an isolated technique of a technological process, whereas fertilizer efficiency depends upon the proper utilization of other products, methods, or processes such as irrigation, crop residue management, methods of weed control, frequency and depth of tillage, use of genetic varieties, management and extent of manure and organic waste use, etc.

The second aspect of the systemic dimension is illustrated by the fact that the technology is applied to specific ecosystems; each cultivated ecosystem has a different, unique rate of nitrogen transfer determined by the properties of the soil, the crop grown, the humidity, the temperature, and, in general, the climate. The whole ecosystem, its elements and processes, are to a lesser or greater extent affected by the technology applied.

Various consequences can also be traced in the socio-economic system: Despite production increase, governments will probably have to divert financial resources for the import of the technology, restricting the import of other products; distributive systems will need to be created in rural areas; investment in water development will be required; and income and land distribution will probably be affected.

The fertilizer case can be extended to the case of pesticides, with the same web of interrelated socio-economic, political, and environmental aspects associated with the use of some pesticides like organochlorine products.

Bunge's concept of technology also includes the idea of control. The above mentioned examples and the historical experiences associated with the use of chemical products reveal that the control mechanisms required for the proper application of technology and its sequence of effects are still insufficient, a shortcoming that aggravates the negative effects and gives rise to additional economic and social costs and conflicts.

Indicators of technological development such as the amount of fertilizer and chemical products used are misleading. A given country can have a lower rate of fertilizer consumption than another, but can achieve a higher rate of nutrient uptake by crops as a result of proper management of the other components of the technological system (e.g. water) or better understanding of the behaviour of the recipient ecosystem, or more effective control. In this case, the country with lower consumption has in fact a higher level of technological development. Or a country may have maximized the use of waste and implemented efficient crop-residue management with the result of savings in the use of chemical fertilizers. Again, such a country can be considered as having achieved a higher level of technological development than one with higher consumption of fertilizer, but poor or non-existent crop-residue and waste recycling practices.

In the case of chemical pesticides, a country that is implementing efficient biological control and integrated pest management would probably have a higher level of technological development than a country with greater pesticide consumption and associated greater problems of contamination, decreasing soil productivity, loss of genetic diversity and other related effects.

The above examples also indicate one of the inconveniences of indicators based on input measures. They can introduce bias toward certain traditions and patterns of consumption and can hide inefficient allocation and utilization of resources.[13]

These comments reinforce the opinion that since technology is a system, indicators of technological development should consist of the combination of input, output, and normative indicators. Levels of technological development can be determined to the extent it is possible to link inputs to results and to establish the connections between means and ends.

One also has to consider the need for disaggregation to be examined from two different standpoints: disaggregation of the specific technology in order to reduce its complexity, or to unpackage a technique for operative purposes, and disaggregation of the effects resulting from technological application in order to assess positive and negative outputs as fully as possible. Obviously, the disaggregation should be performed on the basis of the purpose for which the indicators will be developed, leading to the question: What are indicators for?

INDICATORS FOR POLICY AND PLANNING

Indicators of technological development are needed for two main purposes:

- To describe and facilitate the analysis of specific historical situations, and hence the elaboration of diagnosis, and to help identify inter-

relations between different variables and phenomena where scientific knowledge is applied through technology;
- To be used in policy and planning. In this case the phases of policy and plan formulation need to be distinguished from those of implementation, monitoring, and control, and a distinction also has to be made between the different levels of policy and planning activities: normative, strategic, and operative.

Different sets of indicators are needed in each specific case. However, it is also self-evident that description and analysis are linked with policy and planning by providing factual information about the historical development and present situation of the systems to which the technology will be applied.

Analysis of the situation at any historical moment can provide ideas about the causal relationship between variables, and this indicates strategic points of leverage for policy and planning purposes. The descriptive presentation of the situation indicates the levels and distributions of the quantitative and qualitative elements of those aspects of reality on which it is necessary to act. This information, associated with the historical cause-effect relationship, permits the extrapolation of historical trends as a basis for prediction and consequently makes it possible to assess the extent to which the prevailing dynamics of the system are moving away from the desired pattern of development. The indicators used should also contribute to knowledge of the socio-economic structure and its relationship with its environment, as well as between these and the technological variables and parameters. This phase provides factual information to orient the preparation of the normative phase of the planning process, while the extrapolation of trends permits identification of where and when distortions will appear.[14]

It is, however, in the process of policy design and planning and its implementation and control that indicators are urgently needed. It is not strange that work on indicators has gained momentum *pari passu* with the concept of integrated development planning.

Indicators of technological development should reflect some type of relationship between means and ends and between needs and results. They should give indication of levels of achievement, in both quantitative and qualitative terms. Indicators of technological development must relate not only technological efficiency and economic growth; they must also refer to a more comprehensive, integral concept of development.

Development is a multi-dimensional and an integral concept involving the biological, economic, social, and cultural aspects of a community. According to Johan Galtung, development includes social justice, some level of self reliance through participation, and ecological balance.

Therefore, the indicators used should reflect such a composition as exactly and directly as possible.[15] The environmental dimension should be explicitly included in the development planning process for several reasons, including the fact that the natural system provides the base for sustainable development in the long term and that the quality of the environment is one of the components of the quality of life.

Technological development and application are the main instruments for producing what society needs and for the transformation of nature, and it has profound effects both on nature and on society. Therefore it has a strategic role in the definition of development patterns and life styles and in the implementation of development strategies and concrete actions. Thus, technology variables and parameters must be considered at all levels and phases of the planning process.

According to Azam Ozebkhan,[16] planning has three hierarchical levels: normative, strategic, and operation. Different kinds of problems, of different complexity but clearly linked, must be solved at the three levels. At the normative level, a global goal or objective is identified with a specific pattern of development and translated in a normative model, which enables different alternatives to be analysed when compared with descriptive models of present reality. The two models represent a picture of two situations: one real and current, and the other future and desired.[17]

This level of planning requires two sets of indicators: one descriptive, depicting the situation at a given moment, and another comprising narrative or normative indicators, reflecting levels to be achieved. Such indicators may relate to components of the environment—for example, levels and targets of carbon dioxide and nitrogen oxide concentration in the atmosphere—or to scientific and technological development—fertilizer consumption *per capita* and chemical products used in agriculture. However, these sets of indicators, environmental and technological, do not reflect any relationship between them, nor their dynamics.

At the strategic level, the behaviour of the different elements and subsystems subjected to planning is examined. It is here that the feasibility of plans is determined. What is wanted is now confronted with what is possible, and technological capability is confronted with environmental potentialities. Technology represents the social capacity to optimize the potentialities of the natural system for the benefit of society. But the natural system has at the same time constraints that cannot be transgressed without serious risks of massive environmental disruption or depletion of natural resources. There is thus a confrontation between potentialities and constraints, and different types of indicators are required to describe them. Traditional planning discussed "political" and "technological" feasibility. The concept of sustainable development incorporates the idea of "environmental feasibility," which refers to what is viable in specific natural systems.

The concept of carrying capacity has been mentioned in relation to the incorporation of the environmental dimension in development planning. This concept is roughly defined as the man-land balance which is maintained by the practice of specific production methods. Theoretically, this concept may be applied to any technological system[18,19] and indicates the point beyond which population cannot grow, *ceteris paribus,* without causing disruption of the basic resources of the system. Possible societal responses include: limiting population, migration, restrictive use of natural resources, changes in life styles, and technological innovation.

The concept is rather controversial. It relates to the concept of optimum population, and to some extent shares some of its theoretical and practical shortcomings.[20] From the ecological point of view, difficulties arise from the concepts of ecological regulation and homeostatic function, which are in fact at the basis of the concept of carrying capacity. As Roy Rappaport[21] has noted, there are difficulties in determining which biological variables define homeostasis and how to measure them, while Stephen Brush states that the "principal empirical weakness of the concept of carrying capacity lies in the fact that the theory of homeostatis, inherent to the concept, is neither testable nor refutable." From the point of view of the planning process, the shortcomings arise from the concept's static, deterministic character (the idea of critical limit) and the difficulty of making it operative through definition and measurement of variables. These weaknesses are especially important at the strategic and operational levels of planning.

Some authors have taken different approaches, emphasizing the adaptive capacity of nature and suggesting that the following basic aspects of the natural environment should be considered:[22]

- Selective connections between different interrelated elements of systems;
- Different responses of different ecosystems to same, or similar stimuli, so that the impact of human intervention is not uniform;
- Uncertainty of changes created by human intervention;
- Variability, as one of the characteristics of ecosystems, which gives nature an adaptive self-monitoring and self-correcting capacity that should be considered in planning and managing the use and transformation of the natural environment.

The two approaches mentioned illustrate two positions that can have important consequences for development planning. The first emphasizes fragility and instability, and therefore orients social action toward those activities that minimize the probability of disruption. The second approach tends to orient actions toward the maximization of success, on the assumption that the natural system has a large adaptive capacity.

Which approach is followed is important because it will influence the determination and selection of indicators. Most probably, a combination of both extremes will be the common situation. The environmental viability should be explored vis-à-vis the available and potential technology, and in relation to the goals established in the normative plan.

There is therefore a confrontation between the knowledge and scientific methods and technologies available and the system that society wishes to transform. Indicators need to be disaggregated in order to permit identification of cause-effect relationship between the means to be used and the expected results. In the elaboration of these indicators, instruments such as technology assessment methodologies and a historical experience of past environmental impacts associated with different technologies can provide useful information.

The use of indicators also contributes to the revision of the normative plan by demonstrating the viability or unviability of the objectives adopted. This feedback process is important not only from the point of view of the planning process, but also from the more restricted standpoint of revision, updating and testing of indicators.

Since policy and planning process is basically future-oriented, the use of indicators should contribute to the reduction of uncertainty and risk. They should permit assessment of dynamic processes. Development is a process with actions being implemented and results and unexpected consequences occurring over a certain time span, so indicators should be capable of showing processes of change both in the system affected by the application of the technology and in the development and application of technology itself.

Thus environmental indicators should reflect environmental effects, i.e., processes that are set in motion or accelerated by man's action, rather than environmental impacts, which are the net changes resulting from environmental effects.[23] The quantitative units in which the indicators are expressed should be rates of changes rather than absolute quantitative levels, e.g., rates of increase in concentration of pollutants rather than levels of concentration. Such indicators should be linked in order to show cause-effect relationship.

Cause-effect relationships can be indicated by the establishment of technical coefficients that link inputs with outputs for every particular technology. A process or technology that uses fewer inputs could be considered more efficient and more highly developed. Along the same lines, coefficients can be established that link resources inputs and pollutant emissions or waste generation. In this case those technologies that produce less pollutants and wastes per unit of input could be considered as being more developed. Finally, both types of coefficient can be combined: thus, the most developed technology could be the one that uses the fewest inputs and generates the fewest pollutants and wastes per unit of final good produced.

Many impacts of the social and the natural system are the consequences of past technological choices; there is also a certain consensus that the characteristics of the future social and natural systems are being and will be determined by present and future choices of technology. Thus, the question is: how will these technologies be chosen, and on the basis of what information and criteria?

By making it possible to predict the nature and probable impact of emerging technologies, technological forecasting and technology assessment can make a useful contribution both to the process of decision itself and to the determination of indicators concerning technological development and their probable impacts. Technological forecasting is helpful in the definition of long-range strategies since it involves probabilistic assessments of future technology transfer, including the entire range of vertical and horizontal processes.[24] Technology assessment, being basically a purposeful, systematic study of effects of the introduction of technology,[25] can help in identifying cause-effect relationships, and consequently in determining the most appropriate indicators for strategic planning.

Two additional considerations are worth mentioning in relation to the determination of indicators needed in strategic development planning. The first is that the decision on the type of technology is relevant at the early stages of its development, since once it is developed and transferred, some inertia is introduced in the technological subsystem and the decision-making process may lose flexibility. The second consideration is that concern about technology, especially in the planning process, emerges not from the analysis of a particular technology but from the scrutiny and analysis of alternative technological options. Therefore a set of indicators is a *sine qua non* in strategic planning.

Finally, at the operational level of the planning process,the determination of indicators should be done in a very pragmatic way, focusing on subsets of indicators for specific economic sectors, regions, and policy subjects. In determining them, the horizontal linkages between activities, technologies to be applied, resources of the subsystems in which technologies are applied, and outputs should be taken into account. From these relationships, performance indicators should be developed to be used in the phase of monitoring and evaluation. These indicators establish links between programme outputs and policies, and goals and objectives.

In order to permit this, disaggregation of the indicators used in the two previous phases is required.

Indicators for operative planning and management should measure elements at the productive or at the unit-operations level. They should relate to both inputs and outputs so that efficiency and productivity can be determined. From the environmental point of view, indicators of technological development at this level should reflect, among other things, volumes of wastes and pollutants generated by specific technologies or processes in relation to the amount of natural products used and produced, post harvest losses, loss of arable land, decreasing land productivity as a consequence of specific techniques, etc.

To conclude, the process of development planning should include explicit consideration of the environmental dimension and technology. For this purpose different types of indicators with different levels of aggregation are needed. Input-type indicators alone cannot provide useful information, and may even be misleading. Both input and output indicators will be necessary, for the simple reason that technology is not an end in itself but a means for the achievement of societal goals.

Indicators should form sets and subsets that can reflect the empirical aspects of a specific model. They are the empirical links between reality and the theory which orients action.

The set of indicators so determined should ultimately be used in the process of monitoring and control, which provides elements for the evaluation of activities initiated and for the identification of those that should be corrected, compensated for, or eliminated by new alternative actions. For this reason, the indicators developed should be as timely and as precise as possible and provided with some frequency to allow updating and revision. Indicators of technological development could be a measurement of the development reached by countries and of their potential for further progress; however, they could also be instruments for policy, planning, management, and social control of technology.

NOTES

1. Pablo Bifani, "Ciencia, Tecnologia, Medio Ambiente y Desarrollo," *Ceestem,* El Colegio de Mexico (CIFCA, Cuadernos del CIFCA, No.15, Madrid).

2. Mario Bunge "Epistemologia," (Ariel, Barcelona, 1980).

3. Pablo Bifani, "System Approach to Science and Technology Planning," in **Science, Technology and Development: Options and Policy** (M. Mtewa, Editor) (University Press of America, Washington, 1982).

4. Jacques Ellul "Le Systeme Technicien," (Calmann, Levy, Paris, 1977).

5. Pablo Bifani, "Systems Approach to Science and Technology Planning," op. cit.

6. Genady Dobrov, (a) "La Technologia en Cuanto Organizacion," (UNESCO, Rev.Int. de Ciencias Sociales, 1979) and (b) "The Strategy for Organized Technology in the Light of the Hard, Soft and Org-ware Interaction," *Long Range Planning* (August, 1979) vol.12.

7. Pablo Bifani, "Systems Approach to Science and Technology Planning," op.cit.

8. Mario Bunge, "Epistemologia," op.cit.

9. Bibliography on the Green Revolution is today quite abundant. The following titles can be mentioned.

Keith Griffin "The Green Revolution: An Economic Analysis," (UNRISD, Geneva, 1972).

UNRISD, "The Social and Economic Implications of Large Scale Introduction of New Varieties of Food Grain." (Geneva, 1974).

Lester Brown, "The Social Implications of the Green Revolution," *International Conciliation* (1971).

Barbara H. Tuckman, "The Green Revolution and the Distribution of Agricultural Income in Mexico," *World Development* (January 1976).

Wolf Ladejinsky, "Agricultural Production and Constraints," *World Development,* (January 1976).

Cynthia Hewith de Alcantara, "Modernizing Mexican Agriculture: Socio-Economic Implications of Technological Change, 1940–1970," (UNRISD, Geneva, 1976).

M. Ameer-Ul Huq & G.D. Wood "The Socio-Economic Implications of Introducing HYV in Bangladesh," (Bangladesh Academy for Rural Development, Comilia, Bangladesh, 1975.)

International Rice Research Institute (IRRI), "Economic Consequences of the New Rice Technology," (IRRI, Los Banos, Laguna, Philippines, 1978).

Rene Dumont, "Notes sur les implications sociales de la Revolution Verte en quelques pays d'Afrique," (Geneva, 1971).

Kenneth A. Dahlbert, "Beyond the Green Revolution: The Ecology and Politics of Global Agricultural Development." (Plenum Press, New York, 1979).

Harry M. Cleaver, Jr. "The Contradictions of the Green Revolution," *American Economic Review* (May 1972) vol. LXII, No.2.

Francine R. Frankel, "India's Green Revolution: Economic Gains and Political Costs." (Princeton University Press, 1971).

A. Eugene Havens and William Flinn, "Green Revolution Technology and Community Development: The Limits of Action Programmes," **Economic Development and Cultural Change** (University of Chicago Press, 1975) vol. 23

Inderjit Singh and R. H. Day "A Microeconometric Chronicle of the Green Revolution," **Economic Development and Cultural Change** (University of Chicago Press, 1975) vol. 23

Fr. C. Child and Kiromitsu Kaneda, "Links to the Green Revolution: A Study of Small Scale Agricultural-related Industry in the Pakistan-Punjab," **Economic Development and Cultural Change,** (1975) vol. 25.

G. Blyn, "The Green Revolution," in **Economic Development and Cultural Change** vol. 31 No. 4, University of Chicago 1983.

10. Marc Chapdelaine, "Progress Report on the UNESCO Project on Indicators of Scientific and Technological Development," **Scienta Yugoslavica** (Zagreb 1981) vol. 6, no. 1-4

11. FAO/IAEA, "Effects of Agricultural Production on Nitrates in Food and Water with particular reference to isotypes," (IAEA, Vienna, 1974).

12. J.F. Power, "Nitrogen in the Cultivated Ecosystems," in Terrestrial Nitrogen Cycles- *Ecological Bulletins* 33, F.E. Clark and T. Roswall, eds., (Swedish Natural Science Research Council, 1981.)

13. Paul Streeten and Norman Hicks, "Indicators of Development: The Search for a Basic Needs Yardstick," in **Recent Issues in World Development** (Oxford, Pergamon Press, 1981).

14. Mario Bunge, **Report of Informal Consultations on Indicators of Economic and Social Change,** (Paris UNESCO, May 1974.

15. Johan Galtung & Anders Wirak, "Les besoins et les droits de l'homme et les theories du developpement," (UNESCO, Paris, January 1976), SHC. 75/WS/55.

16. Azam Ozebkhan, "Towards a General Theory of Planning," in *Perspectives of Planning* (Paris, OECD, 1969).

17. Pablo Bifani, "Desarrollo y Medio Ambiente," MOPU (Ministerio de Obras Publicas y Urbanismo, Madrid, Espana 1984).

18. Ezra Zubrow, "Prehistoric Carrying Capacity: A Model," (Cummings, Menlo Park, California, 1975).

19. Stephen B. Brush, "The Concept of Carrying Capacity for Systems of Shifting Cultivation," *American Anthropologist* 77, (1975).

20. Pablo Bifani, "Desarrollo y Medio Ambiente," (Madrid, Cuadernos del CIFCA, No.25, 1981).

21. Roy A. Rappaport, "Commentary," in *Biological Anthropology,* Solomon H. Katz (ed.) (W.H. Freeman, San Francisco, 1974).

22. C.S. Holling (ed.) "Adaptive Environmental Assessment and Management." (John Wiley & Sons, New York, 1978).

23. R.E. Munn (ed.), "Environmental Impact Assessment: Principles and Procedures," (SCOPE 5, ICSU, Toronto, 1975).

24. Erich Jantsch "Technological Forecasting in Perspective," (OECD, Paris, 1967).

25. For the concept of technology assessment, among other titles the following bibliography can be consulted:

Harry Rothman, "Technology Assessment and the Unanticipated Consequences of Technology," in **Science, Technology and Development,** K.D. Sharma & M.A. Qureshi (eds.) (Sterling Publishers, New Delhi, 1978).

Francois Hetman, "Society and the Assessment of Technology," (OECD, Paris, 1973).

United Nations, "Technology Assessment for Development," (New York, 1979) Sales No. E.80. II.A.1.

Derek Medford "Environmental Harassment or Technology Assessment," (Elsevier, Amsterdam, London 1973).

J.F. Coates "Technology Assessment—A Tool Kit," *Chemical Technology* (June 1976).

Richard Carpenter, "The Scope and Limits of Technology Assessment," *Technology Assessment,* (1973), vol. 1, No. 1

Emilio Q. Daddario, "Statement of the Subcommittee on Science, Research and Development of the Committee on Science and Astronautics" (United States House of Representatives, Washington D.C., 1968).

4
Intrinsic Indicators of Technological Development: Preliminary Outline of the Issues Involved

Jean-Claude Bochet,
with the collaboration of Y. de Hemptinne

INTRODUCTION AND OBJECTIVES

The contribution to development made by science and technology is one of the dominant themes of our times. It is the aim of scientific and technological policy to organize and rationalize this contribution in order to render it more effective and, especially, to make it possible to control technical development, which has become dangerously erratic. Such a policy requires tools that are suited for the job to be done; in particular, it must have at its disposal instruments of measurement whereby one can construct **indicators**—thus designated because their function is to indicate a state of development shown by a given degree on a reference scale.

Owing to the fact that scientific and technological knowledge is very difficult to estimate directly, initially there was recourse to "extrinsic" indicators applied to material objects provided by a productive activity since they are easier to measure numerically. However, the information collected provides no indication either to the details or to the genesis of such production. It thus seems essential to look for "intrinsic" indicators of technological development, which are more operative at the elementary level. With a view to finding such indicators, a critical study of production processes is essential, and for more than one reason: theoretically, it might provide an approach to the relationship between the economic value of the finished product and the structure as well as the links in the chain of which it is the outcome; aid by industrialized countries to developing countries could be based more explicitly on the communication of know-how (thus avoiding errors that may have been committed in the past in the area of technology transfers); it would lead technologists to analyse the phases and the structure of a process; and finally, it would promote the search for relationships and analogies— one might even say homologies—between operational technologies whose end-products are quite different. In this connection, it will be postulated later that production processes do not appear in monolithic form, but are rather made up of basic structural elements, which will be called "unit operations." Systematizing these unit operations will make it possible to simplify the impressive complexity of the universe of technology: such is the working hypothesis of this study.

These views have been formulated in some detail elsewhere,[1] and a preliminary feasibility study was carried out by means of surveys done among engineers of two different engineering fields (chemical and civil). Out of the various contacts established in connection with the above working hypothesis, and out of the discussions of basic issues for the preparation of a working programme, there emerged a certain number of questions to be asked, practical problems to be solved (motivation, usage, relevance, efficiency), and concepts to be defined. Indeed, the universe of technology and industrial production is highly diversified and it involves every realm of society.

It was thus felt that it would be helpful to prepare a study bringing together these arguments and discussing the various issues with greater clarity than would be possible in a succinct research proposal. Such a study might also serve as a starting point for decision-makers responsible for the choice of the technological processes and for the unbundling of technological packages offered on the world market. The above-mentioned working hypothesis will therefore be examined below, with a view to exploring the theoretical limits of its validity and, later on, to test its operational applicability.

In the sections which follow, methodological guidelines will be set forth concerning the basic conditions of technology; communication of technology; analysis of technological complexity; problems inherent in the structural breakdown of complex technologies; criteria for defining unit operations; and design of technological development indicators. Needless to say, these guidelines will still have to pass the test of practical applicability and the latter is obviously the ultimate aim of this study. In the meanntime, it is hoped that the methodological guidelines that follow will provide useful insights to technologists by promoting the "internal" systematization of the production processes for which they are responsible.

Producing goods and services is fundamental to the very survival of modern society. Production processes, however primitive, always follow certain rules defining the succession of actions that lead to the desired product or service. Such systematization renders processes transmissible from man to man, be it by imitation only. Production methods have been improved over the years while process reliability and the underlying confidence in causal relations gradually found support from the fast-increasing body of scientific knowledge. The coupling of production technology with scientific knowledge has long remained obscure, despite spectacular breakthroughs in the understanding of the scientific roots of operational technologies that have been achieved from time to time. The respective goals and genesis of human knowledge and production technology are indeed different in essence. For many years, the need to elucidate the coupling of these two spheres of activity was not felt to be of great interest. It was assumed that production and its underlying technology consisted of know-how of a largely empirical sort, while science, on the other hand, was looking for causal relationships and predictive models based on experimental evidence. To be sure, the two lines of development often intersected, yet they remained distinct from one another, and—for a time—everything proceeded as if this situation would last forever.

The increasing mutual impact of the spheres of activity, however, has gradually altered the very nature of their reciprocal interactions and made them more and more interdependent. And while the conceptual simplicity of scientific theories that were believed to be established *ad aeternum* was breaking down, advanced production technologies attained astonishing levels of efficiency and scientific rationality. At the same time, access to these advanced technologies has become more difficult to grasp for the non-initiate, and, owing to the extensive facilities that they require, have been ruled out for industries whose infrastructure or equipment are not adequate. As a result, the technological gaps and disparities between industrial production plants (and between the economies that depend on them) have become so pronounced as to call for a global reappraisal of the situation. Unfortunately, the methods for doing so are woefully inadequate.

This study does not intend to embark upon a detailed analysis of all the dimensions of the problem. It will rather be confined to technological development *per se* (while not losing sight of the arbitrary character of such a limitation) by identifying and systematizing its material processes, and by providing for its measurement by means of indicators that are internal to the technology itself. Underlying this study is obviously the objective of rationalizing technological choices and systematizing technological progress, and to gain a better understanding of these civilizational phenomena with a view to streamlining them with acceptable long-term development goals.

The foregoing preliminary remarks were aimed at reminding the reader of the complex problems that one encounters when technological processes are considered in relation to their socio-economic and socio-cultural contexts, as opposed to the simplified situation one has to deal with—in a first stage—when purely material aspects of operational technologies are considered, as will be done in the pages to follow.

BASIC CHARACTERISTICS OF OPERATIONAL TECHNOLOGIES

Even without undertaking the slightest analysis of socio-economic relationships of operational technologies (which are far from simple), one very quickly realizes that the technological processes themselves are actually multiple-component systems that do not yield easily to reductionist approaches. Indeed, it is not sufficient to consider operational technologies in the abstract, as in a chart or flow diagram; one must also, in fact first and foremost, relate their constituent phases to the basic characteristics common to all operational technologies, i.e.:

- **reliability,** or in other words, the degree of confidence that one can have in the technical modus operandi;
- **automation** of the process: i.e., replacing the action of the human being with machinery;
- the **economic feasibility** of the process: i.e., the production costs which are to be brought down to a minimum through the optimization of key parameters such as labour requirements, necessary investments, the energy used, the number of operations to be carried out, the cost of raw materials, etc.
- operating **safety:** thermal and mechanical dangers, danger of explosion, toxicity of products normally released in the open air or those accidentally released, pollution of the environment, etc.;
- **minimization of the cost** of equipment maintenance: cleaning, repairs to remedy the effects of wear or corrosion, etc.

Fulfilling the above basic characteristics, extending the range of industrial products that are affordable or virtually affordable, and enhancing the mutual contributions of the manifold operational technologies within a country all contribute to raise its level of technological development. The number of dimensions involved in this approach is truly bewildering given the diversity both of the qualifications required and of the constraints imposed by industrialization. Looked at in this holistic way, the sum total of the technological production processes of a country is a complex phenomenon resulting from a never-ending evolution, deriving its driving force from ill-defined sources and sustained by a hypothetical "technological spirit," the more or less remote counterpart of the "scientific spirit." What is at stake in the studying and measuring of the level of technological development of a country can be expressed in a simple dilemma: whether to deal with it synthetically as a whole by embracing all its multifarious dimensions, with the resulting overwhelming complexity; or whether to proceed analytically by going into the technical details of a country's operational technologies, which in turn implies a specific set of methodological challenges. In the choice between these two approaches, one might hesitate. Considerations coming under the heading of "communication" will point to the approach chosen in the present study.

COMMUNICATION OF TECHNOLOGY

Development disparities between countries, viewed here from the specific standpoint of technology, make for a world situation that requires massive aid to the less developed areas. The scope of the task can unfortunately not be compared with the resources that are presently being made available to tackle it as a whole and in all places at the same time. Hence, it might be more effective in the circumstances to serialize the problems at hand, in order to organize the search for rational solutions on a step-by-step basis, with a view to facilitating the choice and transfer of technology.

When describing a situation in terms of disparities, one is irresistibly led to the image of communicating vessels, well-known in hydrostatics. The metaphor very quickly loses its suggestive power, however, as soon as one enters the realm of operational technologies; for, while restoring a mechanical equilibrium is apparently simple in the case of liquids, it becomes an unacceptable approximation when one is dealing with technological development. The latter is only a temporary state, a sort of instantaneous reading along an evolving continuum, depending upon the "technological history" of a society and the nature of its connections with its environment (institutional, anthropological, psychological, etc.). And although it is true that isolated and strictly technical *unit operations* (filtration, drilling, etc.) are in themselves quasi-independent of their human operators, they lose their independence the moment they are integrated into the complete production process of a specific operational (and therefore complex) technology. Any progress accruing from a simple transfer of technology as, for example, in the form of implanting a turn-key factory in a developing country, artificially substitutes a momentary surge ahead for an authentic development in the naive belief that the recipient of the transfer can, in this way, be spared an entire maturing period.

Some learning can of course take place on the job. Nevertheless, temporary outside relief brought for the difficulties that characterize a particular set of circumstances at a particular point in time cannot take the place of delving deeply into the technological problem itself; and this problem is different for each country and for each industrial enterprise. Effective international aid should therefore be aimed at the search for methods that can cope with a detailed analysis of the technological problems at hand independent from time and place of application.

ANALYSIS OF TECHNOLOGICAL COMPLEXITY

Since a frontal attack on the complexity referred to would no doubt lead to a dead end in a multiplicity of isolated cases, it would seem wiser to attempt a break down of the technological processes and to concentrate on the determination and aggregate measurement of their constitutive elements. Such an approach, which is consciously reductionistic in character, is certainly in keeping with cartesian common sense. But here again, one runs into a number of obstacles, both theoretical and practical. The purpose of this study is to identify those obstacles, and to make a start in the research required to overcome them. A first set of questions pertains to the validity of the working hypothesis of this study (cf. p. 78) and the underlying motives of this investigation.

In the first place, one has to question the validity of the break-down-of-technological-processes hypothesis. Some reservations seem in order. Fractionation applied to operational (and therefore complex) technologies—in which empiricism plays a role that is by no means negligible— may seem fraught with difficulty. What is more, it can be alleged that as technology has advanced, technological processes have developed to the point where each one is certain to be one of a kind, and have ultimately become the subject of a complex operational technology. Moreover, the basic characteristics of operational technologies may arouse fear of all the discontinuities that would result from a discursive analysis. Might not the sensitivity of any complex operational technology to any disturbance or disruption actually rule out the existence of constitutive sub-systems in each of them? From a more general standpoint, the hypothesis of reduction of the overall complexity of an operational technology down to the level of insecable elements (an approach similar to the atom-theory in chemistry) certainly belongs to the sort of integral determinism that is now viewed unfavourably in modern quantum physics, but with which it can be argued, operational technology will never be able to dispense. Indeed, a manufacturer cannot content himself with a "high degree of probability" that he will put out a product that corresponds to the requisite characteristics!

While these hesitations are certainly legitimate, they should be allayed somewhat if the reduction in question is stated explicitly. It is not, in fact, a matter of cutting up the whole in order to isolate components, as if one were unscrewing a piece of equipment in order to break it down into spare parts. In such a case, the analysis would be nothing other than reverse construction (and what is more, a construction that has already been completed), assuming that the cohesion of the piece of equipment is being provided by effects relating to mechanics, plasto-elasticity, properties of contact between solid surfaces, etc., all of which are phenomena that are indeed each complex in their own way but do only bring into play the chemical and physical properties of the material. With a technological process, on the contrary, we are dealing with a dynamic set of successive actions exerted on an initial material substrate in order to convert it little by little into a final product, whether what is involved is a chemical, a biological substance, an elaborate device or simply a solid form that answers to precise geometric specifications. Here we are dealing with a macroscopic whole whose actions take place in time and in a certain sequence, but only the end result of which is imposed. It is thus possible to recognize an internal group distribution in each operational technology and thus to attribute a structure to it. Discursive analysis is thus replaced by structural analysis, the principles of which, ideally common to all operational technologies, should make it possible to break them down into insecable elements that, for a given technological process, act as configuration units.

Secondly, one should examine the **motivations** that support a search for a method for breaking up the technological processes distinctive of specific operational technologies. To our minds, such a procedure is justified from a number of different standpoints. In the first place, the explosive aspect of technical progress during recent decades is impressive due to the profusion of means brought into play and due to the specificity of production processes. The extreme scatter of the fragments from this explosion may give the idea—as we see it, an erroneous idea—that each case is unique and that any systematization of knowledge is impossible, in fact as well as in theory. We believe, on the contrary, that while the number of technological processes may be enormous, the number of elements that make them up is limited, and that, therefore, homologies, not to say isomorphisms, are conceivable. Identifying them would be a boon both to knowledge and to technology due to the simplifications that would result from it. What is more, in actual practice the advances made along a given line of development characteristic of one process might suggest another, in a related line (horizontal transfer of technology). In this way, it would be possible to devise new and more fundamental orientations for technological research and experimental development, besides those that are called for by the immediate concerns of an exclusively economic order. It will be noted, and with some interest, that technologists and engineers, who are familiar with the operation and design of production lines, intuitively make the connections suggested here within a rationalized analytic perspective, and will almost spontaneously make use of "elements" that are compatible for the mutual benefit with a view to improving a complex technological process, and even for innovating in the field of process engineering.

The latter remark suggests another kind of question: Why systematize a method for breaking down the complexity of a technological process when specialists seem to do fairly well without it? In our opinion, there are several reasons.

Channeling technological progress. To determine its outcome and not be its promethean victim is clearly one of the major goals for modern society in the years to come. If it is to be achieved, it is by no means certain that the responsibility for such progress should be placed on the shoulders of specialists who, *nolens volens,* are installed within a particular technological discipline and have no immediate reasons to engage in forecasting the societal consequences. The technical solutions are often supplied to them by their intuition or by their habit. The technical workability of these solutions, moreover, is not in question here. It is rather their origin and the paths that their development has followed that are questionable. In our opinion, making the technologist's intuition explicit is made necessary by the need for general technological assessment (ecological, ethical, convivial, etc.), and especially for gaining much greater freedom with respect to customary ideas which, though valid in some respects, are prone to repetition of past errors in orientation. It is also an invitation to open the "black box" of a technological process taken en bloc and familiarize oneself with the handling of its constitutive elements in order to learn how to handle them safely. Along the same lines, it can be seen that, posed in this way, the problem of being able to guide technological development is specific to each country, but it is in no way attached to any particular category of country or to any given level of development. It is a constant interrogation to which there will never be general answers because the critical analysis that lies at its base is by definition particular.

Also, the advantages of structural breakdown of operational technologies reside in the pedagogic, or one might even say autopedagogic, character of the method. When the transfer of a complete technological process is involved (i.e., a more or less complex operational technology), it is first of all postulated that the proposed package is unique; its elementary operations (cutting, drilling, welding, etc., to take an example this time from the field of mechanics) are seen as fundamental components of the package, that is fundamental to the technological process in question, and strictly within the framework of the solution proposed. A structural view of the process, however, calls upon other analytic principles. It does not invite one to be the spectator of a successful achievement built by experts in order to be copied subsequently, but rather spurs the recipient of the technological transfer to examine the elements of the process in light of the basic characteristics of any technology (as formulated above: reliability, economic feasibility, safety, etc.) and to compare them with the elements presently available locally. Understood in this way, technological transfer becomes freed from the framework of an integrated process and becomes the subject of a critical appraisal of the partial objectives to be attained in the various stages of the process.

Finally, the manner of viewing things as proposed here places the engineer in a position of scientific doubt that prevents technological dependency and renders unnecessary the contractual maintenance and troubleshooting bonds with a foreign process that will soon be obsolete if it is merely faithfully copied from the original in its monolithic totality.

PROBLEMS INVOLVED IN STRUCTURAL BREAKDOWN

This section discusses the idea of structure at somewhat greater length by introducing the search for, and definition of, unit operations.

Though the notion of structure may seem clear from the preceding considerations, it is nonetheless necessary to remove any remaining ambiguity. In the true sense of the word, at least in the exact sciences, a structure refers to a geometric complex whose elements are not distributed at random. Here, it is practically through a process of abstraction that it has been taken to designate the form of a technological process (operational technology), because what one had in mind was to consider the process, in its completeness, relating its successive phases to elementary entities established from the outside on a more general basis. To be more precise, the variables of any technological process are not, however, simply those of its symbolic configuration; they are also temporal, inasmuch as the process unfolds in time. This point in no way alters the breakdown hypothesis, but it sheds light upon the properties of the analysis itself. Indeed, the unit operations extracted from the complete process will certainly result in the simplification required for transmission of the process, but mastering each one separately will still not ensure the continuity of their concatenation. This parameter, which is essential, is nevertheless very difficult to apprehend analytically and to dominate rationally. This is why a mere juxtaposition of structural units is insufficient to describe a technological process, even if it consists in a synthesis faithfully constructed like a reverse analysis. The analysis proceeds from the origin to the end product, but the construction of the continuity, on the contrary, proceeds backward, so to speak. It is indeed aimed at anticipating the following stage so that it will have every chance of being performed with the utmost reliability; but since optimizing in this way is always a delicate matter, it is safer to determine the previous stage starting from the end product, and so on, step by step, back to the initial material.

In this way, the make up of the stages, or, in structural language, the make-up of the unit operations, is largely determined by the constraint of continuity: overall dimensions, equipment location, access to material, availability of personnel, transportation means, etc.; and its breakdown is provided by the type of technology in question. In this connection, one might think that such a breakdown has to do chiefly with the responsibility for planning and that its relationship with technology is tenuous. It is quite true that a planning problem does exist, to the extent that planning is the art of forecasting and organizing action on the basis of the forecast; but planning always proceeds in a fashion that is too general and ill-suited for the circumstances with which we are dealing here. Actually, one must go right down to the level of elementary action to establish the detailed concatenations of the unit operations. One can readily imagine the entire hierarchy of importance and priorities to be established with a view to locating the key points in the process. This being the case, one can easily understand why it is far simpler to transfer an operational technology *en bloc,* together with its entire set of original sensitivities, than to bring the transferee to an awareness of the generation of the process.

Thus, if there exists a basic complexity at the level of unit operations, there exists a no less fundamental one at the level of the transitions between these operations—transitions that make for the cohesion of the whole. (By analogy with the cohesion of material systems in the condensed phase.)

These reflections have been aimed at showing that the problems of analysis are tied up with those of continuity and cannot be dissociated from them. Also, the internal structure of each unit operation must be conceived so as to provide for this continuity. It is therefore the result of a compromise, or rather the result of the various ways in which the elementary actions have to be performed to come to terms with the need to be linked together without any discontinuity in a given technological process. The structural-analysis concept combined with that of the continuity of unit operations constitutes, in our eyes, an essential contribution to the discussion of the problems connected with the hypothetical "technological spirit" mentioned above.

The relationship between a structural complex of operational units and the conditions governing the continuity between one unit and the next bring in the aspect of research and experimental development. This multiform activity here takes on its maximum effectiveness precisely because the attempt at structural breakdown forces the technologist to rethink the parameters that characterize a given technological process. A first set of questions is then likely to come to mind, related directly to reliability and aimed at the prevention of trouble and breakdowns that might curtail the efficiency of the equipment or the quality of the final product. It follows that the main thrust of the effort is toward optimizing the process in order to preserve it against any defect or failure. In the event of an interruption or disturbance, this attitude would lead to the question: "Why is the system not operating?" which would compel the operator to ascertain its workability.

However, while this set of questions calls for repairing a fault, there is another that is considerably more profound: "Why does the system work?" which requires a detailed, integrated explanation on the part of the operator. The actual workability of a process and the satisfaction of having overcome the various constraints imposed by production generally seem to make the latter question rather futile. And yet, asking it confronts the operator with an ontological problem and leads him to formulate an objective criticism of the operational technology as a whole, thus shifting his effort from technicalities to system design and conception. This second type of questioning is probably a more powerful stimulus than the first for research and development activity. It reveals that the simplicity of the structural approach is more apparent than real, hence making the operator more receptive, and at the same time more critical, with respect to imperatives such as economic, political, social, institutional and related constraints, as well as those pertaining to urgent societal needs. Establishing an organized structure consisting of unit operations within a process makes it possible to identify certain key questions relating to research and experimental development to be undertaken in connection with the process in question and is conducive to its dynamic integration in the form of a precise operational technology. It should be said in passing that, along the same line of thinking, this approach would be seen to apply to any sequence of actions taking place in time, regardless of their respective natures, right up to the borderline (which now becomes less clear) between technology and art.

UNIT OPERATIONS: THE SEARCH FOR CRITERIA

In the previous paragraphs, a technological production process was considered as an individualized entity. In particular, its structural subdivisions (ultimately, its constituent unit operations) were connected with specific individual situations. It is not reasonable, however, to maintain such specificity at all levels of complexity. Here let us briefly recall our assumptions:

- The number of processes in the various engineering fields (chemical, civil, aeronautic, etc.) is very great, but one can undertake their breakdown into elements referred to as unit operations, which can conceivably be classified typologically for the purposes of systems design and conception, R&D, teaching, statistical surveying and construction of technological development indicators.
- Such unit operations might be obtained through "atomization": i.e., through the reduction of technological processes down to a level of detail that can be considered irreducible (they have been assimilated to configuration units to remind one of the complexity of the initial whole).
- It is possible to identify such units experimentally, in this way establishing a sort of taxonomy of "technology," in the broadest sense of the term.

It would be venturesome, at the outset, to predict to what extent these working hypotheses might all be entirely satisfactory, for a substantial amount of work still remains to be done to develop the basic idea so that it will become an epistemologically acceptable theory that can be experimentally tested. This approach, moreover, was largely influenced by a need for operational simplification for the purposes of technology transfer and support to the technologically less developed areas. However legitimate this objective, it should not lead to minimization of the methodological problems involved. A few preliminary remarks are therefore necessary in order to narrow down the question of laying down criteria for the identification and construction of **unit operations.**

First of all, when one proposes breaking down a technological process, one may wonder where to stop, and the question of what "units" should be immediately arises. Intuitively, unit operations can be defined as those operations that characterize the most elementary actions involved in a given operational technology. This provisional definition can already be considered as workable, and it meets the usual conditions under which the actions take place. Unit operations thus serve here as breakdown limits, which does not mean that they are restricted to a single movement made by the operator. They may even be relatively difficult to carry out and yet still retain their basic character. For example, one might turn to chemical engineering and take the case of distillation. It presupposes that one has the basic equipment (containers, tubes and connections); that one knows how to set it up; that one has means for monitoring and controlling pressure and temperature; that one is in control of fraction purity; and that one knows how to collect these fractions, eliminate residues and carry out the operations of cleaning and reloading. This unit operation is thus far from simple. The same will no doubt be true of the other unit operations of chemical engineering, and obviously, of other engineering fields.

At a higher level of development, one would have to examine how the unit operation fits into a complete technological process. Here, to be sure, it will maintain its unitary properties; but questions inherent in the continuity of the process are to be added. Raising the level still further, the unit operation may be combined with other operations, now becoming a part of a complex ensemble suitable for comprehending the whole technological process and this time acting as a structural unit, in keeping with the remarks in the foregoing section.

It can thus be seen that to each stage of development of an operational technology, there corresponds a set of "tailor-made" structural components. Selecting appropriate parametric dimensions for them would certainly constitute a goal to be achieved by research and development attached to an already acquired technology. Determination of such parametric dimensions is to our minds, desirable and even essential, for characterizing the constituent elements of future structural components. These elements are none other than the unit operations that we have proposed. The term "unit" or "unitary" here takes on its full meaning, because it immediately suggests what the basic constituents of the structural components are. Inasmuch as the perspective adopted in this study is that of the communication of technology, in particular to countries whose level of development is modest, it is clear that, before one attacks structural problems, it is those pertaining to elementary actions that will have priority. Nevertheless, we felt that it would be helpful to situate the unit operations within their functional framework, particularly in view of the fact that they are not always as obvious as in chemical or mechanical engineering. There are technological processes in which defining unit operations is difficult. Consequently, in order to avoid additional complications, we shall address ourselves to operational technologies that are apparently easier to approach and leave aside those which, although widely in use, would quickly prove intractable. It also makes sense, for practical reasons, to maintain for the time being the customary boundaries of economic sectors, though they are of greater significance from the administrative than from the technological standpoint. We shall further admit the existence of the various fields of engineering: electronic, civil, chemical, etc., to which one customarily refers in the industrial production of textiles, leather goods, buildings and public works, transport and communications, plastics, etc.

It is within these frameworks that we shall endeavour to define unit operations within selected operational technologies. This first exercise—although purposefully restricted—will nevertheless be of operational interest, though it may be peculiar to a given economic or industrial sector. It should logically be followed by a second phase, which would ignore industrial or economic sectoriality and aim at general applicability. Relationships might then come to light whereby it would be possible retrospectively to view the sectors as so many languages all conforming, *mutatis mutandis,* to a common syntagmatic structure. Needless to say, this would be achieved only after painstaking empirical study and by virtue of intellectual abstraction. So numerous are the technological entities that one would be tempted to view as grammatical elements (i.e., unit operations) suitable for building up sentences (i.e., operational technologies).

Considering all that has been said, the central problem posed by the definition of unit operations is certainly that of **breakdown criteria.** Here again, it is difficult to say anything without using actual examples taken from activities carried on in various engineering fields. Yet, one can catch glimpses of certain possibilities, some far more satisfactory than others, some already tested and others still in the potential stage.

In a simplified approach to the breaking-down of processes, we managed to get down to the level of the "spare part," and, in the manner of an exhaustive inventory, itemize a petrochemical plant in terms of elementary fractions of equipment and materials. In this way, it was possible to obtain the functional subassemblies of the plant and also a list of components such as piping, supports, valves and fittings, etc. This breakdown was undertaken by engineers who were rather dissatisfied with a technology transfer conceived on the "turnkey" pattern and who had resolved to take upon their own shoulders the full responsibility for the plant. It is manifestly useful for the on-the-job training referred to above, but the form of analysis that it involves does not show the structural elements, which, to our minds, would have a more significant reach. Nevertheless, it must be granted that it has the merit of having opened the technological package delivered *en bloc* and of having extracted from it the material components encountered in numerous other similar installations. Would it have been possible, in any event, to do much more, without any methodology and faced with the inextricable complexity of petrochemistry, which is apparently irreducible?

Another test, conducted this time on the national level, was aimed at measuring the degree of mastery attained by a country in various spheres of industrial production.

Considering industrial operations, such as those of mechanics, for example, a list was made of the principal objects relating to production (graphs and charts, sketches, structures, etc.). Next, the details of their manufacture, which requires a certain number of simple actions to be carried out, were examined. (For our purposes, let us say that they are unit operations, to make things clearer.) These actions are characteristic of one type of engineering, in this case mechanical engineering, and suited to a particular type of production: turning, milling, drilling, thread-cutting, welding, etc. Success in production obviously depends on each one of these simple actions being mastered. Although their concatenation was not examined, it was possible in an initial stage (the one of primary interest to us in this study), to ascertain the level of such mastery in a given process, using an arbitrary scale. By extending this inquiry to all mechanical processes, a set of simple measurements was obtained, the internal distribution of which is a profile of the degree of technological development of the country within the field of mechanics. The same procedure was followed for other engineering fields.

Although this approach takes technology as something given a priority and initially leaves little room for endogenous solutions, it is remarkably efficient as an assessment instrument and promises to be fully applicable to the unit operations and the structural components (or structural units) to which we have referred.

In these first two tests, the **elementariness of the local action and that of the component** would represent the criteria for breaking down technology. One might conceive of others, derived, in particular, from continuity and chronology.

The **chronology** of operations would probably be a safe guide for establishing structural units. Indeed, the successive stages of the construction of an object or of an engineering structure can always roughly serve as structural limits, at least when processes are linear. Such processes exist in well-defined operations, corresponding to recognized trades, and they follow one another in a cursive manner: theoretical discussion, analysis of socio-economic guarantees, planning, starting work on the site, performance of work, finishing, maintenance—these are the main categories of comprehensive operations within which structures must be established, taking specific contraints into account. The chronology of these operations in itself is not absolute, but it is patterned on reality, inasmuch as it faithfully follows the stages of the process itself. The different stages of a chemical synthesis in the laboratory would be a suggestive image of this. This description is simple and it can be applied without difficulty to numerous processes that result in standardized products that can probably not be had by any routes other than the standard production (or construction) itineraries. In these cases, for which some kind of typology could conceivably be developed, the structural units would take on their normative value, analogous to that of an atom of a given element. Despite its importance, however, specificity of this sort represents only one particular aspect of technology.[2] For processes falling within fields of endeavour considered "aggregate" (i.e., more heterogeneous, from a disciplinary point of view), the definition of the unit operation will not be so easy to define. The end product, too, when delivered by a process that is outside the framework of a standard technology, may take on a variety of forms, related to a central concept, but depending upon a host of parameters, not all of which belong to the realm of technology.[3] This is what one observes, for example, with highway structures or other civil-engineering constructions (dams or apartment houses). The general external constraints (holding back water, living in comfort) and the material conditions (being durable, offering guarantees of safety or sturdiness) are unchanging and will continue to exist, but the circumstantial parameters (materials, climate, geography, cost, labour) will determine a particular definition of the end product, which will likewise entail a particular manner of construction. The atomization method will remain valid, but for an object bearing the same name, it will no doubt result in other atoms. It should not be concluded that this involves any restriction on the basic hypothesis, but rather a broadening of its field of application through increased diversity.

Continuity between the stages of the process likewise suggests an array of important criteria, this time from a limitative standpoint. It has been suggested before (practically in the form of a definition), that the linking of one operation to the next was provided by the whole set of precautions to be taken with a view to preventing discontinuities or breakdowns. Given this, one might think of determining the optimum size of a unit operation, taking into account the number and size of its internal elements making for continuity.

Obviously, other criteria will have to be identified empirically in a case-by-case study. For the present, it would be difficult to be more precise because operational technology is, after all, an abstract representation of the action of industrial production which is not connected exclusively with one economic sector of activity such as health, agriculture or transportation.

All of the foregoing considerations relating to the structural units that we are seeking are of a strictly technical nature. However, based on the same observations of complexity made earlier one would also have to take into account the **economic parameters** of technological processes, right down to the delineation of unit operations. This might in turn have a bearing on the search for criteria used in the latter connection. In particular, one might take up the same lines of argument and interpret them in terms of cost, personnel, markets, even policies and other key variables used in deciding whether to adopt a process or in assessing the options to be considered in the interest of the industrial development of the country on the macro-economic scale. The relationship between technological structures and economic variables is no clearer than the relationship between scientific knowledge and this very same technology. At most, one observes mutual limitations that bring about compromises considered to be signs of optimization. Thus, it would not be surprising to speak now from a socio-economic point of view, if one were to be able to define formally the unit operations of a technological process that were different from those obtained by reduction of technological complexity. Unfortunately, owing to the present absence of any unified theory, it does not seem possible to predict any relationship between these two types of operations, not to mention the integration of one into the other, though such streamlining would be extremely useful. For the time being, they should be viewed as complementing one another without asking oneself too many questions about the nature of such complementarity.

APPLICATION TO THE CONSTRUCTION OF INDICATORS OF TECHNOLOGICAL DEVELOPMENT

The purpose of the exercise of breaking technological processes down to the level of unit operations considered as irreducible structures is far from academic. The considerations developed in this study are of prime importance for understanding the unit operation approach among all the activities that favour technological development. These considerations are aimed, in particular, at making it possible to measure technical competence. Such a measurement can be applied directly to unit operations and it would indicate the related level of skill and knowledge attained on an arbitrary scale. The values obtained would then be considered as indicators of **technological development.** How could these indicators be constructed?

The unit operation as defined above is theoretically a structural limit. This view is still valid here, but constructing indicators on such an abstract basis would quickly run up against considerable difficulties. It is therefore preferable—as a first step—to have the indicators in question coincide with the simplest operations of currently used linear technological processes (in the example given above for the field of mechanics: turning, milling, etc.). Certain precautions must be taken, it is true. Mastery over any unit operation taken by itself, for instance, does not guarantee the same to be true when the operation is integrated into a technological process. Again, knowing how to turn a piece on a lathe is not in itself very meaningful: it is necessary to know how to turn a piece made from a certain material. If it is changed, the conditions, too, will change, perhaps with certain complications inherent in the quality of the material (hardness, friability) that would entail consequences in the areas of precision tolerances, surface quality, wearing of the cutting tool, sharpening it, etc. It will therefore be necessary to be specific in describing the circumstances under which the estimate of skill and knowledge has been made.

Indicators based on the simplest unit operations as suggested here thus only partially indicate a level of technological development. In an initial stage, however, they may prove very useful, for they would reflect the capacity of a country or an industrial concern to master elementary operations, regardless of the general (extrinsic) conditions that prevail with respect to a given operational technology (personnel training, availability of labour, presence of competent foremen, access to material, availability of equipment, economic support, suitability of working conditions, etc.). That is where the main interest of such "technological development indicators" lies. And that is why they can be considered **comparative indicators** with respect to the standard technological processes. It is clear that no attempt would be made to turn them into criteria applicable to the assessment of a technological process taken as a whole: the arguments put forward in the preceding sections and pertaining to the structural cohesion of technological processes were aimed precisely at avoiding that pitfall. Attention is simply being called to the requisite skills and knowledge needed to master unit operations. Keeping these remarks in mind, the following definitions can be proposed for a "unit operation":

- **Special:** Considering a simple (linear) technological process (or operational technology), a unit operation would be defined as the most elementary action that at the same time characterizes one of the phases of this process and would apply to other processes in the same engineering field under analogous conditions.
- **General:** Not tied to a specific technological process, the unit operation would be defined as a fundamental element of a given engineering field. Mastery over it, recorded in an unequivocal manner, would constitute an indicator of technological development in that field.

The applicability of these definitions seems to be both very general and independent of the actual level of development of a country. Technological gaps can thus be spotted and this in turn may have a close bearing upon the problems of the selection and transfer of technology. A few comments on concepts that are difficult to grasp and are currently the topic of numerous discussions may be useful in this connection. Firstly, some views expressed in the Vienna Programme of Action on Science and Technology for Development[4] may appropriately be recalled:

Transfer, acquisition and assessment of technology

27. Each developing country should formulate a policy on transfer and acquisition of technology as an integral part of its national policy for scientific and technological development. Such a policy should provide for a technological spectrum ranging from the most simple to the most advanced technologies and for the assimilation and adaptation of imported technology.

28. Further, developing countries should strengthen their capacities for the assessment of technologies from the point of view of their national development objective.

29. Developing countries should develop the capacity to **unpackage** (emphasis added) technologies to be acquired so as to make a financial evaluation of the different elements and an evaluation of the different elements and an evaluation of their technical specifications. In this connexion, developing countries should also develop the capacity:

(a) To know in advance the amount of untied financial resources needed to finance what can be internally procured;

(b) To plan the training of human resources in order to provide needed technological capacities and the establishment of those installations necessary to produce new products and capital goods;

(c) To determine the contribution of imported technology to the development of the national technological base and its effect on the industrial structure of the recipient country and on the environment.

These lines were written within the perspective of aid to be provided to the developing countries, and they encourage those countries to achieve a level of technological competence that will enable them to absorb efficiently the required support. The "unpackaging" referred to above is aimed precisely at preventing the purchase of a "black box" without further ado. But to do this, one must have a method at one's disposal in order to make it useful to break down a technological process or an operational technology, frequently handed over as an entire plant on a "turnkey" basis. In keeping with the approach adopted in this study, it is felt that breaking down technological processes as far as their **unit operation** level makes it possible to open the "technological package." It is to these unit operations that one should refer as a matter of priority in order to initiate and maintain technological development.

Second, among the concepts currently discussed, it should be stressed that the notion of "technological lag" occupies a privileged position. It is clear that, with respect to certain advanced countries, others heading in similar directions (either actually or potentially) might be referred to as lagging behind to a greater or lesser degree. Nevertheless, it must be borne in mind that the greatest diversity reigns among nations, especially in the area of technological development, and in this connection especially, it is impossible to lump the developing countries under a single definition. The levels of technological development are not uniform, any more than those of the technological production processes themselves. Consequently, the highly questionable relevance of certain "technological lines," and the difficulty of finding standards, criteria, zeros and benchmarks impose caution and subtlety in making judgments about backwardness or advancement. The fact is that a lag is due to a multiplicity of intrinsic factors inherent in technology (shortage of material, unreliability, inadequacies in quality control) as well as extrinsic ones (poor personnel training, emigration of labour, planning errors, etc.). These facts are well known and there is no need to dwell on them.

Hence, it is far more constructive to seek to analyze such situations by using simple but easily applicable criteria, and to propose methods for determining such criteria. With a view to raising the level of technological development, it might be more advantageous to strengthen existing resources, skills and knowledge and systematically add to them, little by little, until complete technological processes are constructed. For such incremental evolution, the concept of "unit operations" is certainly an adequate tool since these operations are at the same time reference elements (reference indicators). One is induced to organize the growth of a technological process, one unit operation after the other. By applying such a procedure, developing countries no longer feel in a position of global technological backwardness but are made to confront a spectrum of "unit lags." In this way, the technological development indicator can be adjusted to the overall development level of the country and will never take on that too-easily severe character that comparisons with modern advanced or science-based technologies would have had.

Third, speaking of such technologies, it may be observed that for more advanced countries or threshold countries, where production technologies exist and are already operational, the "unit operations" methodology proposed in this study would remain unchanged. Only the way of measuring would have to be modified. Backwardness would thus be estimated in terms of the time reasonably required in order to bridge the technological gap. In keeping with the view of things, it is the most recent performances that will be taken as points of comparison. Lag categories might be imagined, depending upon whether from one to three years, three to five, five to eight, or eight to fifteen were required in order to catch up with the front ranks. The aim for a country would be to pass systematically from one lag class to the next higher class, process by process, until it equalled or even surpassed the best. It is plain, incidentally, that there will be wide variation in rates of advancement from one industrial sector to another and, obviously, from one country to another. It is by applying such analytical tools to their policy making for technological development that certain developing countries that are now highly advanced achieved spectacular progress in the past decades.

This being the case, the technological development policy of a developing country has to deal with a range of different parameters. It is free to set goals very different from those aimed at competing with the best, if it feels, for example, that the advanced state-of-the-art technology used as a general reference was developed under economic or ethical conditions that do not prevail at home. For this reason, it may very well decide to restrict technological development to a selection of operational technologies belonging to certain economic or industrial sectors and to assign upper limits to such development, considering that it will suffice for the resources that will be available to the country in the coming 20 or 50 years. The fact of the matter is that technical development that is strong in a particular direction rapidly ceases to be independent of the overall technological development of the whole country.[5] In the face of the consequences brought about by technological development, the opportuneness of indicators based on unit operation takes on its full significance. In particular, it makes it possible to seek endogenous solutions which the adoption of a standard technological process would have relegated to the background, be it only for having been considered utopic. In other words, in the light of this second remark, "technological lag" indicators would be unequivocal under certain sets of circumstances only, but this in no way affects the validity of the basic hypothesis.

Aside from the development and systematic interdependence of the various operational technologies, the same concerns for elementariness may be brought into play in the process of selection and acquisition of technology. Here again, it would be wise to rate the relevance of options on the basis of unit operations used as relevance indicators. It goes without saying that such indicators would contribute only partially to policy decision-making relating to the choice of operational technology, in which numerous extrinsic parameters must be taken into account.

In this connection, very advantageous use might be made of inventories relating to the presence and the state of "unit technologies" within the country. The detailed situation of technological processes (whether proposed, partially completed, or already in operation) should be surveyed by means of questionnaires especially designed for this purpose. It would then be possible, based on an analysis of replies, to provide answers to some prerequisite conditions for the country's future technological development. Is it wise to acquire a technology requiring a number of unit operations that is far greater than that which is presently being mastered by the country? Must one not rather ensure the smooth operation of technological processes that are currently becoming operational in the country? What processes should one select in order for newly implemented unit operations to raise the country's technological level, without entailing the need for creating new infrastructures that the country cannot afford at present? To what extent can one be bold without being rash? These questions, among others of the same kind, constitute the grass-root level of scientific and technological policy. Even for countries considered advanced, they should be raised in the same manner, so as to avoid unpleasant, costly surprises. The follow up of this study will therefore, of necessity, include preparation of the relevant questionnaires.

The quantification of indicators based on unit operations itself also poses theoretical problems. Intuitive semi-quantitative estimations, which are often reasonable, yield indicators of little comparative value. On the other hand, inasmuch as the indicators contemplated are based on complex units, they require both a scale of complexity together with a measurement of skilfullness. For the latter, an arbitrary scale might set up with five ratings: nil, poor, fair, good, excellent, in this way avoiding the crudeness of a "yes or no" rating. When extended to various analogous processes, it will lead to a profile of national competence which might be used to stake out the technological development plan. It will be useful in particular for gauging the progress made along a certain line of development, and as a first approximation it will probably be satisfactory for that purpose.

However, one should go further into the particulars of the technological processes themselves, in order to pinpoint the causes of failures, weaknesses or local breakdown. In this connection it is recognized that elementary actions that are reproducible by simple imitation do not constitute a serious obstacle, provided that one has adequate equipment and detailed instructions. The equipment can be acquired, the modus operandi can be explained in painstaking details. Moreover, at the elementary action level, worker skill is virtually the same everywhere. The difficulty appears at the moment when elementary actions are combined with other actions into a "unit operation" and when the latter must be concatenated in time and space with others. It often appears that it is in the internal make up of the unit operations that one must look for the deficiencies or errors. Thus, quantifying the indicator is certainly useful, even indispensable, but identifying and perhaps quantifying the make up of the unit operation would be far more important and fundamental for the development of a country's "technological spirit." Such makeup includes the conditions that have to be met in order to satisfy the basic imperatives of technology: reliability, economic feasibility, safety, etc.). Quantification, effected *in situ,* (i.e., within unit operations) characterizes the actual degree of technological development in a given technological process. One can then step outside of the limited framework of a given technological process and ask oneself whether the faults observed are not also present in another one, *mutatis mutandis.* Through this type of investigation one would finally reach certain roots of the "technological spirit" that ought to guide the conduct of production operations, which, if erratic or faulty, may compromise the success of other development activities.

SELECTION OF TEST TECHNOLOGIES

Up to now, technological processes have been dealt with in the abstract, as entities that one encounters in all the productive activities of society and in connection with its major development goals in agriculture, education, transportation and communication, energy, etc. They will now be approached in concrete form. Since it is impossible to itemize all operational technologies, and since there is as yet no methodology available for synthesizing them, a choice must be made that is a compromise between the importance of the economic or industrial sectors selected, and the resources available for carrying out this research. As a working hypothesis, one might take up the following technologies:

- electronics technology
- chemical engineering
- civil engineering
- mechanical engineering

These generic technologies are of enormous importance in industry, and they reasonably cover the production sectors involving to a greater or lesser extent all of the major societal development goals. Owing to the interdependence of all technologies, it seems difficult for a country to ignore those generic technologies. In what follows, comments will first be made on the nature of these generic technologies and on the teachings that can be culled from breaking down technological processes that involve them. The comments will of course be of a provisional nature since experience alone will reveal the true characteristics of the selected generic technologies and of the break-down method being applied to them.

Electronics technology

The processes of electronic technology offer certain advantages for the purpose of this study. In the first place, during the past few decades electronics has developed at a very fast pace and on a gigantic scale. It nowadays plays a major role in industry as a whole. In the second place, it touches upon numerous fields of activity, such as telecommunications, metrology, data processing, monitoring, regulating, etc. What is more, this technology, far from being attached only to weak currents, is also extendible to power equipment, as well as to the electrical mains (high-tension, traction sector, industrial sector, light and household appliance sector). Most important, however, for the purposes that are of interest here from the methodological standpoint, it fulfills two essential conditions:

First of all, it presents an extremely broad spectrum of complexity, from the simplest to the most sophisticated, with more-or-less continuous gradations, With it one can therefore establish classes of complexity and classes of backwardness, or lag.

Second, its operations are generally carried out in series, following a linear pattern. Furthermore, they are clearly defined and correspond to precise, simple functions both at the elementary action level (rectification, amplification, peak-clipping, and so on) and at the module or assembly level (receiver, transmitter, remote-control stage, repeater, etc.). With these two conditions met, one can foresee that the elaboration of unit operations will not, *a priori,* run up against insuperable obstacles. Up to what level of complexity such obstacles can still be surmounted will of course have to be established as work proceeds.

In this connection, it should be mentioned that everyday electronics operations involve, in particular, the assembly of components and modules already in existence on the market. In routine cases they will mainly consist of connecting and repairing equipment. Aside from these ordinary activities there obviously exist less elementary forms of development. In particular, one might mention special tubes (klystrons or TV tubes, for example) that involve other skills: technology of solid metal surfaces, high-pressure, etc. Being more composite, these operations will in all likelihood also be less linear, and they will result in structural units structures that are not so easy to apprehend.

Lastly, side by side with these multi-component forms, the integrated forms arising from the development of the transistor effect in semi-conductors and other solid-state devices cannot be left aside. A science-based industry includes both the preparation of the material substrates as well as the designing and building of the device. Such processing, though done on a routine basis, is always difficult due to the fact that the electrical properties of the component depend on the crystalline structure of the substrate (monocrystal structure and chemical composition) and especially because operations that are apparently simple when passive elements such as conventional tubes or wire or even printed-circuit connections are involved become far more delicate when one is working with highly sensitive materials for the purposes of miniaturization. With such substrates one reaches the limits of the classic operations belonging to the different engineering fields, while it is not possible to relate them to a single technological discipline. Here we will run into difficulties of comparability and of method **(how far should the breakdown process be pushed?)** since, in the same complete process would be encountered the growing of silicon monocrystals and the preparation of a telemetering device for use in an artificial satellite, for example. Side by side with the characteristic scale of complexity of a process it will probably be necessary to establish a scale of heterogeneity in the very nature of the activities forming part of the operation's make up. What is involved in this case is the contribution that one technology makes to another. From this viewpoint one cannot say whether electronics is simply an exception to sectoriality or whether it is already a technology designed along the lines of the future; yet it is quite possible that structural analysis may enable this question to be answered and thus suggest other avant-garde forms.

Chemical engineering

Most unit operations of chemical engineering have long since been identified and systematized. They gave rise to several of the themes of this study and can therefore be taken as prototypes. We know the varieties: crystallization, distillation, filtration, etc. to which there corresponds appropriate equipment: crystallizing tanks, fractionating columns, filter presses, etc. They theoretically make a structural breakdown of the entire field of chemical engineering possible. It may be, moreover, that chemical engineering lends itself better than others to a reduction of complex sets of industrial procedures. In particular, in relatively simple cases, classic synthesizing processes might come to mind, whereby standard organic functions are prepared (ketones, nitriles, carboxyls, etc.). Here the use of unit operations in their elementary form is everyday fare. It is in fact precisely in systems of this kind that they were identified.

Others do exist, however, that present unexpected difficulties: one need only mention sulfuric acid synthesis, the most classic of procedures. Thus, in the face of the complexity of certain industrial syntheses, it is surprising to find that chemistry, which is at the origin of unit operations, is also the field in which they are often elusive because the processes frequently cease to be linear. The reason for this is that endeavours to lower the cost, one of the chief objectives of the chemical industry, require from processes an increase in yields and the minimization of the energy expenditures involved (thermal or mechanical). Thus synthesis will appear as a complex system in which the reagents are recycled, by-products are collected or destroyed and energy (essentially heat) is redistributed through the system independently of the chronological order of operations symbolized by an elementary diagram or by the basic chemical equation. The process will appear as an integrated whole and its degree of development will often be correlated with its degree of sophistication. Certain processes will even be so elaborate that they will constitute self-contained networks, like gigantic unit operations, such as one can picture in certain petrochemical plants. In order to single out elementary operations from such complexes it will probably be necessary to have recourse to a unique structural analysis derived from economic as much as from technological parameters.

These considerations might lead one to believe that the efficiency of a chemical system depends exclusively on its design. Nothing of the sort. One must not minimize the importance of equipment performance and, in particular, that of quality control equipment during the manufacturing process and of equipment for analysing the initial substances. Thus, to take an example, cement quality (what is meant, by extrapolation, is the sturdiness and longevity of the highway structures built) depends on the precise composition in terms of lime, silica and impurities at the outset. Precise, reliable and rapid analysis (X-ray fluorescence) guarantees such quality without any break in the flow of production. Numerous other similar examples would show a degree of advancement of technology at the level of the elementary action and, indirectly, at the level of the unit operation.

Civil engineering

Civil engineering, like electronics technology, leads to the construction of an object, leaving aside any question of scale. Inasmuch as such construction is carried out through serial actions, stage by stage, it should be possible to pinpoint unit operations without any great complications, in the simplest cases: i.e., those that are linear in structure. The difficulty is rather located at the level of operations planning and concatenation of operations. The construction of a highway would be a typical example. Along the same line of thinking, one will also have to consider the preparation of a network of pipelines (for sewers, or for water or gas distribution). In this there will certainly be a profound similarity with electric power distribution and the building of telecommunications lines. Is it possible that there may be unit operations that are common to all distribution networks?

Analysing the construction of buildings and certain major road structures will probably be less simple, owing in part to the composite nature of the work, and in part to the high degree of dependence upon local conditions, available materials and transport means. To be specific, let us take concrete as an example. Though in the countries of Europe it may play a dominant role in building construction, the same is not true in southern countries, such as those of Africa, for example. For in order to make concrete you need cement, and the economic feasibility of a cement works depends on the nearness of quarries, sources of limestone. But the African soil is poor in limestone and this shortage, coupled with the modest extension of the road and railway networks considerably raises the cost of cement, thus limiting to a great extent the number of concrete structures built. One must therefore think of architectures and structures that consume less of it whenever possible. These restrictions, moreover, rather than slowing down progress, ought to stimulate the search for endogenous solutions that are just as operational as the conventional processes, if not more so, and are in any event less costly.

In this connection one might mention, as examples, the construction of bridges and dams. One standard solution in keeping with a certain conception of technology consists in the unconditional use of concrete, which guarantees that the structure will be sturdy and therefore safe for its users. It does not follow, however, that this is the only solution or that a correspondence between structure and operability of such a structure through interposed concrete is bi-univocal. If what is involved is a dam, the designing of structures that hold back water and use less concrete is perfectly plausible. The correlation between the use of concrete and the level of technological development is thus opened to question. To be more precise: in the classic case, one should speak of concrete technology, and in the case referred to, one speaks of the technology of the engineering structure. The distinction between the end and the means must be respected. It is plainly evident that the concrete structure will be stronger than the other, but only at a certain threshold tonnage. It will thus be necessary to develop a technology of smaller structures which, as a totality, can compete with the single structure. An endogenous solution of this sort comes under another idea of technological progress, and also a different turn of mind, as regards the "technological spirit," from the first one.

Mechanical engineering

This field also covers every degree of complexity, from shop techniques to those of automobile or aircraft assembly lines. Within the context of this study, the unit operations to be considered will rather be those that take care of the maintenance of transport equipment such as motor vehicles or even certain elements of the railroad fleet. The obvious aim is to enable developing countries—in a first stage—not to be tributaries of the manufacturer for spare parts or services. In the particular case of agriculture, the considerable effort scheduled for the coming years for reinforcing mechanization imposes upon one the ability to maintain the fleet (tractors, ploughs, hydraulic equipment, etc.), not to mention the specific means for transporting farm produce from the place of production to agro-industries or distribution centres.

CONCLUSION

The guidelines sketched out in this study will have to pass the acid test of experimental application to operational technologies in the four selected fields of engineering, the principles of which govern operations in numerous branches of industry. These guidelines have several purposes:

First of all, an attempt was made to establish the "problematique" of a method for breaking down technological processes, with a view to defining **intrinsic technological development indicators.** This is why a critical attitude was adopted in some instances with respect to the method itself, in order to forestall possible difficulties arising during the experimental follow-up phase of this study.

In addition, this discussion of problems and issues revealed the need for a set of tools and, in particular, definitions for concepts that are generally hard to approach and often fugitive. Following are some of these definitions, by way of a summary:

- **Unit-operation:** This is the simplest action characterizing both a stage in a given technological process and a type of action frequently encountered within the same engineering field.
- Defined in this way, the unit operation appears as a **structural limit** in a technological process, since the structure of the process is generally complex and cannot readily be reduced to elementary entities.
- Elementary actions are simple operations grouped and combined into these unit operations.

- An **operational technology** is a sequence of unit operations in which the latter maintain most or all of their characteristics and lead to the production of an object following a (usually) linear process.

One will have no difficulty in conceiving of a whole array of cases in which the original unit operations are coupled together in more and more complex processes. For such structures other units will obviously have to be conceived and identified. In this second-generation study, one would endeavour to establish, at the structural level, *unit technologies* analogous to the unit operations established at the elementary level.

An attempt has been made to show the considerable advantages of unit operations for designing technological development indicators:

- Applied to standard situations, they constitute **reference indicators,** without prejudice to the search for endogenous solutions.
- In the case of an analysis of the technological status of a country or an enterprise, they may serve as **technological lag indicators,** in that they indicate, at the elementary level, the af conditions that still need to be fulfilled in order to ensure the operability of a given technological production process.
- For the selection and acquisition of new technologies, they may be used as **relevance indicators,** due to the fact that they tend to force designers and decision-makers to gauge suitability of an option in relation to the simplest technical needs to be satisfied.

From the practical standpoint, a national survey of technological development should be taken through appropriate computerized questionnaires. The principal objects produced by processes in the four engineering fields proposed (chemistry, electronics, civil and mechanical engineering) should be related to the simplest unit operations. To the question, "Have you mastered operations A,B,C, . . . producing X?" the raw answer will simply be 0 or 1. In a more advanced questionnaire, a five-level scale would be used for further specification.

This approach to technological development seems well-suited for developing countries, for it does not stop at a mere overall estimate of the output of a process, but rather attempts to delve into the details of a series of constitutive operations down to the level of the most elementary actions.

Lastly, aside from the objective measurement that one can reasonably expect from such a method, this method may well have the advantage of drawing attention to the possibility of breaking down processes often delivered as "technological packages" in monolithic form. It in fact involves a methodology which allows developing countries to free themselves little by little from their present dependency on technologies brought in from elsewhere, and getting them fully under control.

NOTES

1. See UNESCO document NS/ROU/487 "Problematique et indicateurs du developpement scientifique et technologique. Questionnaire destine a l'identification de quelques questions de base."

2. To continue the analogy with chemistry, it should be noted that there is a considerable difference between the isolated atom and its properties in a molecule, a liquid, a crystalline network or a polymer. When integrated into a composition, the atom loses its individuality through its "bonds" with one or more other atoms.

3. A more integrated view would consist in considering the action and the conditions as dissociable and as constituting the *in situ* technology. While this approach would be closer to reality, it would inevitably run up against methodological obstacles!

4. Published by the Division of Economic and Social Information, DPI.DSI.F.73, United Nations, New York, 1979, p. 9.

5. One of the most significant examples can be given by the setting up of the nuclear industry, which on the one hand constitutes an important solution (and in some instances the only one) for establishing a centralized source of power, but which, on the other hand, requires a technological infrastructure that countries which ought to be the first beneficiaries of it, often do not have at their disposal. This is why a painstaking analysis must be made in order to take stock of the conditions to be fulfilled: first of all, to see to it that native technical staff is involved in the undertaking, and secondly, to make sure that all the consequences of setting up such facilities have been considered at their true value.

5

Scientometric Measures for International Technology Inequitability and Its Field-by-Field Comparison

Hajime Eto

ABSTRACT

This paper analyzes the result of attempts to verify the applicability of the Bradford distribution to international science bibliometric analysis. The Bradford distribution, which is empirically known to be valid for the numbers of scientific articles in journals, applies here to the numbers of scientific articles in a given field across nations. As expected, the Bradford distribution is found to provide useful information for measuring the degree of unequitability or the extent of the gap between developed and developing nations. Furthermore, it is found to indicate, though with some uncertainty, whether the gap is being narrowed or widened. Hence it may serve as an international science and technology index, if not as an integrated indicator, as a part of integrated science and technology indicator.

INTRODUCTION

It is now widely recognized that science and technology are the essential factors for agricultural and industrial development and for the improvement of sanitary conditions. Hence the development of S&T is the crucial task of developing nations. Ironically, however, S&T are very unequitably distributed among nations, more so than GNP or income.[1] Therefore it is extremely important to reduce this inequitability, especially by narrowing the gap between developed and developing nations. This implies that one of the important tasks of S&T indicators (STI) is: to measure the present degree of the inequitability of the gap (Task 1),

Figure 5.1. The Shape of the
Bradford Distribution

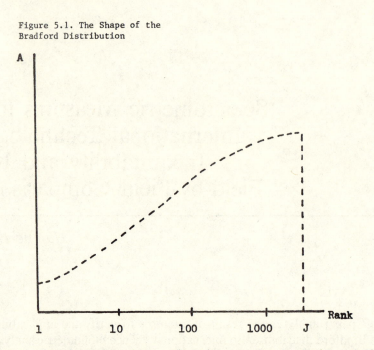

and to indicate whether the gap is being narrowed or widened (Task 2).

The GINI Index has been widely used to measure the degree of inequitability (Task 1). It can also be useful to indicate the trend toward narrowing or widening the gap (Task 2) by its sequential applications to time-series data if it is available. Very often, however, international S&T data are available only for one year or a maximum of a few years. Most statistical analysis methods are incapable of carrying out Task 2 for data covering one or more years. If a method is found to carry out Task 2 under this condition, it will be highly useful for STI. The Bradford distribution is a candidate for this, and the next section will discuss its usefulness for STI and the sections thereafter will show the result of its application to STI and its validity.

THE BRADFORD DISTRIBUTION

S.C. Bradford empirically found[2] that the cumulative number of scientific articles on a given research topic arranged in the rank of journals forms a particular shape (Fig.5.1). Here, journals are ranked according to the number of articles published and are placed on the logarithmic axis while the cumulative number of articles denoted by Ai are plotted on the normal axis. As a cumulative number,

$$A_i = \sum_{j=1}^{i} a_i$$

where i is a rank and a j is the number of articles published in the journal ranked j, i=1, with J denoting the total number of journals.

The following properties, (denoted by Bradford properties) have been found for the graph of the Bradford distribution[2] (Fig. 5.2).

P1. The log-linearity: The middle part of the graph is linear in the semi-log graph. This log-linear line will be denoted by l hereafter. It is explained by the fact that the publication on the topic is not limited to the core journals that first published articles on the topic but is diffused to other journals with a diffusion speed. When the speed is stationary, the associated graph is expressed by l.

P2. The distinctiveness of core: The curve associated with the top-ranked journals is equivalent to above l. These journals are called the core journals. The core journals which first published articles on the topic attract new articles as the authors tend to choose them. This is regarded as having cumulative advantage.

P3. The conditional existence of droop: The curve associated with the lower-ranked journals appears below l when the collection of articles

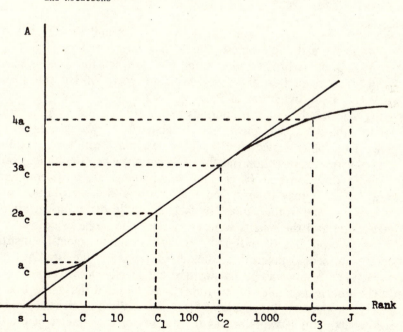

Figure 5.2. Parameters and Notations

is incomplete or when the research topic under investigation is still at an immature stage. When the publication activities on the topic are not yet diffused enough to peripheral journals, the diffusion speed is not yet stationary for distantly peripheral journals.

P4. The equal ratio or geometric zoning:

$$\text{Rank}(c_k) = \text{Rank}(c_{k-1} + cb^k) \text{ for } k = 1, \ldots \text{ with } c_0 = c$$

where Rank (r) denotes the location of the journal ranked r on the logarithmic axis, that is, Rank (r) = log r.

In other words, the number of articles published by the journals ranked from $c_{k-1} + 1$ to $c_{k-1} + cb^k$ is equal to a_c which is the number of articles published by the core journals ranked from 1 to c.

In summary, the number of journals c, cb, cb_2, ... publish the same number of articles. Or formally:

$$\sum_{i=e(2)}^{f(2)} a_i = \sum_{i=e(3)}^{f(3)} a_i = a_c$$

where $e(k) = c_{k-1} + 1$ and $f(k) = c_{k-1} + cb^k$ and (b>1)

P5. The breadth of topics: The X-axis intercept s is large (> 1) when the topic is broad and is small (< 1) when the topic is narrow. P4 may be related to the logarithmic property of P1 and may be explained as an extention of P5.

P6. The number of core journals, which is denoted by c, is usually not less than 3 and is positively correlated to s, which expresses the breadth of topics stated in P5. The curve may shift mechanically to the right upward direction (northeast direction) when the topic is broad.

As the diffusion and the cumulative advantage are quite common in many areas, it may be expected that the Bradford distribution would be seen in many other areas. In fact, a couple of empirical attempts were made and the results were encouraging to some extent.

Information files of individual scientists and of scientific institutes were examined to determine whether they possess the Bradford properties.[3] The result was partly positive and partly negative.

The information files of institutes were found to have the Bradford properties but the information files of individual scientists did not possess P4. This is explained as the macroscopic character of Bradford distributions:[4] The Bradford properties hold at a macroscopic level but not at a microscopic or individual level.

Another empirical examination was made on R&D expenditure of Japanese firms.[5] Its findings were:

- The Bradford properties held to some extent even for a flow such as R&D expenditures;
- P1 held to a limited extent. That is, the middle (log-linear) part existed but the number of firms which belonged to this part and their share in the total expenditures were very small, particularly in less R&D intensive sectors;
- The share of the core firms was about a half of the total expenditures;
- Consequently, P3 of droops held very strongly for an immature or growing area such as R&D of Japanese firms;
- As a result of c) above, usually P4 did not hold because a is too big;
- P5 did hold since s was large in sectors where R&D topics were diversified and was small in sectors where they converged. P6 was also applicable in that c was positively correlated to s though weak, but it did not hold in case of $c = 2$ for several sectors where a couple of core firms had very strong initiatives in R&D.

The limited validity of the Bradford properties on R&D financing of Japanese firms essentially reduces to b), c) and d) above. These three findings mean that a very small number of core firms are very strong and most of the others are far behind the core firms with the middle as a minority. Such characteristics may be due to the following:

- **Immature growth:** The diffusion speed is not stable when the diffusion or the growth is immature and fast like R&D of Japanese firms.
- **Limit of capacity:** The share of the core firms in the total R&D expenditure is not very high when the capacity is strictly limited like the page numbers in a journal; while it is very high when the capacity is not strictly limited like the budgetary limit of R&D of firms.

THE BRADFORD DISTRIBUTION OF
BIBLIOMETRIC DATA ACROSS NATIONS

The Bradford distribution was originally found to be applicable to worldwide bibliometric data across journals. The same or similar data can be rearranged across nations by affiliations of authors. These rearranged data are expected to follow the Bradford distribution to some extent. Meanwhile there is a certain limit to the validity for this problem. The discussion in Section 2 leads to the following hypotheses.

Hyp 1 Shortness of middle part: P1 holds anyway but the middle (loglinear) part is short.

Hyp 2 The strong core: The size or number of core nations is small (i.e., P6 does not necessarily hold), but their share in the total number of articles is extremely high.

Hyp 3 The long droop: The number of droop nations is extremely numerous while their share is extremely small.

Hyp 4 The invalidity of geometric zoning: P4 does not hold (cf. F6).

Hyp 5 The invalidity of topic's breadth indicator: Associated with Hyp 2, P5 does not hold. That is, c is small irrespective of breadth of topic. In this sense, P6 does not hold.

Hyp 5 has to do with the independence of s from breadth of topics, that is, s does not represent the breadth of topic when only particular nations always form the core nations irrespective of topics in international scientific bibliometrics. In other words, whether it is valid to say that the greater the number of journals playing the central role, the broader the topic, is conditional depending on the topic for which journals belong to the core. This condition is usually satisfied for problems across journals.

DATA AND ANALYSIS METHOD

Data are taken from the scientific literature data bases of SCI (Science Citation Index) and COMPENDX. Usually, the computer centre at the University of Tsukuba stores only the latest portion of the data base in order to save memory costs. Hence, only articles published between 1980 and 1984 can be retrieved for our analysis. The 1983 data for chemical engineering are ignored because the degree to which they are updated varies from journal to journal. Limiting data to two years is never a fatal limit to our analysis, and is indeed desirable.[6]

For the purpose of international comparison, broad fields were chosen so that the collected articles cover many countries. The selected four fields are food technology, chemical engineering, nuclear power engineering and ocean engineering. The reasons for this selection were:

Food technology: This covers many non-industrialized and rather agricultural countries, total coverage: 66 countries.

Figure 5.3. Alternatives of
and Associated Parameter Values

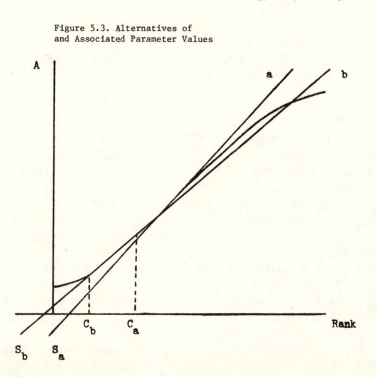

Chemical engineering: This is a relatively old field and hence is already diffused to many countries including the oil-producing countries, total coverage: 57 countries.

Nuclear power engineering: This is a typical high technology, produced mainly in developed countries and hence a contrast to the first two fields, total coverage: 40 countries.

Ocean engineering: This has two complementary aspects, one being a typical new technology evolving only in developed countries and the other being a kind of appropriate technology for fishery countries, total coverage: 35 countries.

As in any regression problem, the way in which l is drawn is somewhat ambiguous. Herein, l is drawn to satisfy the following conditions:

C1. Every middle part is crossing l, which signifies that the number of points on l is not maximized.

C2. l separates the core part from the drooping part where "separation" means that the core part is wholly in one half-space generated by l and the drooping part is wholly in the other half-space (Fig. 5.3).

The drawing of 1 under these conditions makes the middle part shorter than another method to maximize the points on 1 but resolves the ambiguity. Defining 1 in this way, the parameters s, c, c_k and a_c are uniquely determined.

RESULTS

Hyp. 1 to 5 are examined by the method stated in Section 4.

Hyp. 1 is strongly supported. The middle (log-linear) part is shorter here than in the problem of R&D expenditures of firms. The diffusion is far from being matured in our problem and the capacity of the core nations is almost limitless or is far from its limits.

Hyp. 2 is weakly supported. The number of the core nations is 4, 3, 2, and 2 respectively in our four problems, weakly denying P3 which claims that $c > 3$.

Hyp. 3 is strongly supported. There is a large number of droop nations, and the majority of nations belong to the droop section.

Hyp. 4 is also strongly supported. The geometric zoning is impossible because the share of the core nations is higher than 50% for all the four problems. Hence P4 cannot hold.

Hyp. 5 is supported. s is positively correlated with c, which is independent of the breadth of topic. Actually, $s > 1$ for chemical engineering and nuclear power engineering and $s < 1$ for food technology and ocean engineering.

DISCUSSION

The fact that the hypotheses based on the foregoing experiences can all be supported, indicates that such a simple graphical method yields a very stable result or is based on the regularities or lawfulness.

Given a technological field, the Bradford analysis provides a criterion to identify the core, middle and peripheral nations and their numbers and percentage in the total number of nations. It thereby enables us to calculate their shares in the total number of articles in the field (Table 5.1). These data serve as indices of field-by-field comparison on the degree of S&T inequitability among nations or the degree of concentration in the core nations as does the GINI Index. Dominant over the GINI Index, the Bradford analysis provides information on classification of core, middle and peripheral nations and their shares.

Further, its information on the number, percentage and share of the droop nations also indicates the immaturity of the field. This information may be useful for forecasting purposes. For example, in food technology that is already diffused to a relatively large number (66) of countries

Table 5.1 Parameter Values for Fields

Food Technology (COMPENDX, 1980–late Aug. 1984)

Core	2 (3.03)	906 (54.45)	United States, United Kingdom
Middle	3 (4.55)	269 (16.17)	India, Canada, Japan
Periphery	61 (92.42)	489 (29.39)	Federal Republic of Germany, France, Australia, etc.
TOTAL	66 (100.00)	1664 (100.00)	

Chemical engineering (SCI and COMPENDX, 1980–82)

Core	3 (5.26)	2828 (57.51)	United States, Japan, United Kingdom
Middle	5 (8.77)	1252 (25.45)	USSR, Federal Republic of Germany, India, Canada, France
Periphery	49 (85.96)	838 (17.04)	China, Italy, Australia, Czechoslovakia
TOTAL	57 (100.00)	4919 (100.00)	

Nuclear power engineering (COMPENDX, 1980–late Aug. 1984)

Core	4 (10.00)	1735 (73.92)	United States, USSR, Federal Republic of Germany, Japan
Middle	3 (7.50)	397 (16.92)	France, Canada, United Kingdom
Periphery	33 (82.50)	215 (9.16)	Italy, Austria France, Finland Belgium, Switzerland
TOTAL	40 (100.00)	2347 (100.00)	

Ocean engineering (COMPENDX, 1980–late Aug. 1984)

Core	2 (5.71)	877 (70.61)	United States, Japan
Middle	3 (8.57)	200 (16.10)	United Kingdom, Canada Australia
Periphery	30 (85.71)	165 (13.29)	Federal Republic of Germany USSR, France, Norway, Netherland
TOTAL	35 (100.00)	1242 (100.00)	

with the highest diffusion in our four fields, 61 out of 66 nations (92%) belong to the droop section which is much higher than in the other three fields (86% for chemical engineering, 82% for nuclear power engineering and 86% for ocean engineering). This may indicate that food technology is still the fastest in growth among the four fields and the present unequitability will be narrowed in the future.

In contrast, nuclear power engineering is diffused only to 40 countries, which is the lowest among the four fields and 33 out of 40 countries (83%) belong to the droop sections, which is the lowest among the four.

This fact may mean that its future diffusion will be the least among the four and its development will remain confined to a more limited number of countries than that of the other three. In short, this might be the biggest among the four in the future. Remarkably, such information on trend or forecasting are exploited from non-time-series data, a merit of the Bradford analysis.

Another merit of the Bradford analysis is that the data are already available from the existing data base which is updated frequently by the suppliers of the data base. A disadvantage is that, if it is used for detailed analyses on developing countries, the sample size is too small for sufficient reliability. It should thus not be applied to detailed analysis of a single developing country. Its usefulness is limited to a macroscopic analysis or field-by-field comparison to find promising fields or to avoid irrelevant fields.

CONCLUSION

The applicability of the Bradford analysis to STI was examined for four different fields. The empirical results are satisfactorily encouraging. It is found to be useful in macroscopic evaluation and comparison based on evaluations like the GINI Index. Its dominance over the GINI Index lies in its capability to provide trend or forecasting information from non-time-series data.

NOTES

1. M. Anandakrishnan, and H. Morita-Lou. "Indicators of Science & Technology for Development," chapter 1 of this volume.

2. S.C. Bradford, *Documentation.* Crosby Lockwood, London, 1949.

3. M. Bonitz, "Evidence for the Invalidity of the Bradford Law for the Single Scientist," *Scientometrics* vol. 2, 1980, pp 203–214.

4. Ibid.

5. H. Eto, "Bradford Law in R&D Expenditure of Firms and R&D Concentration." *Scientometrics* vol.6, 1984, pp 183–188.

6. B.C. Brookes, "Bradford's Law and the Bibliography of Science." *Nature,* 224, 1969, pp 953–956.

Problems in the Use of Literature-based S&T Indicators in Developing Countries

Davidson Frame

INTRODUCTION

In this paper I will briefly describe some of the practical problems facing analysts who try to utilize quantitative bibliometric indicators to better understand scientific activities in developing countries. Much has been written about some of the specific pitfalls of using abstracts and indexes to garner counts of published scientific papers and counts of scientific citations to research papers. My feeling about these pitfalls is that for the most part, if a researcher is aware of their existence, he or she can work around them. That is, their existence is typically not fatal to the research task at hand. I list some of the most common of these pitfalls in an appendix to this paper.

Rather than focus on what I see to be some annoying but non-fatal drawbacks to the gathering of literature-based indicators, I will here address a number of broader conceptual issues associated with the use of these indicators in a third world context. While there are often reasonably unambiguous solutions to the above-mentioned technical problems, there are no clear-cut answers to the broad conceptual questions.

FUNDAMENTAL CONCEPTUAL QUESTIONS

Question 1. Given the small size of scientific efforts in developing countries, how much of a contribution can bibliometric indicators make to the improved management of the scientific enterprise?

Literature-based indicators are most useful when used in statistical analyses. For example, in comparing the productivity of two cancer research programs, we have some idea of their relative merits when we examine for each program the number of papers produced per researcher, the average number of citations received by the papers, the quality of the journals in which the papers appeared, the number of coauthors per paper, and so on. The larger the sizes of the teams we compare, the more satisfactory the statistical analysis. However, if each program is comprised of only two researchers, then our statistical comparisons lose much of their meaning. In statistics, populations or samples with $N = 2$ are not very interesting.

Most developing countries have very small scientific efforts and publish very few papers. Consider that a scientific "giant" among third world countries (e.g., Egypt) produces only 400 or 500 papers in a year. Harvard University Medical School produces more papers than this. When we leave the list of the top ten third world scientific powers, we face literature production rates of under 100 papers per country. The typical developing country produces about as many papers in a year as a typical scientifically active small college in the United States.

What kind of statistical generalizations can one make regarding the scientific publishing behavior of countries that produce 30 to 50 (or fewer) papers in a year? When these small aggregates are further disaggregated according to research fields and subfields, statistical problems are increased. What meaningful statements can you make about Slavonian entymology—other than "it is a small effort"—if Slavonian researchers produce three papers a year in this field?

It is obvious that this question should be addressed and answered before embarking on programs (in all but ten or so developing countries) to institute elaborate bibliometric data gathering and analysis procedures in the third world.

Question 2. In looking at papers published by third world researchers should we focus our attention only on those appearing in significant refereed international journals, or on those published in peripheral local journals as well?

A large portion of the research that is undertaken in industrial and developing countries alike is not very significant. One way to separate the wheat from the chaff is to read only those journals that have stringent refereeing practices. In these journals, papers are published after they have been subjected to a careful screening process by professional peers. The number of such journals is relatively small. While there are some 25,000 active scientific and technological serials in the world, the British Library Lending Division includes only 10% of that number in its *Science Citation Index* (SCI), which consciously covers only the world's most central journals. Even in the SCI covered journals, one find dramatic variations in quality and importance of journals.

When dealing with developing countries the question arises as to whether we should look at locally published papers as well as those included in mainstream journals. If we look solely at third world articles published in mainstream journals, we see only a tiny fraction of the work being carried out by scientists in developing countries. Counts based on mainstream articles are likely to seriously underrepresent the dimensions of the work being performed. However, by restricting ourselves to mainstream papers, at least we have some assurance that this work meets some minimal international standards of quality.

The resolution of this question depends upon the objectives of those wishing to use science indicators to investigate third world science. If the purpose of the bibliometric indicators is to help in the building of a national scientific inventory telling us what kinds of research are being performed at different institutions, then coverage of local as well as mainstream publications would seem important. On the other hand, if one is primarily interested in investigating third world contributions to world science, then publication counts taken from a restrictive journal set would seem most appropriate.

Question 3. Is the scientific system in a developing country sufficiently well developed to make bibliometric studies of science in that country meaningful?

There is no question in my mind but that bibliometric investigations of the state of molecular biology in the United States can lead to meaningful results. In fact, in many fields—e.g., physics, chemistry, medicine, biology—bibliometric studies can address a large number of issues more effectively than anthropological studies, purely historical studies, anecdotal studies, and so on. I am not so sure that bibliometric studies are as useful, however, in investigating advances in civil engineering, or new developments in the hybridization of corn, or progress in industrial process innovations.

What I am saying here is that bibliometric studies work best in those disciplines where conventional scientific norms prevail—particularly those that encourage researchers to make their findings known to their peers. In industrial countries, these norms prevail in the conventional basic scientific disciplines, and it is here that bibliometric studies are most effective. When the pressure to promulgate one's findings lessens, as it does in the more applied and technological areas, bibliometric indicators begin to lose their power.

I suspect that in developing countries, a significant amount of solid research that gets done is never promulgated outside of a narrow circle of individuals, particularly in areas such as public health, parasitology, tropical medicine, tropical agriculture, and engineering. Some of the forces that work against encouraging publication of research efforts include:

- inability to write in English
- the urgency in certain research areas to solve critical problems and not "waste time" writing and typing of the paper
- lack of clerical support to assist in the actual writing and typing of the paper
- the sense that local problems are not of much interest to the outside world

If this is the case, then bibliometric studies undertaken in these countries may lead to distorted views of national scientific effort, since they do not capture some possibly important work.

Investigations of the social structure of science in developing countries should be undertaken specifically with the view of determining whether publication and citation behavior there is comparable to publication and citation behavior in the industrialized countries. If it is not comparable, then bibliometric indicators may not be appropriate instruments to examine third world science.

Question 4. What do paper counts mean? What do citation counts mean?

Those of us who have been active in the area of bibliometric investigations have been grappling with these questions for years. We have come up with several answers to each of them, reflecting the fact that bibliometric indicators measure more than one thing. Unfortunately, at present we have no clearly formulated statement of the precise meaning of the indicators we use. It is probably advisable that we meet now and again to come to grips with this matter in order to remind ourselves that George's interpretation of a set of bibliometric indicators may differ wildly from Martha's interpretation, and that William may interpret the same data in still another way. One of the principal benefits of international workshops on bibliometric indicators is that it provides opportunities to reassess consciously what it is that we are doing.

Where Do We Go from Here?

I can think of many things that we might do to improve the use of bibliometric indicators in investigating science in developing countries. I will make only one broad suggestion here, however, for fear of losing sight of the forest in the great array of trees. This suggestion arises out of a concern that I have that "bibliometricians" are often guilty of brandishing a tool in search of a use. Remember: to the boy carrying a hammer, all the world is a nail.

My suggestion is this: let us make explicit the objectives we have in studying science in developing countries. If we have poorly formulated objectives, or no objectives at all, then our investigations will be vague, directionless and of little value. Once we have articulated our objectives, then let us determine whether bibliometric tools can help us to achieve them. Some objectives we can address include:

- To better understand scientific communication patterns in developing countries
- To create national inventories of the different kinds and different amounts of research being undertaken
- To model the research system (e.g., compare funding and manpower inputs with publication outputs)
- To identify individual and institutional research performers in the country
- To identify research trends
- To measure scientific dependency on outsiders

Rather than say, "Gee, I have some citation data, what can I do with it?" we now say, "I am interested in studying scientific communication patterns in developing countries—are there any bibliometric tools around that can help me in this effort?"

APPENDIX

Some Specific Problems Associated with the
Collection of Literature-Based Indicators

1. **The homonym problem.** In looking through an index to identify papers written by John Smith, you must be careful not to select papers by other people named John Smith.

2. **The first author problem.** A number of abstracts and indexes only provide author information for the first author of a paper. You must be careful in using such data bases not to overlook the existence of co-authors.

3. **The journal quality problem.** There are tremendous variations in the quality of journals. If you want to take these variations into account, you can weight individual papers published in a journal with, say, Garfield's impact factor or Pinski-Narin's influence weight.

4. **The citation lag problem.** There are substantial field-to-field variations in how rapidly papers get cited. Fast moving fields have short

lags between the time a paper is published and then cited, while in slow moving fields, the lag is considerably longer. If a researcher using citation data is unaware of these field-to-field differences, he or she may misinterpret his/her finding.

5. **The institutional address problem.** Different abstracts and indexes follow different policies in reporting the institutional addresses of authors, ranging from no institutional information to detailed information.

6. **The Abstract/Index Coverage Problem.** Some abstracting and indexing services are very consistent in their journal and article coverage policies. The *SCI*, for example, covers all papers appearing in a well-defined set of journals. Other abstracting/indexing services may be very haphazard in what they cover, including only those pieces that happen to come to their attention in some random fashion.

7

The Effects of Science and Technology on Development: Observations on Strategies for Research

Archibald O. Haller

GENERAL CONSIDERATIONS

The Promise

It is increasingly apparent that advances in S&T knowledge continue to enhance the ability of the richer nations to manipulate nature in ways that are advantageous to their peoples. Naturally, there are adverse consequences, which concerns about toxic chemical and radiological pollution and the increasingly destructive power of modern weaponry make clear. And it seems evident that advanced science and technology is required, though it is not sufficient, to bring the unwanted effects of science and technology under control. This paper presents a number of considerations and experiences of possible use to those who are interested in the establishment of scientific and technological institutions to promote development in developing countries.

Without trying to specify a fully defensible meaning for the terms, it seems clear that scientific and technological knowledge differ from each other. The former is the more complex—knowledge accruing from observation and analysis in the attempt to provide progressively more comprehensive yet ever simpler sets of concepts concerning entities and their relationships, including the variations that such entities may undergo and the proximal causes and consequences of such variations. Technological advances consist of new routines by which to achieve proximally practical ends. The latter—technological knowledge—may be seen as knowledge of proven procedures by which to achieve predetermined goals. Scientific advances consist of new or improved theoretical explanations of phenomena. From time immemorial new technological improvements have evolved from older ones, with or without science.

Science, however, emerged during the past few centuries, and to some extent it too has a life of its own. But these comments do not imply that scientific and technological knowledge are always independent of each other. Modern science depends upon technology to contrive observational and analytical procedures and to disseminate research results. And much contemporary technological knowledge is based upon science. Indeed, one might define the current term "high technology" as sets of practical routines and their material counterparts based largely on recently developed scientific theory. By this definition the electric motors of a century ago were the "high technology" of their day just as computers are today. In the richer nations, S&T knowledge and institutions are thoroughly integrated with each other and they in turn with the rest of the socio-economic structure. In such countries it is obvious that S&T institutions are supported by the national wealth and that they also contributed to it.

With experiences of such nations serving as examples, it is not surprising that many believe the establishment of indigenous S&T institutions could release the people of poorer nations from the constraints of time, distance, natural disasters, poverty, illness and untimely death. Thus the promise of a better life is surely a major incentive behind current efforts to improve the S&T capacity of such nations.

There may be another incentive—a fear of possible deleterious consequences among poorer nations when computerization comes to control the manufacturing systems of the advanced nations. Let us explain. Today, a number of poorer nations are attempting to meet the needs and improve the quality of life of their growing populations by using cheap labour to produce manufactured goods for sale in world markets. These countries appear to use basically literate, but scientifically and technologically unsophisticated, labour in their manufacturing systems. The newer computerized technologies—"brain industries"—that are coming on line in the industrialized nations employ fewer production workers per unit product, and they are apparently more highly specialized than manufacturing and could so reduce the per-unit cost of production as to make the former manufacturing systems—"brawn industries"— obsolete. The manufacturing systems of the newly emerging industrial regions, which employ less specialized personnel, might then fall into obsolescence along with the rest of the brawn industries of the world. If reality turns out to match this scenario, the gap between the rich and poor nations would increase even more than it is now, because the poorer nations would be short of the technological capacity to computerize their plants and would lack the personnel to run them. Apropos of this, preliminary calculations show—not surprisingly—that average secondary and tertiary school enrollment rates of the established manufacturing nations with market economies far exceed those of newly industrializing countries (Brazil, Republic of Korea, Argentina, Singapore, Hong Kong, and Mexico). But it is worth noting that while the value added through manufacturing per industrial worker (VAM/W, an estimate of productivity per worker) increases with tertiary enrollments in the established manufacturing nations, precisely the opposite appears to occur among the newly industrializing nations. There, the higher the tertiary enrollments, the lower the worker's productivity (VAM/W). (Original calculations, from data in World Bank, 1984: 218–219, 231–232, 258–259, and 266–267.) Together, these data suggest that the newly industrializing nations are indeed placing their bets on a relatively uneducated labour force, and that in today's markets the less emphasis they give to higher education the more successful they are. But if in the next decades the brain industries drive the brawn industries out of the market, today's successes among the poor nations will be tomorrow's failures, joining those that never entered the race.

Therein lies the second stimulus for encouraging the improvement of the S&T capacity of poorer nations—to better enable them to be among the producers of a wide variety of manufactured items, consumer goods, and the various productive forces that manufacturing can generate. This may not apply only to manufacturing. Some poorer countries anticipate similar benefits from technologically sophisticated agriculture.

The Practicalities

But are indigenous capacities for science and technology really necessary? Can a poor nation reap the benefits of science and modern technology without going to the expense of building strong science or technology capacities? And even if they were to be built, would they really help to develop the country? These questions are not easy to answer. Some seem to believe that it is the technology that is needed, not the science. Some may think that effective and mutually supportive scientific and technological capacities are necessary but take the expected benefits for granted. Still others may doubt the necessity of either or may want to see evidence of their presumed benefits.

A number of pitfalls or problems are implied by such questions. We shall discuss one set of them at length—the problem of determining whether and to what extent a scientific or technological capacity affects development.

But there are observations that should be noted before entering that discussion. The first concerns real-world differences between science and technology. The others concern the interdependence of S&T, not only with each other but also with the educational system.

First, in the richer nations science not only yields more scientific knowledge, it also breeds technology. And advances in technology often feed into research that enhances scientific knowledge. But technological knowledge is secret while scientific knowledge never is. Technological knowledge is treated as secret or as protected when organizations (occasionally individuals) have a great deal to gain by monopolizing it or a great deal to lose by failing to do so. Private organizations guard their new technologies closely, at least until they have obtained patent rights to protect their monopolies over them. Governments sometimes do so too, and in addition try to keep new military technologies secret as long as possible. Scientific knowledge with obvious consequences for military use also is often threatened with classification by governments. (A recent instance in which a mathematician developed a system capable of breaking the most advanced codes is a case in point.) Beyond this, private firms or even their governments may try to hedge unpatented technologies in secrecy, especially if large profits are expected. This might not be hard to do when such technologies flow from unique and complex applications of scientific knowledge that only a few people understand. Nonetheless it would appear that practically all scientific knowledge and much technological knowledge is presented openly. A considerable amount of agricultural technology is public and fairly easy to employ, although some, of course, will be patented. In the years to come, for example, many of the technologies that genetic engineering is expected to yield will no doubt be protected.

The point is that societies treat the two types of knowledge differently in ways that will be important to the poorer nations. New scientific knowledge often has no obvious applications. Its payoff for development is at best indirect and quite a few scientific advances may not yield any development advantages for the nation. But for those who know how to decifer it, scientific knowledge is usually easy to obtain. In contrast, new technological knowledge is much more likely to yield development benefits—if it can be had. Unfortunately, many manufacturing technologies and even some agricultural technologies are deliberately placed out of reach of all but those who own special rights to them. So countries that want to reap the benefits of many of the new technologies may need to develop the capacity to produce them.

Second, if science is open but technology is closed, some may conclude that scientist-guided institutions for generating new technology are worth supporting but that scientific institutions are not. That is, some of the most promising, potentially competitive new technologies will be based upon scientific knowledge. So it might be thought that a poorer nation should put its scientists in technological institutes so that they can keep track of the emerging scientific literature and translate it into technological innovations. Such a strategy would no doubt be accompanied by another, holding that few scientists and many technicians should be employed in such institutes. The strategy probably will not work without substantial modification. First, most scientists are narrowly specialized, but scientific knowledge covers an immense variety of domains. Most scientific publications will be unintelligible and, for all practical purposes, inaccessible to most scientists: The *Science Citation Index,* for example, covers about 2,500 journals each year, of which 500 or so are considered as "high impact" (Garfield, 1983a). Third, most of the scientific literature such a scientist would read would be irrelevant to the technological aims of his institute. Fourth, divorced from the actual practice of theoretical research, the once well-prepared scientist would soon become obsolete. At best he might turn into just another technician—possibly capable of a bit more penetrating thought than his colleagues, but with a grasp of the advancing state-of-the-art theory that is no better than theirs. Worse, he will not only fail to keep up; he will lose much of what he once knew because he was unable to use it. As their scientific leadership becomes obsolete such institutes will surely lose their creativity.

Yet the basic idea of this strategy may yet be sound. If scientific knowledge, which is relatively open, can be drawn upon to elicit locally relevant new technologies, some of the obstacles to technology transfer might be by-passed. This would require arrangements that facilitate identification and mastery of the relevant fractions of scientific knowledge. A special need is for local scientists to keep up-to-date through significant participation in creative scientific research with equally serious participation in local technology identification and development research. Perhaps scientists of specialized local technological institutes could have ready access to international electronics networks of scientific journal literature and could be actively involved in the research of a major international scientific center while maintaining appropriate involvement in the work of the local technology center.

A third major point is that even if full-fledged, well-functioning capacities for both science and technology were to be established and coupled to effective technology delivery systems, they might not be sufficient in themselves to make much of an impact on the development of the society. This point may be particularly relevant if the nation decides to produce its own high technology and to employ it in mass production. The problem is the shortage of qualified workers. Granted, some high technologies yield manufacturing or agricultural systems that use a certain amount of brawn labour. But they will surely require an increase in the number of personnel who are capable of handling, operating, and repairing the complex equipment that the new technologies yield. This implies that the newly emerging forms of agriculture and industry may require better educated, more sophisticated personnel than formerly, if the benefits of the new establishments of science and technology are to have their greatest effects on the development of the nation. If the nation's labour force lacks the sophistication to take advantage of the production potentials offered by its S&T establishments, many of the expected benefits will never materialize.

As is becoming more and more apparent, capable and diversified establishments for generating scientific and technological knowledge will be costly and may take a long time to bring to the point at which they can serve the development needs of a nation. And as they are built, it may also be necessary to prepare production systems and personnel who are capable of operating them. A fourth point follows from this. Because of the costs, it may be necessary for many countries either to combine their efforts, to specialize them narrowly, or both. A nation's ability to create such establishments will be a function of the size of its total economy. Nations that are rich already have such organizations, many of them, especially those devoted to science, as parts of universities. Populous poor nations, such as Mexico, Brazil, China, India and Indonesia may be able to do so because of the total resources their large populations can generate. By concentrating resources, maybe a few small, poor countries can too. But most of the nations of the world may be too small and too poor to support such units. In some cases, such nations will concentrate their S&T efforts on technical institutes devoted to a few farm crops, ignoring industrial technology. Or a few neighboring countries may join forces to establish technological research units when they are unable to do it alone. It might also be advantageous to encourage substantial involvement of local scientists in research activities of the great scientific centers of the world. It would be expensive to support senior scientists to maintain double careers, one in an indigenous technological institute, the other in a distant center, perhaps even involving payments to host centers to defray the costs of participation. But if it were to raise the rate of useful technological innovation it would be worth the cost.

Summary

In a few words science and technology hold out great promises to the people of the poorer nations of the world, promises abundantly illustrated by the richer nations. Yet the relationships between science and technology and the implications of each for the nation are complex, and the costs of establishing effective S&T institutions will be great. Much is thus to be gained if the development effects of science and technology can be demonstrated. This is not easy. But research on various aspects of the issue are already underway. The next section discusses some of these aspects and provides illustrations of research in which development is the central variable.

THE IMPACT OF SCIENCE AND TECHNOLOGY ON DEVELOPMENT

Those who wish to assess the impact of S&T establishments on development face a formidable task. In brief, to provide secure research evidence it would be necessary to measure the output of the indigenous scientific or technological establishment, the levels of the development variables hypothetically following from these outputs, the levels of other variables which might either function as conveyors of the science and/ or technology outputs on the development variables or as measure of variables offering complementary or alternative explanations of the presumed developmental effects of the science and/or technology variables. It would appear that to date the literature on science and technology for third world development has been devoted almost exclusively to questions of the measurement of science and technology, with little or no attention yet being given to measuring either development or the impact of science and technology on development. In this section we first discuss measurement implications of the differences between science and technology. Next we present one example of research designed to measure the average socio-economic development of populations of regions of Brazil. We present a sketch of a research project now underway in Brazil, which is designed to measure the developmental impacts of variations in the use of traditional and research-based agro-technologies as these have been affected by a central technological research and extension establishment. While these illustrations are far from exhaustive, they may provide a glimpse of the less well understood possibilities and complexities of research on the impact of S&T on development.

Science and Technology Compared

Let us turn to the outputs of science and technology. The yields of science are different from those of technology. Strategies for measuring the effects of each will vary accordingly. The development consequences of innovations in science are normally effected, if at all, through their impact on technology. Thus at most the developmental impact of indigenous scientific centers will be indirect. But the outputs of scientific centers will often be easier to measure than those of technological centers. The immediate output of scientific research consists of published new contributions to scientific knowledge. Citations count data would appear to be the most successful indicators of scientific output (Arunachalam and Garg, 1984; Garfield, 1982, 1983a, 1983b; Blickenstaff and Moravcsik, 1982; Rushton and Meltzer, 1981; Turner and Kiesler, 1981; Frame 1980). Yet some—possibly confusing the outputs of technology with those of science—question their validity when used in developing nations (as reported by Blickenstaff and Moravcsik, 1982: footnote on 135). But regardless of the measurement of science output, the indigenous developmental impact of local scientific research might be impossible to measure in the short run. First, much scientific knowledge is accessible regardless of where it is generated. Second, locally generated contributions to science might have but little impact on locally relevant technology. Third, locally relevant technology would ordinarily be copied or adapted from widely available exogenous technology or generated from similarly public exogenous scientific knowledge. And fourth, spin-offs from science normally percolate slowly into practice if at all. However, as we have seen, science may contribute to the efficacy of technological instititutes. So there might be instances in which long-term effects on technological institutes of varying qualities of scientific establishments could be assessed. The next sections of the paper present research examples pertaining directly to development.

Regional Socio-economic Development. This section is devoted to recent work on Brazil's socio-economic macroregions. It illustrates measurement research regarding one aspect of development and thus shows something of the richness of both the possibilities and problems of developing indicators of this aspect of the research task.

Brazilian scholars and policy makers have long been interested in methods by which to identify Brazil's regions. The nation is so large and so diversified that it is obvious that its natural and socio-economic regions must be taken into account. This has led to many attempts to regionalize the nation. Of course, different criteria yield different arrangements of units such as states, etc., into macroregions. These have been summarized elsewhere (Henshall and Momsen, 1974), and we do not need to go into them. Recognizing in a general way the enormous differences in development levels of the populations of different areas of Brazil, such as Sao Paulo and Rio de Janeiro on the one hand and the Northeast on the other, scholars have recently begun to try to learn how to provide precise specifications of the nation's socio-economic development macroregions.

One such analysis was performed by a University of Wisconsin research team (Haller, 1982, 1983). The analysis utilizes public statistical data aggregated to the level of the macroregion. For some years Brazil has employed homogeneous areal units (municipios and contiguous sets of municipios called "microregions," among others) as bases for regional analysis (IBGE, 1970). On the continent, 360 microregions are so identified. Large numbers of variables have been aggregated to this level and are available for various research purposes. For the present analysis, a few variables were selected as possible indicators of the socio-economic development of the population of the microregions. There are two rational ways to make such a selection. The preferable one is to use variables that are dictated logically by a powerful theory. When no such theory exists, a reasonable alternative is to draw upon the accumulated research experience to suggest variables. This was done in the case we are discussing. For it, two old and powerful lines of research seemed appropriate. One focusses on the economic development differences among nations, the other on household or family socio-economic status. When applied to Brazil's microregional data, the two lines suggest a short, overlapping list of items (each reduced to a per capita rate so as to develop an indictor of the average condition of the data) which were the number of factory employees per worker, the agricultural participation rate, the value of commercial sales per capita, the literacy rate, and access per capita to radios, refrigerators, television sets, and automobiles. The experience of the researchers makes it clear that these would be positively intercorrelated. But their factor structure was not entirely predictable. Two possibilities seemed most likely: 1) that two factors might describe the correlation matrix—economic status, saturating the first three, and household socio-economic status (Sewell, 1940) saturating the last four, with literacy perhaps tied to both; and 2) that one factor might saturate the whole matrix. The first outcome would have argued for the existence of two multi-item variables describing the condition of the population's microregional economic development and microregional household socio-economic development. The second possible outcome argues for just one such variable—microregional socio-economic development. Factor analysis showed the one-factor solution to be correct. This being the case, it was possible to construct a factor-weighted index score indicating the relative socio-economic development (SED) level of each microregion.

The unique aspects of this analysis are two: 1) the systematic non-haphazard selection of socio-economic indicator variables and 2) the use of small units, the microregions rather than the customary states and territories, as the building blocks for the macroregions. When the SED scores of the microregions are laid out on the map of Brazil they show facts that are most interesting, some new, some already well known. The details are presented in the two essays just cited and are reflected in Figure 7.1 (from Haller, 1982:458). As Brazilians have known for years the population of the south is better than that of the north. But conclusions that do not seem to appear in the previous literature include the following: the most marked single SED macroregion is an area of

132

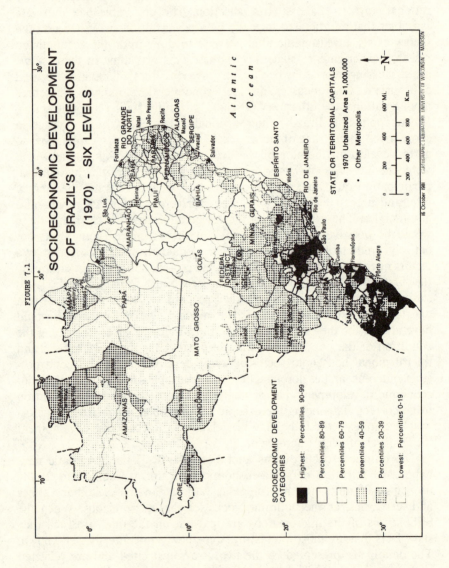

FIGURE 7.1

SOCIOECONOMIC DEVELOPMENT
OF BRAZIL'S MICROREGIONS
(1970) - SIX LEVELS

SOCIOECONOMIC DEVELOPMENT
CATEGORIES

Highest: Percentiles 90-99

Percentiles 80-89

Percentiles 60-79

Percentiles 40-59

Percentiles 20-39

Lowest: Percentiles 0-19

STATE OR TERRITORIAL CAPITALS

● 1970 Urbanized Area ≥1,000,000

· Other Metropolis

0   200   400   600 Mi.

0   200   400   600   800 Km.

16 October 1981   CARTOGRAPHIC LABORATORY UNIVERSITY OF WISCONSIN – MADISON

—N→

uniformly very low SED running south from Sao Luis to near Brasilia and extending from western Pernambuco to eastern Para, encompassing the people of about 20% of Brazil's land surface. As indicated in Figure 7.2, we label it the "Underdeveloped New Northeast." In a way, the most pronounced feature is not entirely old information: the SED homogeneity of the southern areas from the south of Minas Gerais through Rio Grande do Sul. In terms of the SED of the people of its microregions the whole South is perhaps more uniformly high than many have thought. A third, and completely unanticipated, feature is the South's Developing Periphery, a set of microregions of middle-level SED scores that arc across the north rim of the South, from Espirito Santo through Minas Gerais, across southern Goias, through Mato Grosso do Sul and perhaps out to eastern Acre. We labled the whole area the "South's Developing Periphery," and its two sub-areas as the Rim (the area arcing across the top of the South) and the Ray (the area running out along the national border to Acre). The Northeast is a fourth feature. It is composed of a set of continuous near-coastal microregions from the south of Bahia and the northeast of Minas Gerais north through most of Ceara. Its SED characteristic (unlike the former macroregions) lies not in its homegeneity but in its (generally low-level) SED heterogeneity. We label it the "Unevenly Developed Old Northeast." The remaining macroregion is the sparsely populated "Undeveloped Amazonian Frontier." One other observation is useful: while most of the microregions containing the great cities and industrial might of the nation have high SED scores, many of the highest scoring microregions are in the rich agricultural regions of the South, especially in Rio Grande do Sul and Sao Paulo. (Figures 7.3–7.5 illustrate combinations of SED data with those of population density.)

This illustrates an approach to measuring socio-economic development within a country. Other conceptions of development, such as populational health characteristics are possible and might lead to somewhat different regionalizations. In any case, this type of measurement can be performed on countries having the necessary data. Combined with other appropriate information, such data might be used as an element in tests of hypotheses concerning the covariations of science and/or technology and development. Indeed, a Brazilian team has prepared maps of the distribution of modern versus traditional agro-technology that yield delineations of agricultural regions resembling the ones we have just noted (Mesquita, Guzmao and Silva, 1977).

Those interested in assessing the effects of indigenous contributions to science and technology may also note some of the complexities revealed by this illustration. Covariations of the regional distribution of scientific or technological effort or output with development might

FIGURE 7.2

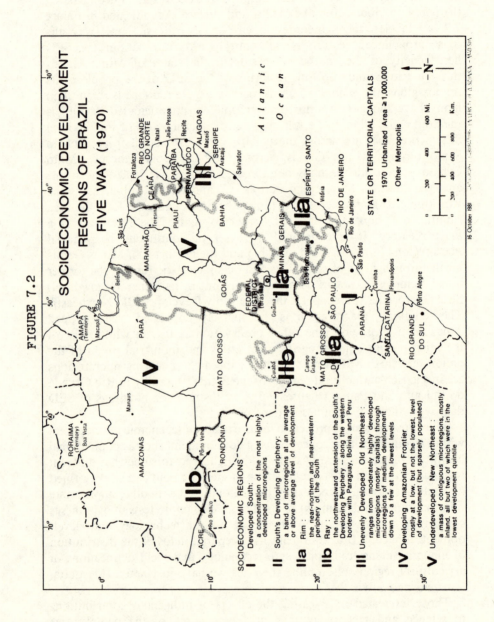

SOCIOECONOMIC DEVELOPMENT
REGIONS OF BRAZIL
FIVE WAY (1970)

SOCIOECONOMIC REGIONS:

I Developed South:
a concentration of the most highly
developed microregions

II South's Developing Periphery:
a band of microregions at an average
or above average level of development

IIa Rim:
the near-northern and near-western
periphery of the South

IIb Ray:
the northwestward extension of the South's
Developing Periphery — along the western
borders with Paraguay, Bolivia, and Peru
down to a few at the lowest levels

III Unevenly Developed Old Northeast:
ranges from moderately highly developed
microregions (mostly capitals) through
microregions of medium development
down to a few at the lowest levels

IV Developing Amazonian Frontier
mostly at a low, but not the lowest, level
of development (but sparsely populated)

V Underdeveloped New Northeast:
a mass of contiguous microregions, mostly
inland, all but two of which were in the
lowest development quintile

STATE OR TERRITORIAL CAPITALS

● 1970 Urbanized Area ≥1,000,000

· Other Metropolis

0   200   400   600 Mi.

0   200   400   600   800   Km.

16 October 1981

—N→

FIGURE 7.3

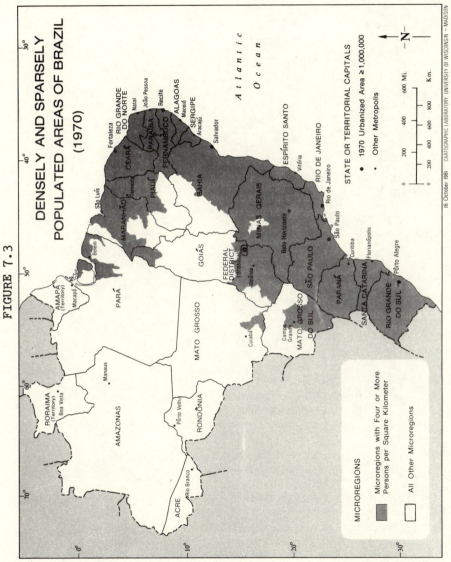

DENSELY AND SPARSELY POPULATED AREAS OF BRAZIL (1970)

MICROREGIONS

Microregions with Four or More Persons per Square Kilometer

All Other Microregions

STATE OR TERRITORIAL CAPITALS

● 1970 Urbanized Area ≥1,000,000

• Other Metropolis

16 October 1981 CARTOGRAPHIC LABORATORY UNIVERSITY OF WISCONSIN – MADISON

136

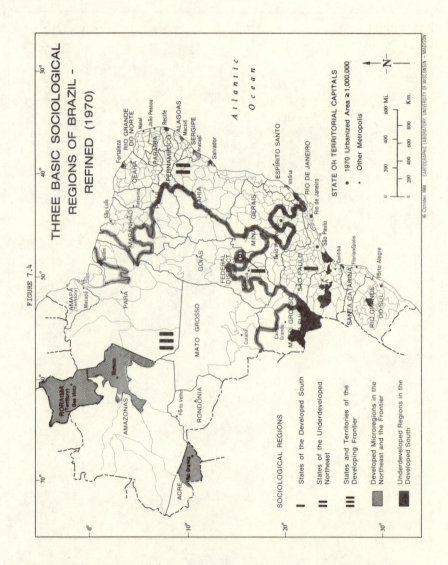

FIGURE 7.4

THREE BASIC SOCIOLOGICAL
REGIONS OF BRAZIL –
REFINED (1970)

SOCIOLOGICAL REGIONS

— States of the Developed South

= States of the Underdeveloped
   Northeast

≡ States and Territories of the
   Developing Frontier

▨ Developed Microregions in the
   Northeast and the Frontier

■ Underdeveloped Regions in the
   Developed South

STATE OR TERRITORIAL CAPITALS

● 1970 Urbanized Area ≥ 1,000,000

• Other Metropolis

—N—

0   200   400   600 Mi.

0   200   400   600   800   Km.

16 October 1981   CARTOGRAPHIC LABORATORY UNIVERSITY OF WISCONSIN – MADISON

Atlantic

Ocean

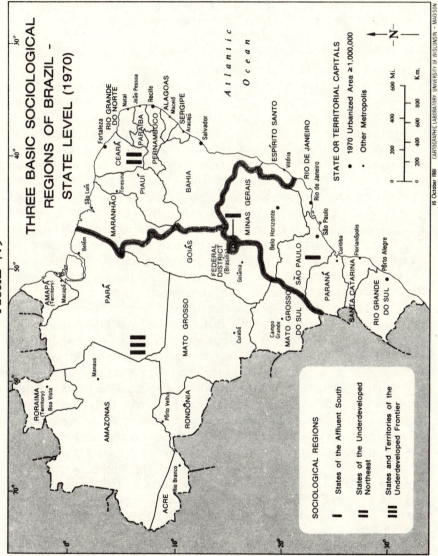

FIGURE 7.5

THREE BASIC SOCIOLOGICAL REGIONS OF BRAZIL - STATE LEVEL (1970)

137

be enlightening. But it might be difficult to demonstrate cause-and-effect relationships. Measures of covariations that specifically incorporate changes in the levels of both classes of variables, allowing for lagged covariations and taking the effects of other covariants into account might help to overcome the problem of identifying causal patterns. In turn this is a reminder of the need to obtain time-series data on the variables to be incorporated into such models.

The Impact of a Local Research Center. It is not uncommon for developing nations to encourage the establishment of specialized technological research institutes. Often these are parts of universities. Some have limited sets of missions, others multiple missions. Some are arms of academic disciplines and are administered by personnel of such departments. Some are large-scale institutes involved wholly in research. Some are small scale. Some are integral elements of a larger research generation and delivery system, and are thus closely tied to extension operations. The present paragraphs sketch one such technology center, its organizational environment and that of the surrounding area, and provide an overview of ongoing research now underway on its effects on agro-technology and those in turn on the development of the region. The research illustrates another approach to measuring the effects of an establishment generating and distributing the results of technological research. The research is far from complete and the present views are those of an observer rather than a participant.

Cacao is one of Brazil's important export commodities. Practically the whole national crop is grown in the tropical coastal lowland south of Bahia. Cacao production was opened up early in the century. The cacao tree has a life of about 60 years and is most productive during its middle 30 years. By 1960 or so the region's production had declined, and shortly afterward the government decided to establish an imaginative agency to restore production. The agency is called CEPLAC (Comissao Executiva do Plano da Lavoura Cacaueira) and it is the main socio-economic support agency in the 89 municipios comprising the Cacao Region. As an incentive, CEPLAC was assigned a budget proportional to the annual sales of cacao and was allowed the authority needed to use the budget in support of cacao production. CEPLAC set up a research center (CEPEC) and an extension division (DEPEX). Over the years CEPLAC has also provided marketing information, helped set up agricultural cooperatives, provided roads and port facilities, and encouraged the establishment of schools. Its central concern is cacao, of course. But it does not ignore other agricultural products of the area. Indeed in one way or another it touches the lives of all the 2.5 million people who live there. As is normal for extension agencies, DEPEX has local offices through the region. One of the main tasks of the CEPLAC system combines the forces of CEPEC and DEPEX. CEPEC is intended to keep abreast of and to provide improved agro-technologies for the region. To that end it is led by Ph.D.s in agrobiological sciences, mostly trained in leading universities in the United States. Its leadership is fully aware that technology operates through people, and CEPEC's personnel include Ph.D.s in rural sociology and agricultural economics. It has several divisions for research and research support, including a socio-economic research unit, a fine computation unit centered on high capacity mainframe, and, of course, biological research laboratory facilities. Its staff includes specialists in computer science and in mathematical statistics. It publishes a multilanguage journal of cacao research. As an agricultural extension agency, DEPEX does not seem especially unique. It is intended to function in part as a technology delivery system, as are most extension services. Its personnel are very well trained by most standards. About 50% of DEPEX's staff have university degrees in agronomic engineering, over 300 in all.

It took several years for CEPLAC to become effective. By about 1970 it was apparent that systematic research should be carried out to determine CEPLAC's effects on agrotechnology and on the socio-economic development of the local population. Accordingly, early in the decade, with the sampling advice of IBGE (the national statistical service), the socio-economic research unit conducted a large number of personal interviews with key personnel of each property selected in two different probability samples. One sample used all properties as its units, the other the properties in four pockets of small farmers. The variables and items were selected by fully trained sociologists and economists skilled in social measurement. Data suitable for developing state-of-the-art multiple-item indexes to measure variations in the use of indigenous non-research-based and research-based CEPEC-proven agrotechnologies were included. During 1985, comparable data are to be collected and used to estimate models of the impact of previous technologies on intervening technologies, and agricultural productivity on a series of social and economic development variables.

Inasmuch as CEPEC is the only research agency operating in the area, since it is specifically designed to seek out, develop and evaluate new technologies appropriate to the region's economy, and since its outputs are channeled directly to producers by DEPEX, it is considered to be the only source of new research-based technology available to the region's producers. Thus any changes in the use of research-based technology can be assigned directly to CEPEC and the net changes in both non-research-based and research-based technology will be attributable either to DEPEX (backed by CEPEC) or non-research based innovation. Confirmatory factor analysis methods (Joreskog and Sorbom,

1981) are to be used to test hypotheses about the causal linkages of hypothetical variables.

To complement these two analyses of property level data, an analysis of 1970–1980 changes in the average socio-economic development (SED) levels of the 89 municipios of the region is also to be conducted, using data from IBGE's files. It is to follow the strategy outlined in the previous section of this paper. The first two projects are expected to provide clear evidence of the impact of the CEPEC/DEPEX system on agrotechnology, production, and the life conditions of the residents of the properties. The third project is expected to show the overall changes of the SED of the population of the region during roughly the same period. Together the three projects should provide convincing evidence of the impact of a technology generating center on the development of its target populations.

CONCLUSION

The two foregoing cases provide illustrations of research strategies for measuring development. The last case goes further than the first by illustrating a strategy for determining the effect of center for generation of publicly accessible new technologies on the development of the surrounding population. By going into such detail, these illustrations may provide a realistic notion of both the complexities and promises of modern socioeconomic research strategies applicable to the assessment of the impact of science and technology on development. The complexities include careful measurements of each variable in hypothetical causal sequences and careful modelling of the various causal hypotheses. They remind us that certain development-related variables may be more affected than others. Agro-technological research will affect agro-technological variables more than others, and may affect rural development variables more than urban variables. Similarly, we would get stronger effect of research on medical technology on health variables than we would on, say, agricultural development variables. And we would expect stronger effects of industrial technology centers on manufacturing than on general development. At least as important, it should show something of the quality of evidence concerning the developmental effects of science and technology that can be addressed. The promise of such research is that it can both provide convincing evidence of the value of investment in scientific and technological research establishments for developing nations and can help guide planning for such establishments.

Taken together, the two main sections of the paper may provide suggestions as to the kinds of evidence that it now seems feasible to obtain regarding scientific research efforts in comparison with those of technological research efforts, and, among the latter, the kinds of evidence that may be feasible, depending upon whether the outputs of the research agencies are open or closed. Perhaps most important of all the paper calls for the measuring of the effects of scientific research on the one hand or technological research on the other. To the extent that these distinctions are valid they may also have implications for the organization of the scientific and technological research efforts of developing nations.

REFERENCES

Arunachalam, Subbiah, and Kailash C. Garg, "A Small Country in a World of Big Science—a Preliminary Bibliometric Study of Science in Singapore" *Scientometrics* 6 (August 1984).

Baruch, Jordan J., "The Cultures of Science and Technology." An editorial in *Science* 224 (April 6, 1984).

Blickenstaff, J., and M.J. Moravcsik, "Scientific Output in the Third World." *Scientometrics* 4 (1982), pp. 135–169.

Frame, J. Davidson, "Measuring Scientific Activity in Lesser Developed Countries." *Scientometrics* 2 (1980), pp. 133–145.

Garfield, Eugene, "Third World Research. Part 1. Where it is Published and How Often it is Cited." *Current Comments*, 33 (August 15, 1983), pp. 5–15.

"Third World Research. Part 2. High Impact Journals, Most-cited Articles and Most Active Areas of Research." *Current Comments* 34 (August 22, 1983), pp. 5–17.

"Mapping Science in the Third World." *Science and Public Policy*, 9 (June 1982), pp. 112–127.

Haller, Archibald O., **The Socioeconomic Macroregions of Brazil 1970.** Nagoya: United Nations Centre for Regional Development (1983).

"A Socioeconomic Regionalization of Brazil. *Geographical Review*, 72 (October 1982), pp. 450–464.

Henshall, Janet P., and R.P. Momsen, **A Geography of Brazilian Development,** London, Bell and Sons (1974).

IBGE, **Divisao do Brasil em Microregioes Homogeneas,** Rio de Janeiro, Instituto Brasileiro de Geografia e Estatistica (1970).

Joreskog, Karl G., and Dag Sorbom, **LISREL: Analysis of Linear Structural Relationships by the Maximum Likelihood Methods,** Chicago, National Educational Resources (1981).

Mesquita, Olinda Vianna, Rivaldo Pinto Guzmao, and Solange Tietzmann Silva, "Modernizacao da Agricultura Brasileira." *Revista Brasileira de Geografia*, 39 (4) (1972), pp. 3–65.

Rushton, J.P., and S. Meltzer, "Research Productivity, University Revenue and Scholarly Impact (citations) of 169 British, Canadian and United States Universities." *Scientometrics*, 3 (1980), pp. 275–303.

Sewell, William H., **The Construction and Standardization of a Scale to Measure the Socioeconomic Status of Oklahama Farm Families,** Stillwater, Oklahoma, Agricultural Experiment Station (1940).

Turner, C.F., and Sara B. Kiesler, "The Impact of Basic Research in the Social Sciences: The Case of Education." *Scientometrics,* 3 (1981), pp. 177–190.

World Bank, **World Development Report 1984.** New York, Oxford (1984).

8

From Social Indicators to Science and Technology Indicators: What Can We Learn?

Ian Miles

THE SOCIAL INDICATORS MOVEMENT

It is almost 20 years since the term "social indicator" (SI) was first applied in a systematic way to the study of social change, as a result of an effort to generate rigorous analytic methods to assess the social consequences of a major technological undertaking—the space programme of NASA. SIs were a major focus of attention of social science in the 1970s, when it became common to talk of a "Social Indicators Movement."

The idea that SIs could **monitor** the consequences of the space programme was rapidly extended to the grander idea that the consequences and direction of overall social development could also be mapped out and **assessed** in the same way as could specific programmes. The SI movement sought to be policy-relevant: the data that were to be employed should be relevant to significant social goals. They might be indicators of progress in attaining goals, or more general measure of underlying processes that have to be taken into account in making policies for these goals—but in either case they would be of normative as well as analytical significance. Some researchers, however, also suggested that SIs would enable social goals to be set by technical experts, circumventing traditional political processes. Certainly social reporting can point to, for example, neglected social or environmental problems and thus be used to challenge national priorities; but this contribution of evidence to political debate is very different from the supplanting of such debate by social-scientific analysis. Inflated claims for the power of SIs did the credibility of research no good in the long run.

The SI movement was launched by the space programme, by the desire to assess the social consequences of a costly technological enterprise whose economic benefits were being brought into question. But the main lines of SI research diverged from what became known as "technology assessment." The latter took two main forms. One was a combination of quantitative economic approaches (essentially elaborate cost-benefit analyses, perhaps combined with some analysis of ecological consequences), and qualitative social impact assessments (typically involving expert judgements of the consequences of technical change, often presented in the form of a range of scenarios), both of which approaches were applied to major technological developments. The other consisted of detailed assessments of local plans and programmes (often carried out using quite idiosyncratic methods).

Most SI researchers, in contrast, tended to focus on the production of new statistics and on gathering together previously unrelated data. A common concern of many of these researchers was to establish ways of making grand comparisons of welfare and quality of life in different settings, and producing equally ambitious compedia portraying changes in social circumstances over time. There were many efforts to improve on the GNP as a development indicator, and much experimenting with social reports.

Both of these directions of SI analysis were concerned with distinguishing between measures of "inputs" and "outputs." The great volume of published social statistics concerning welfare issues had previously been the by-products of the activity of bureaucracies, and reflected these agencies' concern on their expenditure, their personnel and facilities, and the numbers of clients of different types they had catered to. They reported problems only as they were presented to the agencies, not as they were distributed in the population at large. Such data might be relevant to welfare issues, but were as likely to tell observers about the functioning of the agency itself as about the results of its activities, or the significance of these results when viewed in the light of the overall incidence of various problems.

The importance of distinguishing between inputs and outputs is now very widely recognized—including, of course, in the field of science and technology indicators (STIs), where at one time there was considerable skepticism about the possibility of developing output measures. A considerable quantity of SI work became concentrated on social reporting, on documenting changes in welfare-relevant output indicators to supplement data on resource inputs and activities. Indeed, there has been something of a tendency to regard the task of the SI movement as being that of documenting progress toward or away from significant social goals—with rather less attention being paid to the applications of SIs in outlining relevant processes. As well as a diversion of effort away from macro-social analysis, furthermore, there was an isolation of the SI mainstream from project assessment and programme evaluation.

Much of the eager enthusiasm that greeted the early SI movement has now drained away, partly in response to the wild application of the term "indicator" to any statistic, partly in response to the deflation of grandiose suggestions about the imminence of an intellectual SI revolution for policymakers. But the SI movement has also largely been institutionalised, achieving signficant triumphs such as the publication of regular national social reports in many countries, and improvements in data production and the comparability of different data sources. SI research, too, has continued to make headway, though this is now less the province of a clearcut SI movement, being more widely diffused around the social sciences.

LESSONS FROM THE SOCIAL INDICATORS MOVEMENT

One of the rallying calls of the early SI movement was the critique of GNP. A number of arguments constitute a powerful attack on the assumption that GNP could serve as the major criterion for assessing the success or failure of a development strategy. While the current economic crisis may make it seem to be a luxury to criticize emphasis on growth, it is also apparent that existing development strategies have failed to reconcile what growth has been achieved with social welfare and human development. There are obvious implications for those who seek to assess the contribution of S&T to society in terms of purely economic criteria.

The SI movement tended to attribute rather too much significance to the GNP statistic itself, while ignoring the development strategies that facilitated the treatment of this statistic as a uniquely important indicator of national progress. But a number of key problems with this use of GNP were highlighted.

First of all, there was the problem that non-market (or "underground") activities are not included in GNP and associated National Account statistics. GNP is thus a less useful indicator of economic activity for countries with a large informal sector; furthermore, it excludes a host of social production and consumption activities that take place in households as a result of domestic labour. Growth in the GNP might not reflect an overall increase in social production or material welfare if, for example, it was largely a result of the displacement of informal economic activity by market-based transactions achieving the same ends. Thus doubts were raised both about the international comparability of GNP data, and about their value for assessing the overall outputs of even industrial market societies.

Similar problems may be faced by attempts to apply statistics based on measures of formal activity to other types of social production, and definitions based on Western experience may be of limited relevance to third world circumstances. International comparability of statistics is an important goal to aim for, but empirical research is required to specify the degree to which a measure can be assigned the same meaning in different contexts. In the case of S&T, it is likely that research and innovative activities are carried out in quite different locations and by quite different personnel: the R&D laboratories and institutions of higher education that are so important in industrial societies may not be the crucial focus of much inventive activity vital to third world countries. The significance (and content) of formal qualifications may vary from society to society, and even with comparisons of technologies, it is not evident that like is always being compared with like. (Thus the definition of an industrial robot varies considerably across industrial countries.)

A second line of criticism of GNP—at least, as a measure of welfare—contested the usefulness of monetary measures as a basis for aggregating activities of different kinds. For one thing, the same activity may be valued quite differently in different societies. Even in market economies, the purchasing power of money varies from country to country, so that, for example, a given sum of money will typically buy rather more personal services in poorer countries. More fundamentally, radically different activities that are priced similarly are treated identically in calculating GNP, so that the production of poison gas appears to be as valuable as hospital treatment requiring the same level of expenditure. Activities that might be positively detracting from overall welfare, or even reducing national security or the quality of the environment can add to the GNP—while clearly detracting from its value as an indicator of welfare.

Similar criticisms may be levelled against most approaches to aggregating groups of statistics in terms of any single dimension. At least the GNP is calculated according to a clear and consistent rationale— a rationale that is perfectly adequate for national accounting of the formal economy, but is less appropriate to other roles to which GNP has been enlisted. The SI movement invested considerable effort into trying to establish alternative aggregation systems, of which the Physical Quality of Life Index (PQLI) is probably the best known. Because the combination of data in such measures takes place in an arbitrary way— it lacks a rationale like that of economic accounting and a common dimension, like that of money—they have not proved to be readily interpretable, and confound too many distinct items to offer much help to policymakers.

The search for a single super-indicator that can summarize and synthesize data on social progress is misguided. Human and social development are inherently multidimensional affairs, and the assignment of priority to different dimensions is more a political than a technical task. Indeed, this was implicit in the criticism that GNP compounds together data on warfare and welfare, production and pollution.

The SI movement has been caught between trying to establish simplistic summary indicators (more of an exercise in virtuosity than of practical importance) and collecting together masses of data on various social phenomena into social reporting, which has some value, but that typically provides a deluge of information that may obscure rather than highlight policy choices. An alternative to these strategies would be for SI researchers to emulate economic accounting. This would involve developing more limited summary indicators from social accounts. The need to develop social (and environmental) accounting systems along the lines of economic accounts is now more widely recognised; and some researchers are attempting to relate conventional economic aggregations to those based on demographic and time-use data. (Counting heads and hours offers possibilities for aggregating data along common dimensions, just as does counting cash.) Models for the Research-Innovation system such as that proposed by Freeman (1982 a,b) may be a useful starting place for social accounting with respect to STIs.

The third line of criticism of GNP concerned the lack of relation between this statistic and distributional phenomena. Documentation of the "immersing growth" that has taken place in several instances reinforced the obvious statistical point that changes in an aggregate can mask divergence among different population groups. Economic growth might be taking place, but this might be—and often was—accompanied by a deterioration of the standard of living of a large proportion of the population. And even when this was not the case, different groups in the population were often benefitting extremely unevenly from growth— typically with the affluent improving their circumstances to greater extents than the poor. SI researchers argued for less emphasis on the overall economic growth of a country, and for more attention to the economic circumstances of particular groups—or to other SIs (such as those of infant mortality) that might indicate how much improved living standards were reaching lower social strata.

This line of criticism raises the need to consider the distributional dimensions of SIs and STIs. It suggests that it would be as well to investigate approaches to determining levels of participation in the production and consumption of costs and benefits associated with S&T. Data on operative and potential resources may be a useful complement to input, activity, and output data in STIs as elsewhere. Steps have been taken to include distributional phenomena in economic indicators, and since this often involves distinguishing between groups on social rather than economic criteria, they generate material useful for SI construction. The development of Social Accounting Matrices for the analysis of economic development reflects one approach to integrating indicators of distributional change with measures of productive activity in the formal economy, in much the same way that input-output matrices described the interconnections of different branches of production. Social Cost-Benefit Analysis includes distributional dimensions in its assessment criteria; and both approaches can, at least in principle, relate data on stocks to their information on flows. (While flows are considered in the GNP and many other statistics, there tends to be little attention paid to stocks; and where stocks are considered (as in many data on labour forces) these tend not to be integrated with data on flows.) These approaches have been subject to criticism as inadequately reflecting sociological parameters, but they nevertheless demonstrate the possibility and utility of integrating distributional and aggregate data.

A fourth and final criticism of GNP and many other development measures points out that they tend to focus on isolated units of analysis (such as countries or regions), while paying little attention to the interrelationship between these different units, and even less to the system of interaction within which individual units are situated. Economic growth as measured by GNP, for instance, might actually involve increasing dependency upon the political and economic institutions of more powerful countries; it is thus unclear how far GNP is indicative of growing capability to govern one's own national destiny, in economic or other terms. And development strategies tended to be defined in terms of national circumstances abstracted from the world-economy: but perhaps the possibilities for success with different strategies might be determined by location in the latter as well as by one's domestic characteristics.

The growing literature of the last decade has sought to test alternative theories of the relations between "dependency" or location in the world economy on the one hand, and economic and social outcomes on the other. There is considerable controversy about the appropriate indicators and methods of analysis to apply here, and much of the research is more formalistic than substantive. One problem has been that researchers have tended to deal in a rather uncritical way with statistics on such international transactions as trade flows and investment. While they have made rather a good case for the need to consider national and international levels of analysis simultaneously, insufficient depth has been brought to these analyses for them to serve as good models for assessing transnational dimensions of the S&T system. If policy relevant use of STIs is to be made by countries that are in one sense or another technologically "dependent," then it will be necessary to be rather more creative in defining and measuring the important features of the international relations of S&T. As in the case of the inappropriate transfer of Western concepts of the S&T system in the form of STIs for development, STI work needs to be founded on reviews of the experience of different third world countries with the global S&T system.

NEW DIRECTIONS FOR SOCIAL INDICATORS

The SI movement found GNP an easy target—much to the annoyance of many economists, who argued that the GNP statistic was now being attacked for failing to deliver things that had never been within its ambit. But the movement did draw attention to data that cast fresh light on development processes and circumstances. This has resulted in the numerous social reports that are now regularly produced and in the incorporation of SIs into many planning systems.

However, SI work has been hindered by a number of factors. With its focus on outputs (conceived of in terms of human welfare and the quality of life) rather than on the input data that previously formed the bulk of social statistics, the SI movement was able to show how important areas of human life could be charted out. But without some theoretical rationale concerning the processes that result in various outcomes, and without much effort directed toward relating the transitions of people between different social roles to the distribution of costs and benefits, the various SI lists proposed by authors were useful mainly for demonstrating the range of items that could be measured if one were so inclined, and thus were challenges to the ingenuity of social reporting. In our discussion of GNP, attention was drawn to the importance of developing social accounting systems, but this—although explicit in some of the earliest programmatic statements of the SI movement—has been taken up only slowly. (Indeed, the SI movement was not free of the empiricist notion that all that was necessary was to collect sufficient data and the theory would appear by magic—or by computer analyses.)

Of course, an indicator does not have to be part of a fully theorised system to be taken seriously and used to good effect. Data on deaths from respiratory disease in London over one winter, interpreted as an indicator of the effects of atmospheric pollution on the population's health, was important for establishing the Clean Air Acts that made London's famous smogs extinct. While these data derived from a system of medical and mortality statistics, they were hardly part of a social accounting system, or even of a formal list of indicators of the environmental impacts of smoke-producing technologies. But this was a case where the cause-and-effect relationship was fairly clear and uncontroversial, and where it was even possible to estimate the deaths in excess of those which would have otherwise occurred. Such "policy modelling" is far more problematic when the proximate causes are relationships between social groups or the consequences of welfare policies. In the case of STIs, too, it will be easier to demonstrate relationships between specific technological projects and their "impacts" upon their personal and immediate environment than to those between, for example, S&T policies more broadly conceived and innovative performance of R&D. The lesson here is not that every SI has to be part of a social accounting system, but that more effort should be directed to explicating the relationship between the topics for which we are seeking to develop indicators, and exploring the integration of available data into such systems. (This need not necessarily mean elaborate mathematical modelling; when statistical sophistication runs ahead of concern with substantive issues and theory the result is often mere mystification.)

Many economic statistics were valuable for policymakers before the development of modern economic accounting methods, but it is clear that these methods have considerably increased the usefulness of these data—not least in enabling the impacts of policy change to be traced through the formal economy. A system of economic indicators is appropriate to the interrelated nature of the economy, other social sciences are relatively disadvantaged in gaining a role in policymaking, and this partly reflects their difficulties in developing comparable SI systems to capture similar interrelations between inputs and outputs in their fields of enquiry.

As well as aiming more at comprehensive coverage than at accounting, SI researchers have been prone to advocating elaborate SI systems that had more to do with their own concerns and interests than with those of planners and policymakers. In practice this rarely led to severe communication difficulties, for most SI researchers tended to organize their problems into groups of topics essentially similar to the typical functional organization of responsibilities across government departments and ministries. (Thus most social reports present their SIs organized into such areas as health, education, housing, and employment.) However, while most SI systems mirrored the functional discourse of administration, SI researchers were often not sufficiently concerned to demonstrate the policy-relevance of new SIs; likewise, they were often not very interested in the actual mechanics of data production. Thus proposals for costly increases in data production were not accompanied by equally compelling specifications of the benefits of these new data. Because of this, some major initiatives for the establishment of new SI systems—

for example, the innovative programme pioneered by the OECD—have had less impact on national statistical systems than might have been hoped for. And many more proposals for new types of data have met with minimal response because of a failure to consider whether the data could be readily produced within existing surveys and administrative record-keeping rather than requiring expensive new investigations.

Proposals from Western and Western-influenced social scientists that third world countries should attempt to emulate the most advanced SI methods used in industrial countries (such as the attitude-survey measures employed in various "Quality of Life" surveys in the 1970s) sometimes failed to take into account the extreme paucity of even the most basic social statistics in poorer regions and countries, which entails a rather different direction in statistical priorities. The lesson is obvious: while imagination and experimentation are vital for the development of more useful SIs, innovative proposals have to be framed in the light of the existing statistical efforts and capabilities of the countries or organizations concerned. This point applies equally to STIs: the questions of which indicators should have priority in a situation of limited resources and of the marginal costs of preparing new types of data have to be considered. Rather than demand comprehensiveness for its own sake, it is necessary to make a case for particular statistical priorities, and to consider whether more-or-less imperfect data may not be the best that can be hoped for in many circumstances.

Elaborate SI systems requiring major investments in statistical services failed to relate to policy concerns in other ways. Complex SI systems often require lengthy data production and analysis. In planning situations, however, the topicality and recency of data is an important dimension of its quality—a dimension to add to those of accuracy, comprehensiveness, and the various aspects of validity that have been sketched out by social scientists. Methods of rapid appraisal and evaluation were developed outside the SI movement, and it is only recently that these methods have begun to be related to SI approaches. Likewise, planning decisions that involve different projects and programmes, often involving very different geographical scope, require different SIs. No SI system is relevant to all situations, although a good system may well guide one to areas of analysis and types of statistics that should be included in any given project evaluation.

In proposing grand SI systems the SI movement paid insufficient attention to the methodologies necessary to prepare adequate SI measures for more limited planning problems. Only recently, again, have SI researchers appeared to be returning to an interest in social impact assessment. The development of SI capabilities cannot be neglected simply because a set of general SIs is being implemented. It is necessary to be prepared to create new indicator systems appropriate for specific planning decisions—and nowhere is this more true than where technological programmes are concerned.

The SI movement no longer portrays itself as the great hope for revolutionising social science and policymaking. As its positive contributions have been absorbed by researchers and administrators, and its more grandiose claims exposed as hollow, it has lost much of its cohesion. But if we now have more of an SI approach than an SI movement, there is still much work of interest and relevance being undertaken. This essay has sought to identify a number of lessons that the development of SI research may have to offer those interested in STIs for development. Among the key points that have emerged are:

- the need for indicators to be appropriate to the characteristics of the local social system, whether this be the national economy or the S&T system. The different organizations of similar types of activity in different settings means that identical statistics are not necessarily indicators of the same things. STIs that prove useful in industrial countries may be misleading in other regions. Indicator development must be related to research on the concrete characteristics of the formal and informal systems of S&T in the types of society with which we are concerned.
- the need to avoid premature aggregation of different phenomena, for example by reducing all the "impacts" of S&T to an economic cost-benefit analysis, or to some idiosyncratic social welfare function. Related to this is the need to avoid collapsing policy relevant distributional issues into aggregate measures. The participation of different groups in the production of S&T, and in the receipt of its costs and benefits, is a case in point. (Here there is already some relevant work on the role of women in S&T which may be drawn upon.)
- While premature aggregation is dangerous, it is also necessary to avoid data overload. A systematisation of indicators is required, and an integration of data into accounting systems appears to present one valuable way of proceeding here. Elaborations of the Social Accounting Matrix approach are one obvious route to take, but other accounting methods are also potentially valuable. In the shorter term, attempts at national social reporting may be used as inputs to S&T policy, and specialised reporting of S&T may also be of considerable value. Additionally, it may be necessary to prepare specific STIs for the analysis of particular programmes and projects, ranging from the structure of basic research in some

advanced field of activity to the implications of technology based development projects for some locality.

- the need to relate international and national levels of analysis together, avoiding formalistic approaches to understanding the nature of international flows of S&T resources and relations of power in the S&T field. The internal and external determinants of S&T should both be considered, and in particular those that constrain the appropriation of global S&T by third world countries require appraisal via STIs.

- the need to take account of the possibilities for improving the policy relevance of STI research by taking into account the methods developed in parallel fields of impact assessment and rapid appraisal. There is a developing corpus of research on methods for determining the "fit" of alternative technologies to local resource endowments and environmental constraints; more sociological measures might well be integrated into such analyses, making them more relevant to forecasting and monitoring the "impacts" of S&T on local development.

- the need to avoid overambitious claims, and to relate research to specific policy concerns and resource constraints. Again, this highlights the importance of STI work being carried out in close contact with the concrete circumstances for which its use is intended, rather than in the isolation that characterizes some international agencies and national ivory towers.

NOTE

The views expressed in this paper do not necessarily reflect those of the institution with which the author is associated. Nevertheless, I would like to thank my colleagues for information and stimulation which made this paper possible—especially Kurt Hoffman, Ben Martin, Don Scott-Kemis, and Sally Wyatt.

The work reported here is largely based on the results of a project carried out for the United Nations University (in its Goals, Processes and Indicators of Development Project), and which is being published as Miles 1985). Rather than append a lengthy bibliography to this paper, I refer readers to this report, and to an earlier review (Miles, 1985). Carley (1982) provides a good recent overview of the SI field, as does Freeman (1982b) for STIs.

REFERENCES

Carley, Michael, **Social Measurement and Social Indicators,** London: George Allen and Unwin, 1982.

Freeman, Christopher, **The Economics of Industrial Innovation,** London: Frances Pinter, 1982.

Freeman, Christopher, "Recent Developments in Science and Technology Indicators," (mimeo) Fulmer, Brighton: Science Policy research unit. (Paper prepared for the International Development Research Council, Ottawa, 1982.)

Miles, Ian, **The Poverty of Prediction,** Farnborough: Saxon House/Lexington Books, 1975.

Miles, Ian, **Social Indicators for Human Development,** (forthcoming), London: Frances Pinter, 1985.

9

An Assessment Scheme for Science and Technology for Comprehensive Development

Michael Moravcsik

INTRODUCTION, DEFINITION OF TASK, CONCEPTS

Aims

By assessing S&T we mean the gauging of the quality of performance in these fields as judged by a specified set of criteria which may be either internal to science and technology or external to them.

There are very important reasons why such assessment of science and technology is crucial. First, in science and technology, the **quality** of the activity is crucial in order to produce results. There is a broad and also highly skewed distribution of quality in the activities of research and development. The empirically derived Lotka's Law, for example, tells us that measured by the total lifetime contribution to research, the number of scientists in a scientific community producing an amount x is proportional to $1/x^2$. The number of countries producing an amount x of scientific and technological products also follow a similar rule of distribution.

The second reason for the importance of assessment is that S&T are strongly linked to the economic, cultural, social, and other development of countries and hence arouse certain expectations when the meagre resources in these countries are applied to the support of science and technology. These countries want to see measures of output of science and technology relating to their goals and objectives of development.

At the same time, assessing science and technology is a very complex task. For example, scientific **activity** cannot be used to measure scientific **productivity** or **progress** in terms of the various objectives mentioned above. The aims and influences of science and technology are also complex, forming an intricate network, which precludes a simple formula or a lone numerical indicator from giving a realistic description.

For these and other reasons, in developing countries such assessment is practically never practiced. It is ironic that exactly those countries in which resources are most scarce but in which the establishment of S&T is at a most crucial and sensitive stage, the assessment of such activities is absent. This is most regrettable since indicators could form a factual background and a tool for resource allocations, which, in the absence of such a tool, end up being made haphazardly and erratically. In some circumstances the indicators could be valuable for policy making, planning, and monitoring the progress of S&T programs.

One of the aims of activities related to indicators is to create a conceptual scheme for assessing S&T in the context of a given set of development objectives and define those ingredients in such a scheme that need further research. Thus a consequence of this objective is hoped to be the generation of research activities in the coming years that could then be converted into operational prescriptions for assessment and evaluation. The second, simultaneous aim is to use state-of-the-art methods in assessment and evaluation as it exists today and, without waiting for additional research results, to formulate an assessment and evaluation scheme for S&T in the developing countries that can be implemented practically and immediately. In this context, assessment and evaluation mean the measuring of the degree of effectiveness together with diagnosing the defects and the resulting policy recommendations for improvement.

The present effort is focused on developing countries, and so the indicators to be developed must also be selected to be appropriate in that context. While science and technology have a large universal component, and hence some indicators are likely to be also universally applicable, the different **context** of S&T in the developing countries, that is, the different stage of development, the different infrastructural conditions, and the different capabilities and realities outside S&T may call in many situations for different indicators, or at least indicators specially adjusted and modified to fit the different context.

Goals of Science and Technology

(1) **Science** is closely tied in with **technology,** which in turn is strongly linked with modern **production** and hence the bettering of our material life.

Scientific research has increasingly used technological gadgets for creating the circumstances to be studied and for converting the direct signals from the phenomena into signals perceivable by our human senses. Simultaneously, technology has turned to science for knowledge of new phenomena with which we had no direct everyday experience and hence on which we could not use the trial-and-error method of constructing gadgets. Thus, science and technology have been mutually dependent on each other to a high degree. The relationship is complex and subtle. For example, by no means all of new technology is directly related to the latest scientific results: New technology may, at least in part, be based on older science. The connection may be through actual application of scientific concepts and results in the design of new technological products, or in terms of the measuring instruments used in technological development, work, or through auxiliary handling of data or information, or through any of many other contributory elements in technological development work. The same holds for the dependence of science on technology. New technology often opens up new problem areas for science and creates new scientific subdisciplines. The complexity and multidimensionality of these connections, however, must not obscure the fact that almost all of present day technology is dependent, one way or another, on science and vice versa.

(2) Science and technology are paramount non-material human aspirations in the 20th century.

In the 20th century, one of the primary human aspirations is the extension of scientific knowledge and of technological capacity. In the context of the dichotomy of "developed" and "developing" countries, science and technology are the keys to breaking the strong dependence on other countries and serve as indicators of the extent to which the country participates in the overall efforts of humanity.

Even in the 20th century, aspirations vary from culture to culture. In some cultures the aspiration for engaging in scientific research is not as strong as in others, and similarly, the aspiration toward utilizing technology may also be weaker in some than in others. In some cultures people who consider themselves elite shy away from getting involved in technology. In some cultures the educational policy may stress the humanities more than the natural sciences and technology, while in other cultures it may be the reverse. Similarly, the balance of emphasis between commercial activities and manufacturing activities may vary from culture to culture. In short, the value system inherent in a culture will determine the value in that society attached to the pursuit of science and technology.

(3) Science and technology form an important influence on man's view of the universe and of his place in the universe.

Science and technology do not form a whole culture by themselves, since they are not concerned with many questions that are part of cultures, but nevertheless science and technology have a major influence on cultures with which they come in contact. For example, a basic tenet of science is that knowledge is open, that there is much we do not know yet, and that there is a well defined procedure whereby such new knowledge can be acquired. Together with technology, science also believes that such new knowledge can be used to change man's standing in the world and hence influence its well-being. Science and technology emphasize change as a fundamental characteristic of the world.

In the developing countries, where modern science and technology began relatively recently, the impacts of science and technology on people's thinking and attitudes are also just beginning to assert themselves and may, in some countries, still be limited to only a small fraction of the population, including some scientists and technologists and perhaps some intelligentsia. The extension of the impact of science and technology to the thinking and attitudes of the whole population is, therefore, a major motivation for science and technology in the developing countries. In particular, the extent to which the popular utilization of the thinking and the attitudes of science and the popular participation in the affairs of science and technology will grow depends upon the development of perception and interest at various levels, not only within the science and technology community but also among the media and the general public.

Multidimensionality

In analyzing the structure of science and technology both internally and in relationship to their goals, it is absolutely essential to keep in mind the multidimensionality of the system. The opposite of multidimensionality is one-dimensional thinking, in which elements of the picture are visualized in terms of a single dimension, and hence arranged in a linear chain. In such a one-dimensional world, ranking according to some quality can always be done unambiguously, and cause and effect can always be neatly separated out.

In contrast, in a multidimensional model of the world ranking becomes much more complex and is predicated upon defining relative weight factors for each of the dimensions that form the overall basis of the comparisons. In it, cause and effect are much more subtly manifested, with everything having many contributing factors and everything contributing to many other factors.

More specifically, in a multidimensional model the links within the science and technology system of a country and the links of this system to external entities become an involved network of connections in which it is of little practical significance to consider only one link connecting two isolated factors. Correspondingly, the finding of a single evaluationary indicator, or even of a small set of these, becomes an illusory goal from the very beginning, and hence efforts are directed from the outset toward a more involved and larger system of indicators which, among them, taken together, offer a realistic method of assessment of the S&T system.

In S&T assessment, complexity and sophistication are signs of deeper understanding of the S&T system and are therefore absolutely necessary. The S&T infrastructure is a complex system, in which the laws governing the system consist of more than just a linear imposition of the laws governing the interaction of any two components. Such systemic analysis is also becoming more prevalent nowadays in the natural sciences themselves, such as in the study of strong interactions in high-energy physics, in the study of composite biological systems, or in the study of behaviour patterns in psychology.

A consequence of multidimensionality is that in terms of the varied set of aims and objectives of science, the quality of activities in science and technology cannot be assessed alone by criteria internal to science and technology. For example, if a research scientist, no matter how successful in his research by the customary scientific criteria, fails to convey his expertise and knowledge to the country's technologists who in their development work need such interaction, then the overall assessment of this scientist in the context of the comprehensive development objectives of the country cannot be altogether positive. The recognition of this and its incorporation into the assessment procedure and into the set of indicators used in it marks a crucial difference between existing approaches and the new initiative aimed at in this report.

Types of Indicators

Indicators used in the assessment of S&T can be of various types, and so it might be worthwhile to make some *a priori* choices as to which types we want to utilize in our evaluation scheme.

(1) Input vs. Output

In applying traditional input-output approaches to the assessment of S&T, it quickly becomes evident that it is much easier to measure input than output. For example, one can measure the amount of funds invested in research, the number and kinds of buildings constructed for scientific activities, and number of scientists trained and employed for research, etc. On the other hand, the output of science knowledge is rather intangible and hence hard to gauge. In case of technology, its product may be somewhat more concrete, but gauging its quality is also difficult. Even in describing input, however, some difficulties arise. For instance, although it is easy to give a simple headcount of the number of scientists employed, it is much more difficult to describe the quality distribution within such scientific manpower. As mentioned earlier, Lotka's Law exists for just such purpose, but so far its empirical validity has only been tested on rather large groups of scientists working in scientifically advanced countries, and whether it holds for each institution separately and under the contextual conditions for science and technology in developing countries is quite unknown at the present.

Moreover, the classical input-output analysis suffers from many limitations, including the difficulties of measuring proximate output and of relating input to output. It is possible, for example, that the output of one system may be the input of another. Human resources in R&D is the output of S&T education but the input to R&D activities. Publications are the output of R&D but the input to technological development work.

To circumvent such difficulties, it is sometimes assumed that the output will be closely proportional to the input, and hence input indicators are implicitly used to measure the output. We know, however, that at least in those cases when the input-output relationship in S&T has been studied at all, the above assumption is a very misleading one to make. It is true, for instance, that very roughly the GNP of a country is proportional to the overall "scientific size" of the country, but such very rough measures are, for most purposes, quite useless in practical problems of evaluation and assessment.

For a functional and realistic evaluation of the S&T system, output indicators must be measured directly and not through input indicators. Of course, in doing so, we would run counter to the practices of the overwhelming majority of studies, statistics, and tabulations produced in the past by national and international sources, since such material contains almost exclusively input indicators.

(2) Quantitative vs. Qualitative

Indicators can be strictly quantitative, thus assigning a definite number on some definite scale to describe some aspect of the S&T activity. For example, by giving the number of scientists working in a given institution or on a given project, we use a strictly quantitative indicator. In contrast, an indicator may be predominantly qualitative. Through peer review, we may come to the conclusion that the existing scientific manpower in country X is (or is not) sufficient for carrying out a meaningful and productive research related to the project.

Strict quantitative indicators have a definite intellectual appeal, giving the impression of being more objective, more precise, and more reliable than strictly qualitative impressions. Indeed, one should work toward the goal of developing quantitative indicators for as many aspects of S&T as possible. Yet, a quantitative indicator is no better than the reliability of the set of assumptions and models on which it is based, and no better than the reliability of the generation and collection of data used in arriving at the quantitative mark. Furthermore, some very crucial elements in the S&T complex may not be amenable to quantification, or may not yet be so. Indeed, in the scholarly community of the "science of science," those who disapprove of the research areas in this field, scientometrics (the quantitative study of science as a human activity), make their case exactly along such lines, claiming that, at least at the moment, only the most superficial and trivial aspects of S&T can be quantified, and hence restricting oneself to quantitative indicators alone amounts to disregarding some of the most essential aspects of the overall problem.

In the present efforts, therefore, both quantitative and qualitative indicators should be used, wherever possible.

(3) Activity, Productivity, and Progress

In describing what we want to find indicators for, it is useful to distinguish among the three concepts of scientific (or technological) activity, productivity, and progress. Productivity would mean going a step further from activity and assessing whether all the activities involved in a particular setting actually advance the attainment of an eventual goal or not. That is, we would have to ascertain that the activity carried out is in the right direction and is done well enough to move toward the given goal. Finally, progress would consist of measuring the degree to which all the productivity described brought us closer to our task. It is clear from this picture that while what would matter most is the measurement of progress, what is easiest to do is the measurement of activity.

In our efforts, we will, if at all possible, strive toward creating measures of progress, or at least of productivity, while realizing that in some cases, at least temporarily, we may have to be satisfied with mere measures of activity.

(4) Quality, Importance, and Impact

Another useful distinction to be made among indicators is along another trichotomy: quality, importance, and impact. The **quality** of research describes how well it has been done, whether it is error free, how elegant, general, and intriguing the results are, etc. It is a relative indicator and may be judged differently by different people and at different times. **Importance** denotes the potential influence on related research activities under ideal conditions, extrapolated into the unknown future. **Impact** means the actual influence that piece of research will have on the course of science and its various aims and utilizations in the future, something that may be influenced by many factors, many extraneous to science and its various aims and utilizations.

As before, our ultimate goal here would also be to find indicators for impact, but often we may have to be content with having indicators only for importance or only for quality.

(5) Functional vs. Instrumental Indicators

We can develop indicators for certain **functions** of S&T activities (e.g., for research results), or we may want to evolve indicators for certain **tools and instruments** that are used in the S&T infrastructure (such as for the repair of scientific equipment or for management methods of scientific research). To illustrate this, let us consider an analogy. If we want to assess or evaluate a given car, we can look at its fuel mileage, which is a functional indicator, or we can look at the pressure in the cylinders, which is an instrumental indicator. Note that both of these are output measures, so the output-input dichotomy has nothing to do with the functional vs. instrumental dichotomy.

While in the ultimate analysis what matters more are the functional aspects of the S&T system, for diagnostic purposes instrumental indicators may be very useful and in fact even superior to purely functional ones in that they may more readily point at various remedial measures that can be taken to eliminate certain deficiencies. Thus we will allow both functional and instrumental indicators into our overall system of evaluations.

(6) Micro vs. Macro Indicators

Finally, a distinction is also made between "micro-" and "macro-" indicators. The latter may pertain to the S&T system as a whole, or to the performance of large parts of it, while micro-indicators would describe some small, partial component of the whole system. For example, the number of scientific publications produced in a given country in a given year can be regarded as a macro-indicator, while the number of scientific visitors from abroad per year may be a micro-indicator, pertaining to one aspect of scientific communications, which, in turn, is only one part of the infrastructure needed to create scientific research in the country.

Another type of micro-indicator is that restricted to one particular area of science or technology. This is important because although the development of different areas of science or technology may proceed at quite different rates, the different disciplines and areas are interrelated and influence each other. Thus, retardation in one area may have serious consequences for many other areas. A micro-indicator pertaining to a particular scientific or technological area can be an important diagnostic tool for spotting deficiencies in the interwoven structure of science and technology as a whole.

Another macro- or world indicator is concerned with the international distribution among countries; that is, with competition. Patenting is an important manifestation of international competition, international trade is another. Clearly, how "macro" something is may depend on the point of view. It is, nevertheless, useful to make such a distinction.

Validity and Reliability of Indicators

It is desirable to be able to check the validity and the reliability of indicators. Frequently, indicators are obtained from compilations of statistics, some of which are not reliable due to the method by which the data were collected, to implicit assumptions that may not be appropriate, or to other reasons. The validity and reliability of an indicator may be gauged by checking for consistency with other indicators. For example, it is known that there are a number of relationships among manpower indicators and financial indicators. If a set of indicators shows large deviations from the expected relationship, validity and reliability may come into question. This calls then for deeper probing into the reasons for such a deviation, including possible errors in methodology or possibly dubious assumptions made in the course of data collection. Further analysis may not always yield a concrete answer, but at least a certain degree of critical assessment of the data is provided.

A MAP OF THE SCIENCE AND TECHNOLOGY SYSTEM AND OF ITS LINKAGES TO COMPREHENSIVE DEVELOPMENT OBJECTIVES

In this section an attempt is made to reproduce the structure of the complex S&T system, with parts and interconnecting links. We will do this in a set of "maps" of various scales, some showing the overview of the whole system without details, some showing only small parts of it but in detail. Some of the detailed maps will accentuate links between parts of the system, some others will emphasize the local vs. worldwide dichotomy.

The links are of special importance since many of the indicators that have been developed for S&T are indicators of the links from which we can also derive something about the parts connected by the link. For example, bibliographic indicators, nowadays very popular, are based on the assumption that in order for a piece of science to be effective at all, it has to be communicated from the originator to other scientists. As another example, in order for a technological innovation to be influential there must be a tie somewhere between the technologist and the entrepreneur who will carry the innovation over into production.

While the links among the components of the S&T system itself have received much attention in recent research in the science of science, the links connecting S&T to the various objectives of comprehensive development have been treated much less extensively. Yet, in the policy making for a country, S&T policies cannot be treated in isolation but must be linked with the cultural, economic, social, and other goals of the country, so that the evolution and utilization of S&T in the country harmonizes with the external determinants. This chapter therefore is intended to illustrate the various functional linkages not only among the parts of the S&T system itself but among these parts and the comprehensive development objectives.

Anybody wanting to create such a map of the S&T system immediately runs into the question of the extent to which details should be incorporated into the map. One may approach this question in two ways. One way is related to the set of nested macro- and micro- indicators already mentioned in the first section. One can find certain macro-indicators that measure the functioning of a larger subsection of the whole S&T system. If such a macro-indicator suggests serious deficiencies, we turn to more micro-indicators pertaining only to that subsection, and thus disaggregate the operation of the faulty subsection into smaller subsections. This procedure is then followed until the units causing the deficiency are located and the reasons for the malfunctioning are diagnosed.

Another way to answer the question is through decentralization. The assessment system we formulate contains, as a fundamental component, the requirement that various levels of assessment be done on various levels of decentralization. One could conduct a series of indicator applications, going from macro to micro, with each of these applications made on a different level, involving in each case the person in the most appropriate position to pinpoint the trouble on that level.

Depending on whether we want only to ascertain a defect in the scientific-technological infrastructure or whether we want to trace down the causes and institute remedial action, we may use different methods and indicators. Purely quantitative and data-based indicators alone would not be able to serve these purposes adequately. Indeed, in many cases we might be dealing with intricate aspects of the social administration and organization.

Most deficiencies in the S&T systems of developing countries cannot be traced to one single cause. Multidimensionality, discussed earlier, reigns also in this respect. Thus, the S&T system must have sufficiently imaginative and knowledgeable personnel on all levels to devise assessment methods for particular situations on each particular level.

The objective of this report is to describe the overall structure of the S&T system, give samples of micro-maps on several levels, and

Map 9.1. Overall Map of the Six Areas

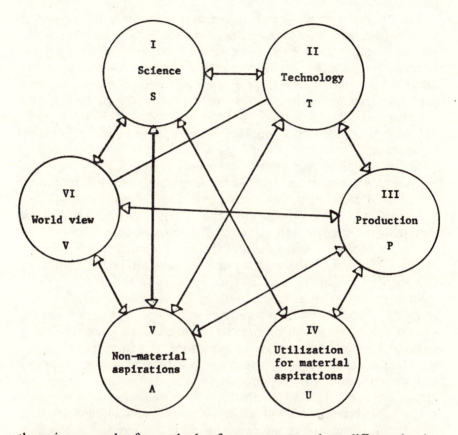

then give examples for methods of assessment on these different levels. Comprehensiveness will not be sought.

Map 9.1 shows the overall view of the S&T system we want to analyze. The six elements shown in this diagram correspond to the three fundamental aims of S&T discussed in the first section. The connecting lines are those we want to include in the assessment system. Note that not all of the 30 possible connecting lines appear in the diagram. Those links that are outside the scope of assessment techniques directly linked to S&T are not included.

The links on this overall map actually represent a whole set of links between respective subcomponents of the six areas. Consider an example. An indicator of the science-technology interface is the number and type of references to scientific articles appearing in patents. This indicator would therefore be one of the I-II indicators. On a map showing the detailed structure of science and of technology, this would actually connect one type of scientific publication with one type of technological publication.

The I-II link may also be characterized as forming a new branch of technology called "basic engineering." The distinction between it and applied scientific research can be expressed by saying that, while applied scientific research has its roots mainly in science, basic engineering draws its inspiration from problems encountered in engineering that need clarification. In these terms one can then suggest that science (whether basic or applied, or whether worldwide or local) is more universal in its problem choices than is technology and hence also basic engineering.

Map 9.2 includes four of the six elements in Map 9.1 and shows the relationships among them. It is, in the terminology of the first section, a functional rather than an instrumental map. It again distinguishes between local and worldwide, and the thickness of the arrows in it represents the strength and extent of the connections.

The map shows, among other things, something that is very essential to the assessment of the functioning of a scientist in the developing countries. Note that the pool of scientific knowledge utilized by local technology is created predominantly by worldwide and not by local scientists. This is simply because well over 99% of the new science created around the world will have its origin outside a given developing country, a percentage that has been growing in past years. Thus, the most important function of a scientist in a developing country is not directly through his own personal research, but rather through his capacity of a selector, digester, interpreter, and transmitter of new science created elsewhere. No one but the local scientist can fulfill this function.

Map 9.3 depicts the connection between technology and production, again emphasizing the local vs. worldwide dichotomy. One of the important aspects of this map is the flow into local development of free technological information from outside the country. This link is usually overshadowed by the politically more burning issue of the link with the patents, also shown in the diagram. Assessment of the relative importance of free technological information over patents is made difficult by the fact that at the moment, the free information is very poorly utilized by the developing countries, and so its potential impact is hard to estimate.

Map 9.4 gives a micromap of communication in science. This is not the most detailed map one can imagine. For example, under the heading of "journals," there is a large number of different items, such as the availability of back volumes of international journals, the refereeing system used in publishing journals, etc.

Map 9.2. Overall Map of Four Areas,
Emphasizing Local Versus Worldwide Manpower

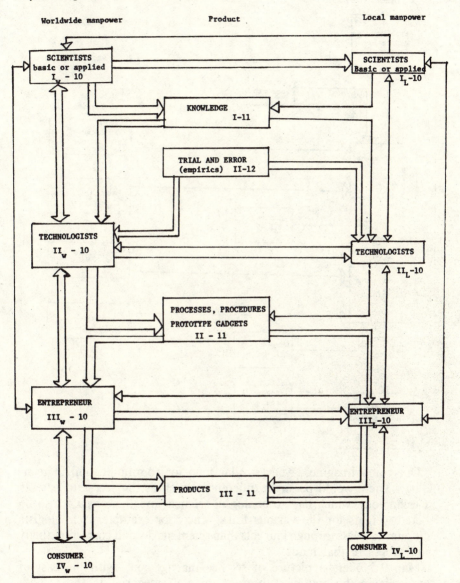

Map 9.3. Medium Level Map of the Links Between Technology and
Production, Emphasizing Local Versus Worldwide

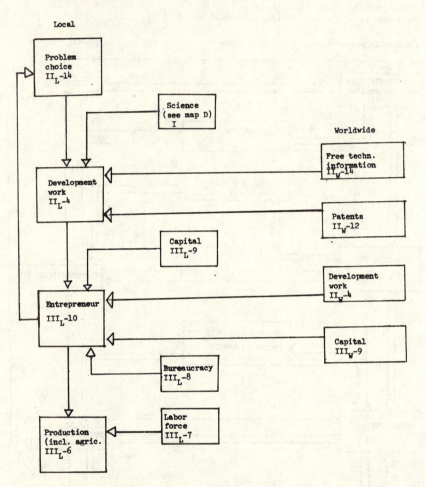

One could imagine a very similar map for communication in technology. There would be slight differences, such as the access to patents
in technology, which has no analog in science, and there would also be
altered weights for the various links, since, for example, technologists
communicate less through journals than scientists do, and correspondingly
publish less in that mode.

Map 9.5 offers a picture of science management, with the cast of
characters in the first line, the instrumental categories in the second,
and the functional elements in the third.

Finally, Map 9.6 depicts some elements of socio-economic development, particularly those that interlink between the social and economic
spheres.

Map 9.4. Detailed Map of Modes of Communication
by a Scientist

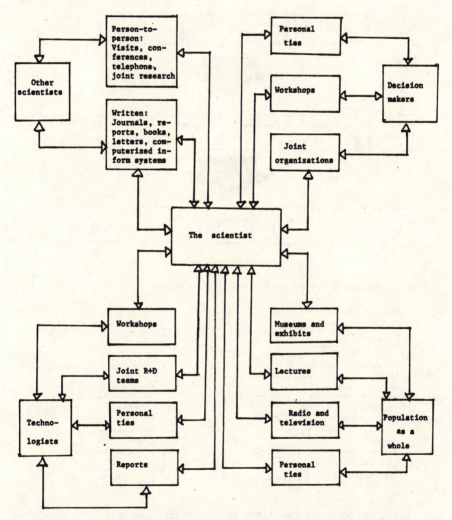

Without having exhausted the set of maps that one can draw of the science and technology system, we now turn to the listing of indicators that can be used to assess the many aspects of these maps.

THE STATUS OF INDICATORS

The aim of this section is to list the indicators that are available to assess the elements in the maps of S&T presented in the previous section.

Map 9.5. Detailed Map of Science Management

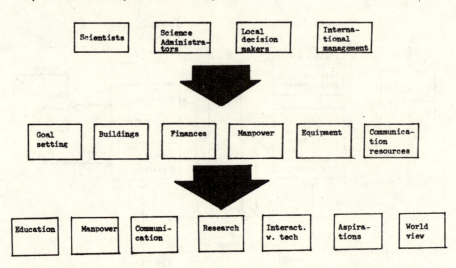

Map 9.6. Some Elements of the Socio-economic System

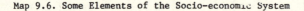

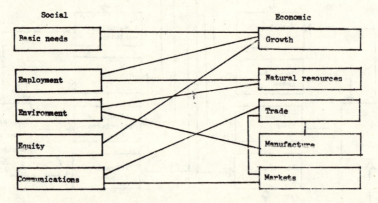

There are basically two kinds of indicators. The first kind, which we will call "data-based," utilize various and mostly quantifiable measures obtained from basically statistical data describing the operation of the S&T system. The second type, which we call "perceptual," feature the opinions of knowledgeable persons on the part of the S&T system being assessed. The second type is also called "peer review," though the knowledgeable persons may not always be peers in the strict sense of the word.

It would, of course, be operationally preferable to be able to formulate an assessment system consisting only of data-based indicators. Such a system could be applied inconspicuously, easily, and by a staff trained only in statistics, and would yield "hard numbers"—or at least it would appear to do so. How "hard" those numbers could possibly be may however be argued, since such an indicator is no better than the theory underlying the selection of the indicator, the collection of the data, and the interpretation of the results. But that is not the most serious defect of a purely data-based indicator system. The main objection to it is that, at least at this time, we are very far from being able to measure through data-based indicators all the important elements of the S&T system.

While this dispute does not concern us in detail, the overall conclusion is clear: In formulating an assessment system we must be ready to use both data-based indicators and perceptual ones. Since the latter involves the consulting of many scientists, technologists, and possibly other professionals and involves on-site visits, we must conclude that assessing an S&T system from a remote location using data-based indicators alone is not possible. The human element is an indispensible part of any realistic and functional assessment system.

Let us now turn to the indicators themselves. Following the recipe proposed in the previous section, namely that of starting with the macro- and going toward increasingly micro-indicators, let us first take Map 9.1.

In it we find altogether 22 connecting links, which can be used to gauge the output of the elements from which they emanate. Let us take them one by one, starting with the most conspicuous pair—the links between science and technology. The output of science, from the point of view of technology, is scientific knowledge useable in technological development work. Some of this knowledge will be generated in the developing country itself, while a much larger part of it will be generated abroad. It is, however, the function of local scientists to transmit both kinds of science to the technological development workers.

Indicators for the scientific knowledge generated in the country itself are easier to find. New science is almost always published in one form or another, thus enabling us to use the number and quality of these publications as indicators. Indeed, such bibliometric indicators are among the best-developed ones in the field. From the point of view of the developing countries, however, the form of these bibliometric indicators that is customarily used may be somewhat inappropriate for at least two reasons:

- The computerized compilations of data on publications are prepared in the advanced countries and may use criteria for selection of publications to be included that do not give a full picture of publications originating in the developing countries.

- Bibliometric indicators cover only the formal journal literature and hence omit publications in the form of reports and other, more informal media, which, however, may be significant in the case of research in the developing countries, particularly when it comes to more applied research.

To circumvent these two deficiencies, it has been suggested that the developing countries, or groups of them, establish their own bibliometric statistical systems. This is, however, easier said than done, not only because of the financial resources and the scientometric expertise that are needed for such a task, but also because of the necessity to deal with some conceptual questions, such as what a "scientific publication" is. In other words, the question of quality and not only quantity must be dealt with.

Let us now look at the reverse link, that going from technology to science. Here there are two major elements. One is the role of the technologist in determining the domain of applied scientific research. In as much as the applied scientific research in a given developing country pertains to some technological areas that are directly connected to the country's specific problems at that particular time, the technologist needs to participate in circumscribing the areas of research that may be useful from a technological point of view. Such a feedback from technology to science is also likely to occur through informal channels and verbally, thus making it not easily accessible to data-based indicators.

The other important function of the technologist is to collaborate with scientists in scientific instrumentation. Some scientific instruments come directly from production, but many are too special and too novel to have been produced in standard manufacturing operations. Thus such instrumentation is usually built in cooperation between scientists and technologists. Such direct cooperation, through "mixed teams" of scientists and technologists, also occurs in R&D projects. Both in national laboratories and in the laboratories of private companies, such mixed teams play an essential role. Measuring the effectiveness of such mixed teams in the developing countries would give us an additional indicator for measuring the link between science and technology.

Let us turn now, still in Map 9.1, to the pair of lines between technology and production. First, in the link from technology to production, the function of the local technologist is twofold: to provide the local production facilities with new technology, and to transmit the technology created abroad to the local production facilities.

Especially in developing countries, only a tiny fraction of technological development work will appear as patent, and technical journals will contain only a certain fraction of the remainder, thus leaving a substantial part unrecorded in written form. So here again, more so than in the case of science, we have to supplement bibliometric indicators with indicators of verbal communication, including indicators based on questionnaires and opinion polls.

The reverse link, going from production to technology, again provides a double aim: To supply technology with hardware, and to guide technological development work toward areas easily useable in local production. It is, therefore, an important indicator to ascertain how often and to what extent technological development projects are initiated after consultation with potential users. There is no appropriate database indicator to gauge this, so it has to be done by perceptual indicators.

In further exploring Map 9.1, let us turn to the links leading to or originating from aspirations and from the world view. Here we encounter an even greater gap in present day practices. The United States National Science Foundation Science Indicator series, for example, provides some such information in the domestic United States context through the results of public opinion polls, but there is no corresponding information available for the developing countries. Furthermore, even the data for the United States pertain more toward the aspirations than toward the world view, in that very little is revealed on the way science influences people's attitudes and practices in conection with everyday tasks.

We see, therefore, that on this macro level, many of the 22 links in Map 9.1 have no ready measures at the moment. Of those that might, the majority can be evaluated best through perceptual indicators. Only a few can utilize data-based indicators, and even those are marked by some problems and imperfections.

Consider Map 9.2: How well is the inflow utilized by the local entrepreneur? Studies for such links have been made in some cases, mainly through perceptual methods. The link may pass through the local technologist who, at least in principle, can be expected to be up to date on what has been done around the world in a given area of technology; but then many local entrepreneurs in developing countries may not be in contact with such technologists at all, or may not care to utilize the last word in technology, turning instead to a much less sophisticated process that nevertheless assures quick profit in the absence of competition.

Or consider the link between products and consumer. Research on consumer reaction to products may or may not exist, partly depending on whether there are or are not incentives for pleasing the consumer. This, in turn, depends on many factors specific to the country.

The situation of the entrepreneur is also shown, in greater detail, in Map 9.3, which also includes elements like capital and bureaucracy. The links pertaining to capital can be measured reasonably well by data-based indicators, but that does not describe the whole story. Obtaining capital often involves extensive dealings with the local bureaucracy, so that the difficulty of actually acquiring capital is not at all fully expressed simply by the amount of capital that is available.

Let us turn, as an illustration of maps on a more micro level, to Map 9.4, in which scientific communication is pictured. As mentioned earlier, some aspects of this can be well measured by data-based indicators, such as the corpus of scientific journals **de facto** available to the scientist, or the number of scientific visitors, or the number of joint R&D teams involving scientists and technologists, or the amount of time devoted on the local radio to programs on science. But even in these areas, the purely quantitative, data-based indicators can be very misleading.

In Map 9.5, it is easier to find data-based indicators for the second row, which gives the perceptual decomposition, than it is for the third row, which gives the functional subdivision. At least as far as quantitative measures are concerned, we can provide data-based indicators for the construction of buildings, for the amount of equipment available, and for the amount of money that is available. When we consider the functional elements, however, we again run into the inadequacy of purely data-based indicators, because such indicators have great difficulty in measuring quality, and in such functional elements measurement means little unless it includes an indicator of quality.

To illustrate the way these maps include S&T issues frequently discussed, let us consider two such problem areas.

The role of multinationals in technology transfer: This aspect of S&T is represented in Map 9.2 and in Map 9.3. In both cases the role of multinationals is only a part of those links, and hence, in order to study the specific effects of multinationals vs. other influences from the worldwide technological community, one would have to refine, subdivide, and make more detailed links in those maps. Indicators in the study of those links may be the number of licencing agreements, licencing royalty and fee payments, etc., between unaffiliated enterprises in the developing countries and multinationals.

The degree of S&T dependence of developing countries upon developed countries: For this purpose Maps 9.2 and 9.3 would be used, and one would use as indicators the ratio of "local" to "worldwide." The same can be done with Map 9.4, which in that case would have to be refined to distinguish between communication with local vs. communication with worldwide sources. Probably data-based and perceptual indicators would have to be employed.

In connection with Map 9.6, let us elaborate on the social and economic elements in comprehensive development. If science and technology are to contribute effectively toward the fulfillment of these particular development objectives, it would be useful to define those economic and social functions in which S&T are particularly strong influences, though even in these cases, factors external to S&T must also be taken into account in order to assure success and hence in order to utilize scarce resources wisely. In particular, it is important to distinguish those areas of economic and social development in which S&T are necessary preconditions, that is, in which a lack of S&T will be an inhibiting factor.

Among those elements of economic and social development one would want to consider, there are those dealt with specifically in the International Development Strategy for the Third United Nations Development Decade. This list includes self-reliance, patterns of production, consumption and trade, and effective control over the natural resources of the developing countries; the development, management, and utilization of natural resources; manufacturing activities; expansion of all energy resources; prevention of environmental degradation; provisions for basic shelter and infrastructure for all people; and the improvement of the competitiveness of natural products produced in developing countries with synthetics and substitutes. Map 9.6 shows those elements in this list that are thought to be particularly closely linked with S&T.

Let us summarize what we have found. We have investigated maps on various micro-levels and pertaining to various aspects of the science and technology system in developing countries. We found that a considerable number of links can be measured in terms of data-based indicators. These include quantitative measures of finances, manpower, equipment, industrial production, formal modes of communication (particularly written ones), and many others. We also found, however, that for many of these links, the purely quantitative aspects that can be measured by data-based indicators need to be supplemented by measures of quality for which data-based indicators at the moment do not exist and probably will not exist for some time to come, since we do not know how to create them. Therefore, for these qualitative aspects we must rely on perceptual indicators. Finally, we also found some links that, at least at the moment, can be assessed only by perceptual indicators. Some such cases could be handled by the type of peer review that already exists in the scientifically advanced countries, which therefore could be created in a similar way for developing countries. For some other links, like the assessment of the effectiveness of the link between working scientists and science administrators, new methods of perceptual assessment may have to be evolved.

WHERE DO WE GO FROM HERE?

Since the aim of the present discussion is to suggest directions for future research and to specify the way a practical indicator system could now be implemented, we now have to use the conclusions of the previous three sections to satisfy these two aims.

As far as future research is concerned, the agenda consists of two parts: The improvement of the internal quality and performance of the S&T system in developing countries and the development of methods to assess the linkage of the S&T system with the comprehensive development objectives of the country. Both of these tasks should be advanced in two ways, namely through data-based and through perceptual indicators.

The discussion of the first of these two has received, relatively speaking, a fair amount of attention, and hence the discussion of it here will be brief. The improvements needed include a sharpening and uniformizing of the definition of quantities to be measured, greater emphasis on output quantities as compared to input quantities, a more functional categorization of these quantities to conform more closely to the essential questions in the building of S&T, improving the methodologies for data collection, a closer analysis of the extent to which the data-based indicators used in the scientifically advanced countries needed to be modified for use in the developing countries, and several other aspects. For example, it would be of great importance to organize a small and brief but intense workshop, involving not more than 25 well selected participants, lasting three or four days, and preceded by an extensive period of preparation by the participants, to determine whether the presently used bibliometric indicators (mainly those originating with the Institute of Scientific Information) are appropriate in the context of the developing countries, and if not, in what way these bibliographic indicators need to be modified to serve the purpose better. Items on the agenda like this one, while pivotal, are very inexpensive and easy to organize.

The task of evolving qualitative indicators is a much more challenging and neglected task. Problems exist along all fronts. In most developing countries, the local scientific community is too small and not sufficiently diverse to be able to carry out perceptive assessment and peer reviews on its own. On the other hand, developing countries are often reluctant to turn to the international scientific and technological community for assistance in these reviews for several reasons. It is sometimes felt that selecting peer reviewers randomly from the worldwide S&T community will result in opinions that do not sufficiently take into account the special circumstances surrounding the practice of S&T in the developing countries. Moreover, the personnel in the offices of science management in the developing countries often are not sufficiently familiar with the particular areas of science or technology to know whom to turn to. Those reviews that involve on-site inspection may be too costly for some developing countries. These are only some of the factors that discourage developing countries to make use of international peer review.

A number of international agencies have sent review teams to developing countries in connection with specific projects. That mode encounters other difficulties. The organization of such reviews is often very costly, time consuming, sometimes inflexible, and can result in not having access to the most suitable people.

Some modes of peer review participation may not even require on-site visits. For example, local scientific journals in the developing countries are often in dire need of a body of referees from the international S&T community for the purpose of judging the manuscripts submitted to the journal. There are no ready mechanisms to handle such situations.

It is sometimes claimed that review systems are so riddled with deficiencies that they may not be worth utilizing. Yet, the opinions and insights generated by review systems of this kind do contribute a most valuable element in the overall assessment of the S&T system. Most of the large scientific and technical journals considered to be excellent and most influential in S&T utilize elaborate referee systems, and most S&T funding agencies in many of the scientifically advanced countries do the same. The peer review system plays an essential role not only in improving decision making in an objective sense, but also in forming a consensus within the S&T community.

In view of the great importance of peer review, and in view of the various grave difficulties in the utilization of such a system in the developing countries (and the resulting extreme under-utilization of the potential of this type of indicators), a concerted effort should be made to improve the situation. The logical bodies to get involved in such undertakings are the professional societies and agencies in the advanced and developing countries. The initial pilot work would involve some conceptual research into the best format or formats such review systems could take, followed by one or two experimental projects that test some of these ideas based on opinions gathered through the direct involvement of the scientific community in the developing countries.

Let us now turn to the second part of the agenda, namely the assessment of the links of the S&T system with the economic, cultural, social, and other development goals of the country. Among the tasks to be accomplished are the creation of assessment methods for S&T

coverage in public communication media; for the relationship between scientists and technologists on the one hand and the policy and decision makers on the other; for gauging consumer reaction to products created with help from the local S&T system; for the contribution of S&T to the growth rate of the country or of the trade of the country; for the impact of S&T on creating employment opportunities, improvements in living conditions, development of natural resources, etc.

The prescription for an assessment procedure that emerges from our discussion is summarized as follows:

- Specify the part of the S&T system and its connections that should be assessed. This also includes specifying the level of "micro-ness" of the assessment.
- Specify the purpose of the assessment, that is, whether it is for description, for implementing remedies, for planning, etc.
- Specify the way in which you will control the multitude of other variables that influence that objective in the multidimensional network of connections, especially when the assessment of S&T is with regard to some objectives that are related to S&T through a network of indirect and perhaps even remote links. This point is particularly pertinent in the case of some social and economic objectives.
- List indicators that appear relevant, functional, and implementable in view of the specifications given before.
- Use a combination of data-based and perceptual methods to acquire information on the indicators specified above. Make provisions for redundancy in order to have some consistency checks.
- Specify the way in which you will interpret the information obtained from the indicators, keeping in mind the purposes specified earlier.

We saw in the previous sections that by a combination of data-based and perceptual indicators a substantial part of the S&T system can be assessed. This, however, is only a theoretical statement since no country has so far utilized such a system of indicators to actually try to get a description of its own S&T system. It is, therefore, our suggestion that as a pilot project, such an assessment of one or two countries should be undertaken. For this a country should be selected that is very much interested in undergoing such an assessment; is of medium size in terms of S&T, so that the task is not too huge and statistics-based indicators can be applied; has some local resources and personnel in the area of science management so that the assessment process can become a truly cooperative undertaking; and has some industrial production in addition to agriculture so that a broader spectrum of links between S&T and production can be explored.

These pilot projects could easily be undertaken by extramural research groups and organizations as well as by international organizations themselves. It should be mentioned, without at this stage suggesting specific names, that there are in existence such extramural, independent groups of researchers well equipped to handle such research who have demonstrated by past research results their preparedness for the task. No organizational or manpower difficulties are expected, therefore, in following up the suggestions made in this report.

The task should thus be delegated to an individual or small research group with proven record in this field, who, with chosen associates (including people from the country to be assessed), would first prepare a detailed proposal, taking into account the special situation of the country selected for the assessment project. A small grant would cover the expenses connected with this preparatory phase of the project. Once the proposal has been received, refereed, and perhaps critiqued and modified to include suggestions, a group of financial sponsors for the assessment project itself would be acquired. Once the financial basis of the operation is assured, the project would start, and would probably be completed within two years. The results would then be made the subject of thorough discussion by a small workshop consisting of perhaps 20–25 carefully selected people known for their interest and experience in such assessment problems, who would assess the success of the project and make suggestions for further activities in the field of assessment in view of the practical experience gained from the project.

Such a pilot project, representing a first in assessment of S&T in a developing country, would be of invaluable significance in shaping future assessment activities. S&T management is not yet a science, and is, at the moment, an art that gains wisdom from the time-honored trial-and-error process. Such small pilot projects which actually try out some of the ideas proposed and discussed at international meetings and in the literature, would lead to further progress. In the process, practical difficulties not anticipated might be discovered, new methods of assessment may be invented, internal consistency checks on systems of indicators could be made, etc. In addition, the country being assessed would gain from the results of the assessment, something that would help in the country's own efforts in building S&T. Finally, such a project would also represent, simultaneously, an element in the first aim discussed in this section, namely the ongoing development of increasingly better systems of indicators to measure the development and functioning of S&T systems in the developing countries.

As a consequence of this initiative, or parallel to it, a number of competent institutions and scholars should be encouraged, both in developed and in developing countries, to devote their attention to addressing the methodological as well as programmatic points raised in this paper.

The objective of such a new international initiative would be to promote a network of interested institutions and scholars to focus and enhance their research efforts on indicators of science and technology in the context of comprehensive development; to monitor the worldwide developments in such indicators; to seek support for a series of projects designed to develop and use such indicators in the context of developing countries; and to organize training courses and workshops to promote a mutual exchange of experiences.

10
Problems Concerning Comparison of Economic, Scientific, and Technological Development Levels

B. Saltykov

In the last decade, R&D became a specific sector of a national economy as well as the main source of technical and socio-economic development. This is the reason for an overall world-wide interest in the study of the impact of science on different aspects of social development, which also reveals ways of speeding up economic development by adjusting resources devoted to science and technology. The efficiency of such an approach is observed by a number of countries, where significant structural changes were anticipated by adequate shifts in technologies used and even before that by changes in priorities of scientific studies.

In order to formulate a reasonable scientific and technological policy and to make decisions concerning priority determination in research and development, and redistribution and accumulation of scientific resources, it is necessary to make a qualitative assessment of the consequences of those decisions. There are at least two difficulties in getting such assessment.

The first is the complexity and multilateral character of socio-economic systems due to the existence of numerous links between different variables. Any impact on scientific potential[1] simultaneously influences many other human activities.

Second, there exists a very high degree of uncertainty in predicting R&D results. It is therefore practically impossible to estimate accurately science and technology impacts on economic and social life. Science that produces new knowledge as well as utilizes it in technological innovations was created on the boundary between higher educational and industry sectors. Science in these sectors is interlinked, but its impacts have spread widely. The priority given to research areas dealing with human life is a good example, demonstrating an increased interest of society to such problems as improvement of population health, quality of nutrition, environment, labour conditions, etc. The priority designation is accompanied by certain management decisions such as increases in financing in the priority areas.

At the same time, given the specific character of S&T, it may not be possible to find an answer in the foreseeable future to such question as "What should be the increase in financing and/or in research in biomedical research areas in order to increase the average lifespan of population per year?" However, it is useful to study the traditional (technological) impacts of science on economic development and economic growth.

Although there is no clear correlation between such parameters as expenditures on science and national income, a relationship does exist between the level of economic development of a nation and the level of its scientific potential.

The efficiency of S&T development or the efficiency of diffusion of innovations may be practically nullified if the necessary conditions for their adoption such as the availability of raw materials, scientific personnel, infrastructure, consumer readiness to adopt innovations, etc., do not exist. For some countries this means comprehensive and balanced socio-economic and S&T development is a necessity, but it also poses the problem of measuring the factors involved.

Different approaches to this problem can be considered. The first can be illustrated by A. E. Varshavsky (1983), where ranking of scientific and technological potential for certain industries by means of numbers (or points) is proposed.

The following indicators of S&T potential are taken into account:

- the professional level of personnel working in the industry (the composition of engineers and technicians, the composition of personnel graduated from higher school, etc.);
- the technological level of production (the percentage of mechanization, productivity per worker etc.);
- and the quality level of the produced items.

An average level of indicators for a given set of industries is analyzed. Then each industry is rated against the set average. If an industry exceeded the average number it is rated 1, if it was equal to the average it is rated 2, if it was lower than the average number it is rated 3. Then the identified ranks are summarized, and the industries are grouped in accordance with those summarized ratings.

The scientific potential of an industry can be estimated in the same way. Selection of indicators would be based on the assumption that the results of scientific and technological activity depend on the availability of resources and the professional level of the personnel conducting R&D.

As a result, all the analyzed industries may be divided into four groups:

- those at a high technological level (for instance, the electric and energy sector);
- those at an average level (machinery and metal processing, chemistry, fuel, etc.);
- those under average level;
- those at a low level (lumber and lumber processing, etc.).

Some qualitative conclusions can also be made on the basis of that analysis.

An insufficient level of scientific potential in a number of industries largely explains their low level of technological development and is one of the main reasons for technological lag of other industries consuming their production items.

In some cases the expected high productivity (or capacity) of new equipment has not been attained. This often happens in those industries where a balance has not been maintained between the increasing complexity and capacity of new equipment on one hand and the maintenance/repair system and the professional level of the labour force (general level of technological potential) on the other.[2]

The problem of balancing different development aspects on national and regional levels differs very little from this sectoral or intersectoral balancing of S&T potential components.

As a rule, the goal of such studies is to obtain a typology of countries in accordance with different partial and aggregate elements of socio-political and economic (and to a lesser extent S&T) development.[3] Initial information about different countries includes a wide range of partial indicators based on official statistical data. Different methods are available for analysing such data. Comparative analysis is based on an assumption that there exist typical correlations among variables describing socio-political, economic, scientific, technological, and other aspects of national development.

Factor analysis methods permit the aggregation of a large number of partial indicators to a limited number of factors that may be interpreted as certain generalised characteristics of an object or a process.

Interlinks could be established between some indicators characterizing science and technology by conducting comparative analysis of a number of regions (republics) of the USSR. The method of external parameters grouping[4] was used as an instrument for such an analysis. Initial parameters included in one group strongly correlated with each other and parameters of different groups had a weak correlation. For each group a random value (generalized factor) was then established that strongly correlated with other parameters of that group. The method of external grouping provides simultaneous grouping and formation of generalized factors due to certain objective function.[3,4]

For preliminary experiments a limited number of macro-parameters (indicators), mainly characterizing scientific and economic resources in a region during a year, were taken. Economic indicators used included total population, the number of workers occupied in the socialized sector of the economy, the primary source of production funds, and national income. Scientific indicators included the number of researchers, the number of topics under study, the number of theses adopted, and the total expenditures allocated to research.

In some experiments, the following indicators were added to the initial ones: the number of professors and doctors; the number of personnel with a university degree, the total urban population in the region. Due to the small number of indicators it seemed reasonable to divide all of them into two groups and consequently to form two generalized factors, which could be interpreted as economic and scientific potential. Because of significant variations in the size of regions and consequently in the absolute value of parameters, those parameters were calculated as a ratio per capita.

In the first experiment the group of socio-economic parameters included: total number of employed in the economy, the primary source of production funds, and national income. The increase in the number of parameters led to the inclusion of the total urban population and the number of people who have a university degree.

The second group included so-called scientific parameters: the number of researchers, the number of theses adopted, the total expenditure for scientific research, and the number of R&D projects.

The correlation coefficient of parameters inside one group was quite high. Simultaneously, generalized factors were formed, the value of which was used for classification of regions in accordance with their economic and scientific potential.

All the regions were divided into three classes and each class included regions with close value to each factor. The resulting classification done is shown in Fig. 10.1. One should note a distinct group of regions in the upper right part of the figure (regions with a high value for both factors, region numbers 1,2,3,8,10,15) and a group with relatively lower value for the factors (region numbers 4,11,12,14). The diagonal location

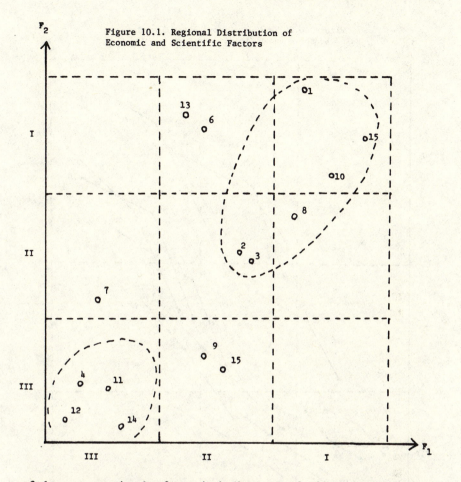

Figure 10.1. Regional Distribution of Economic and Scientific Factors

of these groups in the figure is indirect proof of interlinks between economic and scientific-technical potential (more exactly between the growth of resources allocated to the economy and science).

In both groups there are regions with a total of ten times or more population differential.

Despite the approximately equal value of economic factor for each of the four regions (numbers 5,6,9, and 13), two regions (numbers 6 and 13) may be grouped together, having a value of scientific factors as compared with another group of regions (numbers 5 and 9).

The group (6,13) is characterized by a very high concentration of researchers in the population, and this indicator shows the most significant impact on the scientific factor (0.966).

In order to increase statistical reliability and to get a dynamic picture of regional development, almost the same initial parameters are exper-

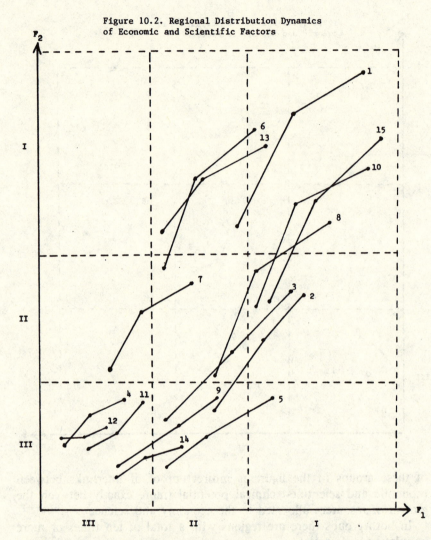

Figure 10.2. Regional Distribution Dynamics
of Economic and Scientific Factors

imented with but for different years. (The time interval between extreme
points was ten years.) Although the classification sustains its main
features as in the previous case (Fig. 10.2) one can notice the trajectory
of regional development in the generalized factors through special coor-
dination.

In the more developed region groups one could notice higher rate of
economic growth as compared with scientific factors in the second time
interval (region numbers 1,6,13,10,15,8). In the group with a lower factor
value there are regions with different development dynamics (regions
11 and 12).

The results of these calculations cannot be interpreted without taking into account the constraints that are determined by the chosen parameters. The constraints mainly reflect the resource characteristics of science (inputs) and partly of economy. The introduction of results (outputs) as well as structural indicators (different indicators characterizing availability of resources, funds and assets, ratio of high professional personnel in R&D, etc.) may substantially change the classification and development dynamics.

In the scope of "macro-indicators," it is necessary to take into account existing differences in resource requirements for certain R&D areas. Scientific specialization in regions may result in misleading assessments of the development level of their scientific potential made on the basis of macro-indicators analysis. In this case a preliminary elaboration of so-called conditional norms of resources consumption for certain research areas may be quite helpful.

Shifting the focus to the problem of elaborating "development indicators," it becomes a necessity to have not only macro-indicators, but indicators of the next level such as distribution of research personnel and expenditures among different areas and stages of R&D, structural indicators of science for different research areas, etc.

A similar level of detail is also necessary for some socio-economic indicators (for instance, employment, productivity, etc., for different industries). The countries with different levels of socio-economic development have different types of interlinks between indicators. Therefore the analysis of interrelationships between variables must be done in two stages.

At the first stage the typology of countries (regions) should be made in accordance with the factors under study, and at the second stage regression correlations among factors should be analysed for certain homogeneous groups of countries. The absence of necessary statistical data may be a serious obstacle to solving this problem.

NOTES

1. M. Anandakrishnan and Hiroko Morita-Lou. "Indicators of Science and Technology for Development," Centre for Science and Technology for Development, United Nations, New York, 1983.

2. A. E. Varshavsky, "S&T Potential Development Problems," Izvesdtija Ac. Sci. USSR Economic series, 1983, N 5.

3. V. M. Zhukovskaya, and I. B. Muchnik, "Factor Analysis in Socio-economic Studies," Moscow "Statistica" publ. house. 1976.

4. E. M. Braverman, "Methods of Extremal Parameters Grouping and the Problem of Determining Significant Factors," *Avtomatica i Telemechanika*, 1970, N.I.

11

Conceptual and Methodological Problems in the Development of Science and Technology Indicators

Giorgio Sirilli

INTRODUCTION

Any enterprise at large—one employing hundreds of thousands of scientists and engineers and commanding important shares of national budgets—is subject to calls for accountability of its performance and to justification of the national investment in terms of returns that the funder (the taxpayer at national level and the shareholder at company level) can appreciate.

In other words, at national and lower levels, concerned observers are asking how well the scientific and technological system is performing and whether it is getting better or worse, how it arrived at its present condition, and what can be done to improve it if that is necessary.

The study of science indicators, which was started in the 1960s in the United States, was in part motivated by concern in the scientific community and elsewhere about the apparent decline in the comparative performance of the United States in science and technology. Politicians, administrators, and economists, who were skeptical of subjective judgments and anecdotal evidence about the supposed decline in the United States position, pressed for more quantitiative indicators of what was happening.

Therefore a fresh effort was made in order to make available a battery of science indicators that were expected to play a role similar to that of social indicators in helping scientists, policy makers, administrators, and the general public to assess the present state of science and technology and to anticipate the consequences of rapid technological change.

The purpose and function of science indicators is then to follow changes in the scientific enterprise and its components over time, and thereby to reveal strengths and weaknesses as they begin to develop.

Such indicators, updated regularly, can provide early warnings of trends and, taken together, can make decision-makers more aware of the interrelationships of the many variables that describe a scientific system's effort. Hence they can assist those who set priorities for the enterprise and allocate resources to it.

Besides the connotation of an instrument for the measurement of change, science indicators are to be thought of also as tools for confirmation or refutation in handling questions, hypotheses, and theories that interest scholars and practitioners concerned with the state of sciences or engineering from their various platforms in science policy studies, the history or sociology of science and the like.

The definition adopted by OECD (Y. Fabian, 1979) talks in fact of science and technology indicators as series of data designed to answer a question or series of questions about the existing state of and/or changes in the science and technology enterprise, its internal structure, its relationship with the outside world, and the degree to which it is meeting the goals set it by those within or without.

The establishment of a comprehensive system of science indicators involves the investigation of potential indices, expansion of the underlying data base, improvement of methods for measuring the impact of science and technology, development of analytic approaches for interpreting the measures, and demonstration of their utility across several audiences.

If science indicators are to be used to stop or reverse undesirable trends, time lags may become crucial. It takes time before indicator data are collected and published; it takes time before they are studied; and it takes time before they lead to actions, presumably administrative decisions of some sort. And it then takes time before these decisions are carried out and take effect. Unlike other types of measures that achieve their purpose the minute they are implemented, actions in support of science need time before they mature. Conceivably, the sum of these delays could make certain undesirable developments irreversible.

MODELS

Indicators in general and science indicators in particular may serve as models in which to shape knowledge, to mediate perception, to order values, and to handle ambition. According to these general lines, and in more concrete terms, science indicators may be thought of as a system of indicators for describing the state of the entire scientific endeavour and to chart its changing state.

Indicators, by definition, describe a particular facet of a complex reality. It is therefore necessary that an explicit model of scientific enterprise, both in itself and to the rest of society, be available. Such an ideal model would help fix the significance of each indicator and would enable the various indicators to be correlated.

A number of experts have pointed out the difficulties in constructing a general model of the science and technology process. Others point out the need for better theories about science and technology processes or believe that better models are necessary to guide the construction of indicators useful for policy action.

At the present, one must rely on less formal notions of the cause-effect relationship that holds between "input" and "output" indicators, as well as on less definite notions of the exact significance and precise impact of each individual indicator.

Different models of perceptions—of science, of the linkage between science and society—will produce a spectrum of different indicators, as well as different views of the limitation inherent in some indicators or of the way in which indicators are functionally dependent on the input and output expectations.

H. Averch (1980) points out that, if a model has to be used to make a reasonable contribution to science and technology policy, no general model of science and technology process may be feasible, or persuasive. Even if persuasive in some descriptive or explanatory sense, it may not contain policy variables. Policy makers must have variables or instruments whose application can be improved by more information or by more precise indicators, and models that do not relate policy variables or instruments to outcomes may be of interest, but are not directly relevant for policy purposes. Averch's criticism is essentially linked to the difficulty of endogenizing policy variables in the model.

There is another difficulty of a structural nature, namely, the difficulty of devising an accurate predictive or cause-effect model. It stems from the viewpoint that science and technology are regarded as instrumental, and hence one should measure their contribution to "national goals." But the timing and direction of these contributions are essentially unpredictable and therefore the model should provide for pluralism, in other words, the possibility that a range of actions are taken so that good bets are not overlooked. Moreover, one should take into account the fact that in pluralistic societies, there is little consensus on national goals, and hence little consensus on what is expected from science and technology.

The limits of models in general as a sort of *loci* or of synthesis of conflicting forces are to be taken into account, too. C. Freeman (1969) expresses general reservations about the idea that somehow science ought to be able to provide all or most of the answers to societal needs, and in particular that the social sciences could somehow or other transcend the clash of interest groups and the passion of ideological conflicts.

Recently, this idea has often emerged in the form of a new technique such as systems analysis or computer modelling, or in an appeal to "Popperian" logic and scientific method or positivism in social sciences.

There are some epistemological aspects that should be dealt with in any attempt to make indicators. They have to do with the problem of measurement, on which even contradictory attitudes may emerge. Let us cite an example:

> When you cannot measure it, when you cannot express it in numbers, your knowledge is of a meagre and unsatisfactory kind.
>
> Lord Kelvin

> When you can measure it, when you can expres it in numbers, your knowledge is still of a meagre and unsatisfactory kind.
>
> Jack Viner

The entangled process of scientific theorizing and measuring is efficiently discussed by Einstein, in commenting the attitude of putting data ahead of an explicit theory:

> ... it may be heuristically useful to keep in mind what one has actually observed. But on principle, it is quite wrong to try founding a theory on observable magnitudes alone. In reality the very opposite happens. It is the theory which decides what we can observe ... from the phenomenon to its fixation in our consciousness we must be able to tell how nature functions, must know the natural laws at least in practical terms, before we can claim to have observed anything at all.

Although the paradigms of natural sciences cannot be transplanted *in toto* to the social sciences, it is certain that the reasoning in establishing science indicators looks very much like the setting up of a physical measurement. One must admit that while at present an increasing amount of observation of aspects of science and technology are becoming available, the discussion on the underlying theory is falling behind.

In practice, if at an early stage the plausibility of some data for use as indicators may be acceptable, eventually there must be some explicit theoretical base for choosing some data, discarding others, and noting the absence of needed data. What happens is that an implicit theory, or theories, are adopted that descend, in different degrees, from disciplinary approaches, values, or policy pressures.

Talking about a model, in reality one thinks about a conceptual scheme that rests on an integrated portrait of the functioning of science and technology; such a portrait allows one to identify which variables are of relevance, and how they should be weighted.

Problems of measurement arise also because little of the output of science and technology emerges in units that are comparable and countable.

Ideally, the process should begin with the search for indicators and the construction of indices after having clarified the indicand, the object to be measured. In practice, the search for or construction of indicators often has begun without such clarification and one postulates, or tries to establish, the relationship between indicators later.

INDICATORS, INDICES, DATA

Some writers underline the difference between data, indices and indicators. G. Holton (1978) proposes that the term "indicator" be properly reserved for a measure that explicity tests some assumption, hypothesis, or theory; for mere data, these underlying assumptions, hypotheses, or theories usually remain implicit. Indicators are the more sophisticated result of a complex interaction between theory and measurement. In illustrating the difference between data and indicators, the author puts forward an analogy: the measurement of the rapidly declining blood pressure of a patient remains as data until it is seen by someone with enough understanding of physiology to recognize it as an indicator of a change in the state of health.

Y. Ezrahi (1978) points out that, as a rule, we use the terms "indicator" and "index" interchangeably whenever we gauge the dimensions of an object (indicand) that is not itself directly accessible because the physical task would be difficult or because it lies in the future. The author goes on to say that it may be useful to distinguish between indicators and indices and reserve the latter term for custom-made measures, such as the Intelligence Quotient (I.Q.) and the Consumer Price Index (CPI), which aim at measuring complex objects and have by themselves no separate significance; and to reserve the term indicators for measures that have such a separate significance and are in addition indicators of another object to which they stand in some numerical relationship: barometric pressure to the weather; infant mortality to national health; arrest rates to police efficiency.

It is our opinion that, whereas the distinction between data, indexes, and indicators may be heuristically relevant, one should keep in mind that it is the systematic selection of aspects of "reality" that are interesting and relevant that guides the collection and interpretation of information— be this regularly collected data, indices calculated on an *ad hoc* basis, or indicators constructed for specific purposes. What is then crucial is to have a theoretical model—possibly an explicit one—which guides the selection and the interpretation of indicators.

SOME CRITIQUES

One of the critiques made about science indicators as they are produced at present concerns the aspect of aggregation. Enterprises such as the making of economic indicators or science indicators—almost by definition and surely by virtue of the vastness of the task—tend to gravitate to the use of aggregate, composite indicators, or to bulk or gross measures rather than to attempt to look for fine or detailed structure.

This tendency is certainly justified by the fact that, in the infant stage of a theoretical process where the science of science is of very limited help, the choice was made to focus first the great aggregates in a macro approach for which statistical data were either available or could be collected through *ad hoc* surveys.

Holton (1978) however, points out that this attitude may be dangerous because aggregates tend to hide phenomena of non-homogeneity and therefore there is the danger of mixing together incommensurable populations. Also Shumpeter, constantly aware of the limitations and dangers of abstract generalizations and models, emphasized how misleading aggregative statistics could be in economics, since they frequently conceal, rather than reveal, the underlying processes of change in the productive structure.

To illustrate the tendency toward bulk measure and the predominant influence of "lumpers," Holton cites both the fact that the majority of publications on science indicators show aggregate figures even when more detailed "spectroscopy" data is available, and, more clamorously, the fact that, even though the whole exercise regards science and technology indicators, the term currently used is "science indicators."

AN EXAMPLE OF INTERPRETATION

From what has been said up to this point, it is clear that indicators and models are intended to be an heuristic tool and, at the same time, an instrument to be used in science policy making and analysis. Various studies and comments on the scientific and technological enterprise underlie the aspect of cooperation, whereas others emphasize the proprietary status of results.

When the stress is put on science, it is apparent that knowledge is something produced by a network of people and institutions, scattered throughout the world, who work in a framework of cooperation and free exchange. On the other hand, technology is the outcome of scientists and engineers whose end-product obeys normal property laws. In other words, the final outputs of technology are economically valuable goods and services; the outputs of science are typically publications into the world system of scholarly information. The characters of cooperation and competition are of crucial importance for the setting up of science policy and science indicators.

An illustrative case is that of the debate that has been taking place in the United States and in the United Kingdom about government support to fundamental science with a relatively low commercial payoff. Some observers (McCulloch, 1980) are worried about the fact that, as the output of this activity has become available to other nations without major investments on their part, the United States and the United Kingdom may have paid a disproportionate share of the total cost of these advances. In a nutshell, too many Nobel prizes and too little economic performance.

By the same token, H. Brooks (1980) suggests that the United States should probably rejoice rather than complain at the closing of the technology gap between the United States on the one hand and Europe and Japan on the other. A possible way of interpreting this may be that the rapid progress of science and technology in Europe and in Japan rather than a decline of United States science and technology can be a good thing, at least to the extent that the progress of world science and technology is a social good from which all societes derive benefit.

In the same vein R. Vernon (1980) points out that today most major innovations entail the dovetailing and adaptation of complex systems. In these cases it is beyond the capacity of any innovating institution to draw wholly on its own internal innovative capabilities, and it therefore becomes desirable to find the needed subsystems that exist in foreign environments. If it is in a country's interest to measure its capability for innovation, and therefore for collecting and applying scientific and technological knowledge, one should be able to measure how the national institutions are rounding up the needed inputs in a framework where the ideal condition is no longer self-sufficiency but the ability to exploit world knowledge.

In this case even the same indicator—one measuring the flow of technology between countries—will be interpreted in quite different ways.

PROSPECTS AND FUTURE WORK

Holton is optimistic about the usefulness and prospects of the science indicators effort. According to him, there is no doubt that the studies available already mark the significant beginning of an important enterprise that will have repercussions on science policy, on scholarly work in the history and sociology of science, and above all on the life of science itself. However, he poses the question of whether science indicators, in addition to giving a wealth of data, show that the sciences and technologies, their quantities and qualities, can be "measured" in a meaningful way. The answer is that what is reported in publications in the area of science indicators leaves one with the overwhelming feeling that, although a positive answer to the question is not yet guaranteed, it is highly probable.

Brooks is also on the whole optimistic. He thinks that, to the extent to which science indicator publications were a response to the pressure for more quantitative understanding of what was happening in the United States it was on the whole a success, regardless of what the critics may say about the measuring of input indicators or the questionable relevance of international comparisons within an enterprise which resembles a world cooperative effort more than a horse race.

In recent years the use of science indicators has led to the raising of the quality and of the explanatory power of both input and output indicators. In particular, it should be mentioned that patent statistics, the technological balance of payments, the trade in high-technology products, and bibliometrics have gone ahead well. Also, statistics on innovations have been developed in some countries, but further work is required before they may be used on a wide scale.

SCIENCE INDICATORS FOR DEVELOPMENT

The preceding discussion covers some key conceptual and methodological issues concerning S&T indicators. These issues are very general in nature and are thought of as a prerequisite to setting the stage for the construction and the development of indicators for the assessment of strengths and weaknesses of the scientific and technological capacities of countries, either at an aggregate level or at the level of sectors, scientific disciplines, technologies, and socio-economic objectives. In this perspective, and at this level of generality, the distinction between developed and developing countries is not very relevant.

However, this distinction becomes quite relevant when, having taken stock of the inherent limitations and the real capacities of indicators, one wants to use these tools—bearing in mind that their development is a contribution to the process of evaluation and not a substitute for it—in the various phases of planning, monitoring, and assessing.

In fact, within what may be considered a paradox, it may be noted that, whereas scholars concerned with science policy in the developed world tend to concentrate attention on the more intimate aspects of the inventive/innovative process, their colleagues in less-developed areas usually address broader issues.

This state of affairs underlies the limitations of the use of S&T indicators developed in the industrialized world for purposes of analysing the developing world, in particular because of the need, in the latter case, to have access and control over a greater number of variables in the multidimensional network of connections in a greater scientific-socio-economic system. In other words, in developed countries the *coeteris paribus* condition may more often be accepted, whereas in developing countries the task is more complex because some structural variables such as development objectives should also be encompassed by the model.

A case in point is the linkage between R&D and production. In industrialized countries these two activities may be considered as working in a fairly efficient way, whereas in developing countries a less efficient functioning is the manifestation of larger structural problems that must be tackled contextually with scientific and technological development objectives.

It seems clear, therefore, that at present, methodological problems concerning the establishment, the collection, and the use of S&T indicators still deserve particular attention and that in this context the difference between developed and developing countries appears to be more quantitative than qualitative in nature, in other words more a question of emphasis than of content.

REFERENCES

Averch, H., "Science Indicators and Science Policy," *Scientometrics,* vol.2 No.5–6, 1980.

Brooks, H., "Science Indicators and Policy Analysis," *Scientometrics,* vol. 2 No.5–6, 1980.

Ezrahi, Y., "Political Contexts of Science Indicators," in Y. Elkana, J. Lederberg, R.K. Merton, A. Thackray, H. Zuckerman (eds.) **Toward a Metric of Science: the Advent of Science Indicators,** J. Wiley & Sons, New York, 1978.

Fabian, Y., "Conceptual and Methodological Problems in the Development of International Science and Technological Indicators: The OECD Science and Technology Indicators Systems," Seminar on Research Needs and Applications for Indicators Based on the Scientific and Technical Literature, Institute for Scientific Information, Philadelphia, 1979.

Feller, I., **The Measurement of Industrial Innovation,** Papers Commissioned as Background for Science Indicators—1980, vol. 4, National Science Foundation, Washington D.C., 1980.

Freeman, C., "Measurement of Output of Research and Experimental Development: A Review Paper," **Statistical Reports and Studies** No.16, UNESCO, Paris, 1969.

Freeman, C., **The Economics of Industrial Innovations,** 2nd edition, F. Pinter, London, 1982.

Freeman, C., "Recent Developments in Science and Technology Indicators: A Review," Science Policy Research Unit, University of Sussex, mimeo, November 1982.

Garfield, E., "Is Citation Analysis a Legitimate Evaluation Tool?" *Scientometrics,* vol. 1, No. 4, 1979.

Garfield, E., **Citation Indexing—Its Theory and Application in Science, Technology, and Humanities,** Wiley and Sons, New York, 1979.

Griliches, Z., "Economic Problems of Measuring Returns on Research," in Y. Elkana, J. Lederberg, R.K. Merton, A. Thackray, H. Zuckerman (eds.) **Toward a Metric of Science: the Advent of Science Indicators,** J. Wiley & Sons, New York, 1978.

Holton, G., "Can Science Be Measured?" in Y. Elkana, J. Lederberg, R.K. Merton, A. Thackray, H. Zuckerman (eds.) **Toward a Metric of Science: the Advent of Science Indicators,** J. Wiley & Sons, New York, 1978.

Kochen, M., "Models of Scientific Output," in Y. Elkana, J. Lederberg, R.K. Merton, A. Thackray, H. Zuckerman (eds.) **Toward a Metric of Science: the Advent of Science Indicators,** J. Wiley & Sons, New York, 1978.

Mansfield, E., Comments on "International Indicators of Science and Technology," *Scientometrics,* vol. 2 No. 5–6, 1980.

McCulloch, R., "International Indicators of Science and Technology: How does the U.S. Compare?" *Scientometrics,* vol. 2 No. 5–6, 1980.

Narin, F., "Corporate Technological Performance Assessment Based on Patents Citations," Workshop on Patent and Innovation Statistics, OECD, Paris, June 1982.

National Science Board, **Science Indicators** 1972, 1974, 1976, 1978, 1980, Washington D.C. various years.

OECD, **The Measurement of Scientific and Technical Activities: Proposed Standard Practice for Surveys of Research and Development,** Frascati Manual, Paris, 1981.

Rosenberg, N., Comments on "Indicators of the Impact of Research and Development on the Economy," *Scientometrics* vol. 2, Nos. 5–6, 1980.

Sirilli, G., **Manual for Statistics on Scientific and Technological Activities,** UNESCO, Paris, September 1980.

Vernon, R., "On Science Indicators 1978, Papers Commissioned" as Background for Science Indicators—1980, vol. 1, National Science Foundation, Washington D.C., 1980.

12

The Establishment of an S&T Indicator System in the People's Republic of China

Xu Zhaoxiang

INTRODUCTION

The aim to set up indicators for the socio-economic and scientific and technological developments of the developing countries is a very important yet complicated and difficult task. This is also a new area that has only recently become active in China.

For the developing countries, it is very necessary to formulate a fairly complete system of socio-economic development objectives as well as a fairly complete system of indicators. The latter should be able to reflect the needs and requirements of the objectives so as to ensure their successful realization.

A comprehensive indicator system should include:

- not only economic indicators, but also social, S&T, environmental, and quality of life;
- not only these indicators *per se,* but also relationships among them, especially the impact of S&T on socio-economic developments;
- not only indicators of quantitative measurement, but also qualitative indicators of socio-economic benefits.

The establishment of such a comprehensive indicator system is certainly not an easy task. It can only be established and improved step by step. Recognizing the practical conditions in developing countries with regard to the availability and reliability of statistical data, the organizational framework, the costs, etc., the first set of indicators should be limited and closely related to the needs/priorities of the developing countries. It should reflect matters of utmost concern to decision makers of developing countries in formulating their development strategies and objectives.

China has just started to establish an S&T indicator system to monitor the coordinated development of S&T and the economy. A brief introduction of its status and main considerations for China is given below.

CHINA'S DEVELOPMENT STRATEGY

China is a developing country with a population of over one billion. In spite of its many achievements in economic construction and S&T undertakings since the founding of the People's Republic, it is still relatively backward in S&T and economy. The per capita national income and the number of S&T personnel per population are still among the lowest in the world.

For a long time China had not formulated a correct and stable policy for the development of its national economy and S&T undertakings; the linkages between the producer and the user organizations have been inadequate, and R&D funding, especially that used for the technological development, has been insufficient. While there is a general shortage of S&T personnel, their sectoral and regional distribution has been very uneven and unreasonable. The result is inefficient utilization of both human and natural resources.

Since 1973, when the focus of the work of the Party and the government was shifted to economic construction for socialist modernization, China has set itself a strategic goal to quadruple the gross annual output value of industrial and agricultural production in two decades—from 710 billion yuan renminbi in 1980 to 2800 billion in 2000. (One Yuan renminibi is approximately equal to half of a United States dollar.) The strategic policy guideline has been: "Relying on S&T progress to vitalize our economy." Under this guideline, the stress of China's S&T activity has shifted to the advancement of production technology, including the technological transformation of existing enterprises and major R&D programmes oriented toward the requirements of new construction projects, on the strengthening of the S&T capabilities of factories, mines and rural areas; on the technology transfer both from abroad and within the country; and on management system reform to provide a better climate for technology progress. In the meantime, research in basic science is to be enhanced gradually on a stable basis.

In the past few years, quite a number of national conferences and workshops were held to discuss such topics as China's development strategy, reform of the management system, and the specific development objectives and technology policies of various economic sectors. Over a dozen national conferences on technology policies in such fields as agriculture, energy, transportation and communication, machine-building, materials, computers and Ic's, construction engineering, consumer-goods production, and environmental protection, etc., were held one after the other in 1983. Tremendous work had been done by experts to investigate the actual conditions and to collect data for these conferences. The proposals and conclusions made at these conferences have been considered by the authorities and adopted as government policy or as a part of the national economic and S&T plan.

PRELIMINARY RESULT OF THE STRATEGIC TRANSITION

The formulation of a new guiding principle for the development of S&T, oriented to the needs of economic construction, is the beginning of a strategic transition through which the wide application of technological achievements plays an increasingly important role.

During the period of 1979–1982, the gross industrial and agricultural output value increased at an average annual rate of 5.9% and 6.6% respectively. In 1983, industrial and agricultural output increased 10.2% as compared with 1982.

Case studies have shown that the implementation of the new policy guidelines, the management systems reform and the improvement of management capabilities, and the R&D achievements and the transfer of the technology achievements to the production sectors, are the main factors influencing the economic growth. Hence, technology progress is crucial in China's socio-economic development. For example, incomplete statistics have shown that among the 428 major technological inventions that have won National Invention Awards, 358 were widely disseminated and applied in production, with good economic results amounting to 17.5 billion yuan over the past few years. The result of the extension of the use of hybrid rice alone brought China an extra 4 million tons of rice in 1982.

In February 1984, the 2nd National Workshop on Evaluation of the Role of Technology in Promoting Economic Growth was held in Tianjin. The preliminary result of its assessment, based on the "residual explanatory factor of the production function theory," is that the contribution of technology progress to the growth of China's gross industrial output value during 1979–1982 was 26.2% of the total growth, the average rate of technology progress during that period was 2.4%; during the Cultural Revolution (1966–1975) it was 8.7%.

The figures are, of course preliminary and still controversial. There are too many variables and uncertainties. But it is interesting to note that

- among various cities and provinces, the rate of technology progress and its contribution to economic growth in some advanced regions (e.g., Shanghai, Beijing, Jiangsu Province, Zhejiang Province, etc.) has been higher than most of the other regions. Yet, some of the medium-sized cities that were backward in industrial production and lacked S&T personnel are now catching up through their policies of encouraging the transfer of S&T personnel and technology from the advanced regions. The contribution of technology progress to their industrial production has been as high as 50% or more during the past few years.
- among the economic sectors, we may also find that some (textile, construction material, food industries, etc.) have a higher rate of technology progress and a higher percentage of S&T contribution. We may also analyse the potential of raising the figure in other sectors.
- compared with advanced countries, these figures are very low. Actually we still rely too much on increases in capital investment and the labour force to increase our industrial output.

There are now approximately 400,000 industrial enterprises in China. A great number of key enterprises were built in the mid and late fifties. Most of them have not undergone all-around technology transformation since then. The technology transformation of existing enterprises is one of the strategic measures in realizing our national goal of modernization. By using proper techno-economic indicators and making international and regional comparisons, we may find that there is great potential to increase productivity with less investment.

THE ESTABLISHMENT OF A NATIONAL S&T INDICATOR SYSTEM

In 1983, the National Bureau of Statistics (NBS) established a S&T Indicator System that will be revised after its trial implementation in several cities and provinces. The content of the statistics will include such items as

- the number of research institutions, grouped according to their affiliations and according to their research fields,
- the number of R&D personnel, grouped according to their qualifications, etc.,
- major research achievements,
- academic exchange activities, including the number of professional learned societies, etc.,

- funding for research,
- and S&T investment used for trial manufacture of new products, pilot plant-scale experiments, and subsidies for major R&D projects of national priority.

There are also other indicators that are not classified as science and technology but are closely related. Educational indicators are an example.

Along with the establishment of the statistics reporting system, the building of a computer data base was started in 1983, and the National Statistics Act was approved by the People's Congress earlier this year.

The S&T Indicator System (still at a preliminary stage) established by the NBS is slightly different from the S&T statistics now handled by the State S&T Commission (SSTC) in that the former includes social sciences and the activities of professional learned societies, while the latter does not.

Both the NBS and the SSTC statistics system list "major achievements" as the main indicator for R&D output. SSTC has established a nation-wide system of reporting, identifying, registering, and awarding major R&D achievements. Of the major achievements identified and approved at the local, provincial, ministerial, or national level, the most outstanding ones may apply for national awards. The general criteria for the National Science Award are significant importance, the first of its kind initiated domestically, and proven to be advanced and applicable in China.

Therefore, the major achievements listed in the S&T statistics should have been identified and approved at a certain level, in the registration form the name of the institution responsible for the identification should be listed, and the result of the application of the achievement, including its socio-economic benefits, etc., should be reported. If it has been awarded at the national level, the grade of the award—i.e., Special Award, 1st, 2nd, 3rd, or 4th Award, will also be recorded in the registration form.

The contribution of R&D achievements to our socio-economic development is one of the most important concerns in China, and it is put in the S&T indicators as such. In 1982, some 4100 major achievements were registered and 149 items of important inventions were awarded, an increase of 24% over 1981. In 1983, there was an increase of 44% over 1982. As mentioned before, case studies on the economic benefit brought by the extension of the use of the achievements have been made.

The "input" side of the indicator system is also a matter of concern for policy makers. For example:

- the total number of S&T personnel in all state-owned organizations in 1982 was 6.26 million, an increase of 34.3% within three years. Yet the proportion of S&T personnel per million people is still very low—only 6200. At present, the number of S&T personnel is estimated to be approximately 6.8 million, of whom about 400,000 are engaged in R&D.
- the total number of new entrants in higher education institutions as undergraduate students was 278,800 in 1981. The figure rose to 420,000 in 1984.
- in recent years, there has been a steady increase in R&D funding which now accounts for about 1% of the gross national industrial and agricultural output value. Since the Chinese government has decided to merge national industrial and agricultural output values into the national income figure in our future statistics, the percentage of R&D funding will be a little higher. It is China's decision to gradually increase this percentage.
- funding for natural science, education, culture, and health in the national budget has also been increased in the past few years. The 1984 figure of 3.16 billion Yuan R.M.B., is an increase of 80% within two years. The increase in the funding for education has been especially remarkable.
- the S&T indicators show the sectoral and regional distribution of R&D resources, from which one can find that the S&T capacity on the forefront of industrial and agricultural production is particularly weak. S&T personnel in coal industry for example, constitute only 1.96% of its total work force, even though coal is the primary source of energy in China with an annual production of over 600 million tons. That is why the present S&T policy calls for the strengthening of S&T capacity in the factories, mines, and rural areas, and in the S&T indicator system, those S&T investments that are used for trial manufacture of new products, pilot plant tests, etc., are particularly emphasized.

As it is only the beginning of the establishment of S&T indicators in China, we are looking forward to further improvements. For example, in addition to the Science Award and Invention Award mentioned, a regulation on a Technology Progress Award is being drafted to include more achievements due to improvements in managerial capabilities, efficient technology transfer, and other S&T activities; and the Patent Law has now been approved by the People's Congress. All of these will be useful for the measurement of the outputs of S&T activities.

Many other S&T indicators for the measurement of the impact of science and technology on socio-economic development are being studied or proposed.

INDICATORS MEASURING THE NUMERICAL CONTRIBUTION OF TECHNOLOGY PROGRESS TO ECONOMIC GROWTH

The residual explanatory factor of the production function theory has been studied and debated for a long time in the developed countries. In China, this problem has been picked up only in the past two years or so. Some think that it would be useful if, through further study and improved methodology to suit our own conditions, some sort of indicators could be established.

- the annual rate of technological progress:

$$a = y - \delta K - BL$$

where y is the rate of increase in gross output value, K is the rate of increase in capital and L is the rate of increase of the labour force. δ and B are the parameters to be determined.
- contribution of technological progress to economic growth:

$$E = a/y$$

where a is the rate of technology progress and y is the rate of increase of the gross output value.
- Technological Progress Index:

Let the Technological Progress Index of a certain year = 100, then the Technological Progress Index after t years:

$$A_t = A_{t-1}(1 + a)$$

where a is the rate of technological progress, A_{t-1} is the technological progress index one year before the year t.

OTHER POSSIBLE INDICATORS FOR POLICY DECISIONS

With the aim of realizing the national goal of quadrupling the gross I&A output value in two decades, quite a few problems become a matter of common concern, including

- the saving of capital investment per unit of the output growth. In past years, the ratio of capital investment to gross I&A output is estimated to be roughly 1:1. With such a high ratio of capital investment, it is impossible to quadruple output by the year 2000. Only by using advanced technology, by improving the quality of the labour force, and by raising the level of managerial and S&T capabilities (relying on technology progress in the broader sense), can we have higher economic growth with less investment. Hence, the indicator for capital investment per unit economic growth can reflect to some extent the impact of S&T on economic growth.

- the saving of energy and raw materials consumption per unit gross national product (or I&A output). It is estimated that energy production in China can possibly reach the equivalent of 1.2 billion tons of coal, about twice the amount of energy produced in 1980. How can we achieve the goal of quadrupling output by only doubling the energy supply? The answer is only by adopting advance technology and raising the ratio between GNP and energy consumption.

IMPACT OF HIGH TECHNOLOGY ON SOCIO-ECONOMIC DEVELOPMENT

With the rapid development of high technology in the developed countries, developing countries are facing new challenges as well as new opportunities. The wide use of the latest technology will greatly improve productivity, reduce energy and raw material consumption, and help the process of development of S&T capabilities; and the integration of high technology with traditional ones will give rise to an entire new series of products. The direct and indirect economic results of the application of IC's, computers, etc., have been and will be increasingly evident. Perhaps it is also necessary for the decision makers in developing countries to take notice of some special indicators relevant to the development and use of high technology. Statistical figures reflecting the change of the economic structure and organizational structure of the production system, the number of IC's and computers used in various areas and their economic results, and the S&T input necessary for the efficient application of high technology, including training and other technical services, are examples that may be useful for developing countries.

The Chinese community is a huge, dynamic system of complicated structure and with many interactive factors. It is important for China to use modern methods of statistical data collection and modern methods of system analysis. The envisaged S&T Indicator System in China is still in its trial stage and is simple compared with that of the developed countries. For policy analysis, many more indicators need to be explored and discussed actively in China. Only part of the ideas have been illustrated here just to show the main trend of considerations for further development of the S&T indicator system.

As to the work on the establishment of the indicators for the measurement of the impact of S&T on socio-economic development of the developing countries, more might be done to indicate what the major policy issues are and how the results may be interpreted in terms of these issues.

Generally speaking, the technology development of most developing countries is still in the stage of learning and mastering advanced achievements already made in the world. The rate of their national economic growth depends heavily on how effectively it uses foreign and domestic technology and this may not be measured well by such indicators as R&D investment and the number of publications, citations, etc. Much research work done in the developing countries may often be "just for research's sake," with very little connection with production sectors and national socio-economic development objectives. The technology gap between the developing and the developed countries is, first of all, in the field of organization and management. Education efforts and S&T activities that will enable the masses to manipulate and assimilate advanced technologies are perhaps more important than purely academic research activities.

The result of the technological transformation, i.e., the restructuring of the production system, should not be underestimated either. One of the objectives of technological transformation is to improve the infrastructure, including energy, transportation, communication, microelectronics, marketing, and services for technological development.

The proportion of these "modern sectors" in the production system is an important indicator of a country's technological progress or transformation. It is also the result of its effort to reduce the technological gap in comparison with advanced countries. As a late-starter in industrial modernization, developing countries will be able to choose those modern technologies that will be more efficient in capital investment and energy utilization. It has been reported in a study by B. Elbek that in 1975, the energy consumption per dollar of output of the industrial sectors in middle-income countries was almost four times as high as that of the high-income countries. This is chiefly due to the obsolete technology and equipment used in industrial production in the middle-income countries. This is a good example of the influence of S&T on economic development and is an important factor to be considered in formulating development strategies. Another study by ESCAP points out that in Japan, for every $100 worth of imported technology, about $125 was spent in local R&D efforts to digest these technologies with a success rate of about 50%. Japan's past experience has important current implications for most developing countries.

A review of what such indicators show will be helpful for developing countries to consider their own problems and set up corresponding indicators.